City Limits

City Limits

Paul E. Peterson

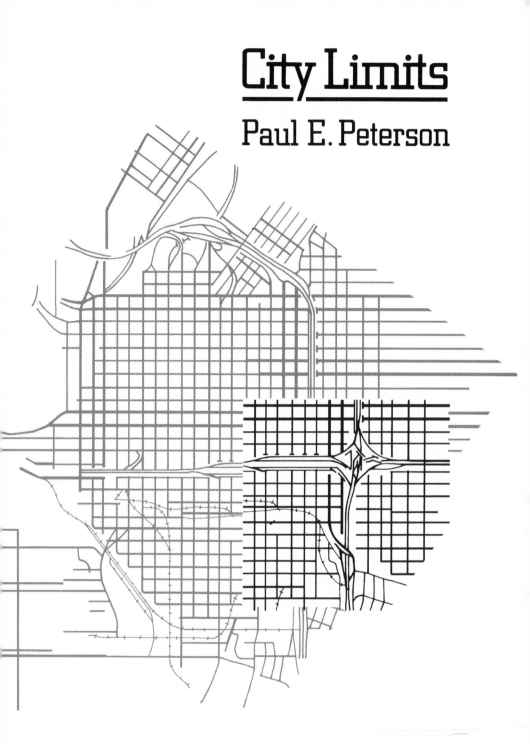

The University of Chicago Press
Chicago and London

Library of Congress Cataloging in Publication Data

Peterson, Paul E
City Limits.

  Bibliography: p.
  Includes index.
  1. Municipal government—United States.
2. Federal-city relations—United States.
I. Title.
JS341.P47   320.8'0973   80-29043
ISBN 0-226-66292-6   AACR1
ISBN 0-226-66293-4 (pbk.)

The University of Chicago Press, Chicago 60637
The University of Chicago Press, Ltd., London

98 97 96 95   7

To Carol

Contents

Preface

Of the prewar work on local government, only that of Harold Gosnell, and perhaps of Charles Merriam, still merits examination even by specialists. But for a short generation after World War II the study of local government was able to transcend its traditional concern with administrative efficiency and structural reforms and consider questions of central concern to industrial democracies. Not only did Robert Dahl, Edward Banfield, Morton Grodzins, and Norton Long lend their prestige to this new field of study, but it was in large measure through the examination of local political life that they gained their professional ascendancy. A second generation of scholars, including James Wilson, Nelson Polsby, Aaron Wildavsky, and Theodore Lowi, then paved the trail that their seniors had prepared. Urban politics became a mainstay of the professional panels of the American Political Science Association and its regional affiliates. Departments added courses in urban politics and local government. New graduates found exceptional opportunities in what came to be the fastest growing segment of the discipline.

The issues which dominated the study of urban politics were central to political science as a whole. Who had power? In what sense were cities democratic? How could the public interest be secured? What were the political relationships among social classes? What was the significance of ethnic politics? Could race conflict be managed more peacefully in this century than in the last? Political scientists did not answer these questions, but they at least addressed them, and in so doing gave vitality to the study of local politics.

It is now clear that these days have passed. Urban political analysis has been removed once again to the periphery of the political science discipline. The field must struggle to gain representation on professional panels, course offerings in the area have peaked, and its attraction to graduate students has begun to wane. Although scapegoats can be found, one need look no further for an explanation than the field's own loss of intellectual vitality. Academic courtesies are such that colleagues refrain from saying plainly to local government specialists that the leaders of this academic empire have no clothes, but their nonverbal behavior speaks as clearly as any small boy's remarks. Yet my metaphor is misplaced, for emperors no longer can be found nor are there claimants to the throne. Instead, a multiplicity of feudal barons each encapsulated in remote and insignificant provinces till fields of little concern to the larger world. We no longer have students of urban politics. Instead there are specialists in transportation, health, education, welfare, housing, and all the other departments of local government. More than that, there are specialists in all the aspects of minority politics: black politics, Chicano politics, Puerto Rican politics, and Native American politics. One also can find experts in local referenda, local courts, local taxation, local expenditures, local bureaucracies, and municipal unions. And then there are the geographical experts: the students of suburbia, of the central city, of Western cities, of the South, and especially of New York City. There is no harm in these specialties; on the contrary unless one knows well some things in particular, one is not likely to say anything much in general. But the hope remains that it might somehow be possible for urbanists of the eighties to address the central concerns of political life with the vigor and conviction with which it was possible to address them two decades earlier.

I have spoken thus far about the center of the discipline, that large body of practical scholarship which is not particularly reflective about its philosophical underpinnings or ideological thrust. This mainstream is not exceptionally fastidious about justifying its research topics, its techniques of analysis, or the policy implications of its findings, because its work is sanctioned by the century-long practices of the social science professions. Some may call it positivist, but the fact-value distinction is honored more in the breach than in the observance. It probably is more correct to call these social scientists pragmatists, because their normative assertions usually depend on values and judgments which themselves require justification. And it must not be forgotten that the social sciences as a whole, and political science in particular, budded in the self-conscious pragmatism of the Progressive era. If contemporary scholars find much about the Progressives that they dislike, their passion for discerning the mistakes of those early reformers

only betrays their own ultimate dependence on these same pragmatist values and beliefs.

Such pragmatist scholarship is so suited to American political
theory and practice that it will long remain the dominant center of
the intellectual work of the country's scholarly community. At least I
hope that to be so. But at those moments when the pragmatist tradition loses its intellectual élan, it becomes particularly susceptible to
onslaughts from the more ideologically atuned and philosophically
self-conscious tribunes of the right and the left. And so it is not
surprising that the forces driving the study of urban politics in the
late seventies and early eighties are the utilitarians, masquerading as
welfare economists, on one side, and structural Marxists, on the
other. Both perspectives speak to crucial problems at the heart of
urban politics, and both speak with a certainty that compels attention in what otherwise is an aimless drift.

Welfare economists approach the study of politics armed with all
the powerful assumptions of neoclassical economics. The components of the system are individuals; each is a rational, value-
maximizing voter-consumer; the political market is more or less
competitive; and except for stipulated restrictions, outcomes are the
product of strategic interactions in an utterly fluid political game.
With a sincere conviction that outsiders can only admire, many of
these analysts are able to state what should be the range of responsibilities assumed by the government; significantly enough,
their comparative standpoint is the perfectly competitive marketplace which God has yet to devise. Still others are able to concoct
solutions to racial and ethnic conflict, a favorite proposal being racial homogeneity in decentralized settings where differing tastes can
be satisfied in mutually isolated settings. The power and daring with
which these Pareto-optimal individualists discern solutions to central problems commands respect—increasingly so when the dis-
ciplinary center is unable to propose alternatives.

Vigorous alternatives are now offered only by a robust left that in
the United States has for the first time discovered a reasonably persuasive version of Marxist thought. Structural Marxism, as this new
variant is called, has a particular appeal to a growing body of Western academics, because it resolves two difficulties confounding earlier writers in this tradition. First, Marxists previously had not been
able to specify exactly in what sense the state was the executive
committee of the bourgeoisie. For decades this claim generated massive research efforts on the social backgrounds of decision makers
and great controversies over exactly where decisions were being
made and policy was being formulated. If the state were the execu-

tive committee of the bourgeoisie, then individuals from appropriately middle-class backgrounds must be participants. But particularly in urban contexts overt politics has been quintessentially proletarian. In response to this difficulty, the structuralist now denies the significance of the social characteristics or even the political orientations of policymakers within capitalist systems. What counts instead is the structural embrace of the state by capitalism, which compels state attentiveness to problems of capital accumulation and system legitimacy. The most well-meaning socialist—indeed, even Communist party—leaders are constrained by these objective requirements of the capitalist state. Second, earlier Marxists had failed to explain the durability of Western industrial democracies and the increasing affluence of their working populations. But with structural modifications to the theory, Marxists have focused increasingly on the system maintenance properties of capitalism. Although contradictions in society continually become manifest, the state is eufunctional. Sometimes acting even against the expressed wishes of particular capitalists, the state discerns and acts upon the long-range interests of the capitalist class as a whole. Contradictions are papered over, workers are appeased, and underlying schisms lie dormant until revealing themselves in still another form. What these Marxists fail to realize is how much their own analyses owe to the work of Talcott Parsons and David Easton.

As readers will soon discover, I am indebted to the work of both Pareto-optimal individualists and Marxist structuralists. Aside from more specific debts acknowledged in the text, I learned from the former that neither city residents nor city leaders are fools. On the contrary, they can be expected to think about their situation and take reasoned positions on the problems they face—within the limits of the information available to them. From the latter, I learned that all is not possible in politics. Especially in urban politics, the social and economic context within which the city is embedded limits choice.

Having said that, my largest objective is to offer an analysis of urban politics within the pragmatist tradition which is convincing enough to sustain further research from a perspective that is neither utterly individualistic nor conditioned on a belief in the historical inevitability of a particular utopian vision. The autonomous individual acting with complete freedom to maximize his own tastes was a fiction unconvincing even in the late nineteenth century. Interdependency is now all the more apparent, as the welfare economists' own concern with externalities, neighborhood effects, and collective goods amply betrays. And even after the Marxist structuralists have introduced system maintenance into their historical vision, their certainty that class interests are paramount and that these will reveal themselves in predictable forms still requires a faith to which few practicing social scientists can subscribe. Social life consists of the exchanges among individuals in ever changing contexts. These exchanges are structured so that individual choice is limited, but the shape of these structures is not so fixed that we now can know what their future shall be. Such is the context for urban politics as for other political relationships. It remains to give content to the structures of urban political life.

Acknowledgments

I am grateful to the individuals and institutions who helped make the preparation of this manuscript possible. I owe most to the Social Science Division of the University of Chicago, which continues to provide a marvelous setting for scholarly research and teaching. More particularly, I am indebted to the division for the small grant it supplied me at the initial stage of my thinking on these matters and for the partial support of a sabbatical in 1977–78. Partial support also came in the form of fellowships from the John Simon Guggenheim Foundation and the German Marshall Fund. During this sabbatical I was privileged to be an academic visitor to the Department of Government at the London School of Economics, which generously provided space, access to a fine, well-maintained library, stimulating conversation, and many other resources.

Without the critical advice of students in my seminars on urban public policy at the University of Chicago, this manuscript would be much the poorer. I had more specific research assistance from Barry Rabe, Mark McCue, and, at LSE, Deborah Woods. I am especially indebted to Margaret Weir, who is coauthor of the chapter on New York City, and to Susan Karpluss, who, besides much other assistance, executed the data analyses reported in chapters 3 and 4. Many typists and "word processors" worked on this material, but Carol Forster preserved my sanity during the most difficult period.

I also benefited from numerous conversations with friends and colleagues. Terry Clark, Jay Chambers, Stephen David, Benjamin Page, J. David Greenstone, David J. Olson, L. J. Sharpe, Peter Self, Paul Kantor, Nelson Polsby, George Jones, Henry Levin, and Frederick Wirt all made helpful suggestions in writing.

Acknowledgments

Portions of the manuscript have appeared elsewhere. An earlier version of portions of chapters 3 and 4 was published in the *British Journal of Political Science* (July 1979), pp. 281–314 (copyright 1979 by Cambridge University Press), and reprinted in Dale Rogers Marshall, ed., *Urban Policy Making* (Beverly Hills, Calif.: Sage Publications, 1979), pp. 147–82, under the title "A Unitary Model of Local Taxation and Expenditure Policies in the United States." Chapter 9 is a revised version of "Redistributive Policies and Patterns of Citizen Participation in Local Politics in the USA," in L. J. Sharpe, ed., *Decentralist Trends in Western Democracies* (Bevery Hills, Calif.: Sage Publications, 1979) (copyright 1979 by Sage Publications Ltd.). Various portions of the manuscript were also included in a report submitted to the Committee on Evaluation of Poverty Research, National Research Council, Assembly of Behavioral and Social Sciences, National Academy of Sciences, which has been published under the title "Federalism and the Great Society: Political Perspectives on Poverty Research," in Vincent T. Covello, ed., *Poverty Research and Public Policy* (Cambridge, Mass.: Shenckman, 1980).

Finally, I am grateful for the continuous, daily support provided me by my wife, Carol, and my children. Since most of the manuscript was prepared in a city and country which has found a way to create decent, enjoyable environments even when economic "limits" must constantly be respected, I am happy that the burden on them was less than it otherwise might have been. Any burdens the text imposes on the reader are my (and, in chapter 10, Margaret Weir's) responsibility.

1

An Alternative Theory
of Urban Politics

_____

One

City Limits and the
Study of Urban Politics

Too often cities are treated as if they were nation-states. What is known about the politics of nations, it is said, can be applied to the politics of cities within them. And what is known about politics within cities can be applied to the politics of nations. Cities are little political systems, or miniature republics, or national politics writ small enough to be studied with ease. For the quantitatively inclined, nation-states have the disadvantage that they are few in number and difficult to study. Cities, on the other hand, are numerous enough that one can identify systematic patterns of variation, through the application of statistical controls, to data collected on a large number of cases.[1] And the more qualitatively oriented of empirical political scientists have, if anything, been more enthusiastic about the city. Every political scientist lives in a city, in a town, or at least in a village; by studying the politics around him, he can—with only modest research resources—gather the rich contextual information necessary for high-quality interpretive analysis, which he then generalizes to the nation as a whole.[2]

In the hands of most analysts, the factors shaping urban public policy are internal to the city. The rivalry among groups, the patterns of coalition formation, the presence or absence of competitive political parties, the power of local elites, or the vagaries of political campaigns are what influence policy outcomes. Moreover, parties, groups, the news media, bureaucracies, and other political institutions function similarly in local and national contexts. Generalizations about the behavior of these political entities at the local level, it is maintained, are applicable to the national level, and vice versa.

It is the burden of my argument that local politics is not like national politics. On the contrary, by comparison with national

3

politics local politics is most limited. There are crucial kinds of public policies that local governments simply cannot execute. They cannot make war or peace; they cannot issue passports or forbid outsiders from entering their territory; they cannot issue currency; and they cannot control imports or erect tariff walls. There are other things cities cannot do, but these are some of the most crucial limits on their powers.

Because cities are limited in what they can do, the powers remaining to them are exercised within very noticeable constraints. Moreover, even their political processes take a shape very different from that taken by national political processes. City politics is limited politics.

Because cities have limits, one explains urban public policy by looking at the place of the city in the larger socioeconomic and political context. The place of the city within the larger political economy of the nation fundamentally affects the policy choices that cities make. In making these decisions, cities select those policies which are in the interests of the city, taken as a whole. It is these city interests, not the internal struggles for power within cities, that limit city policies and condition what local governments do.

This approach differs from four literatures that have shaped the study of urban politics and intergovernmental relations: the debate over community power; the analysis of the conflict between political machines and reform movements; the literature on comparative urban policy; and studies of federalism. In their own way, each of these studies has taken the city as a more or less autonomous decision-making unit with all of the characteristics of the nation-state. In most cases political forces within the city are treated as the fundamental elements explaining what cities do. As a result, scholars have engaged in needless controversy, misinterpreted their findings, and failed to appreciate the full significance of their material. There nonetheless remains in these literatures much that is of considerable value, and I shall not hesitate to invoke their findings when pertinent to this analysis. What is offered in subsequent chapters must be understood as supplementary to the rich literature on the internal politics of American cities. To ignore internal factors altogether would be as misleading as to treat urban politics and policymaking solely in terms of them. It is only because the studies reviewed here have elucidated one aspect of urban politics so clearly that they are worth critical review.

The Community Power Controversy

The postwar study of urban politics owes much to the prolonged and still fascinating dispute over the distribution of power in local communities. The dispute became central because it focused on a question of enduring significance but about which it was impossible to reach a satisfactory conclusion. The dispute was significant because its resolution had important implications for the country's claim to a democratic form of government. Yet the issue could not be resolved, because to know the distribution of power was to understand the causal forces determining government policy. To have a complete theory of political causation is to have an empirical theory of politics, a remarkable achievement likely to escape the wit of social scientists for some time to come.

The three sides to the debate are too well known to require lengthy introduction.[3] Those who saw a local "power structure" said that communities were controlled by a small group of leading businessmen and financiers, who together with mayors and trade union leaders beholden to them determined the community's future.[4] Those who saw pluralist decision-making processes treated urban policies as the outcome of events in which diverse groups competed.[5] A third view accepted the complexity of local political processes but then argued that overt political events in the community were only one manifestation of the distribution of political power, and not the most important one at that. To understand power required an appreciation of the forces that kept issues off local agendas; once this was achieved, the hands of an almost invisible elite would be detectable once again.[6]

In my view, all three positions are correct as far as they go. More exactly, all three positions have captured one aspect of local politics, and when put together (in chapters 7, 8, and 9) the three interpretations give a quite convincing portrait of the local political landscape. But before such a synthesis can be realized one critical error common to all three approaches must be appreciated: each of the three sides believed that the politics of communities could be understood roughly in the same terms as the politics of nation-states. All assumed that cities had few, if any, limits. When "power-elite" theorists identified a small group of power holders, they regarded the decisions this group made as the primary factors determining local policy. In fact these leaders were largely responding to factors external to the community that were quite beyond the control of the "power elite." When pluralists saw widespread and diverse participation in local politics, they believed that the choices being debated were the issues local residents regarded as most significant. They assumed that any question which divided community residents soon became a matter of controversy. But we shall see that many problems important to the well-being of most people seldom became issues for public discussion at the local level. And when they are raised, supporters are too scattered and ineffectual to have more than transitory impact.

Does this not then imply that the most important issues are kept off the local agenda by a ruling elite that contrives a local consensus? At the very least, are there not rules and procedures that "bias" the issues that become the stuff of local politics? The answer can only be, "Yes, but . . ." Yes, in the sense that structures always limit the choices available to political systems. However, the qualifying "but" is exceptionally significant. The issues screened out of local politics are not eliminated by local electoral devices, bureaucratic manipulations, or a one-sided press. Nor are the issues removed from local agendas necessarily eliminated from the country's politics altogether. The demands that do not arrive on the agenda of local politics are those that fall outside the limited sphere of local politics. Only if local politics is treated as equivalent to national politics can one claim that one has discovered something significant about power in American society simply because one has found an issue that does not appear on a local agenda.[7]

Consider the most obvious example, national defense. No American city has seriously considered taking strong defensive measures against the possibility of attack from the Soviet Union. From that, one might conclude that a Communist elite keeps certain issues off local agendas. Yet one might also conclude that national defense is the responsibility of the central rather than local government. We shall see in chapter 4 that not just defense and foreign policy questions but many domestic issues have qualities that make them more appropriate for national than local resolution. Yet the "other face of power" school treats their absence from the local agenda as a telling fact about power. In doing so, they make unwarranted inferences about power relations in American society.

Political Machines and Urban Reformers

The prototypical conflict in urban politics has for decades pitted partisan political organizations against nonpartisan, good-government groups calling for the reform of City Hall. Political machines consolidated their political power through patronage, attention to the demands of competing ethnic groups, and the provision of government services through partisan channels. Reformers uncovered misappropriations of public funds, promoted civil service recruitment by merit criteria, and sought to standardize the distribution of services to all parts of the city.[8]

The standard interpretation of machine-reform conflict has been in terms of a class model of local politics.[9] It has been stated most persuasively in terms of the conflicts between the "ethos" of the machine, as representative of working-class immigrants, and the "ethos" of the reformers, who represented upper-class, silk-stockinged, Anglo-Saxon businessmen and professionals. The issues that divided machine from reform were rooted in two political cultures competing for dominance in the urban North. On the one side, the Catholic immigrant, whose culture emphasized family, neighborhood, and friendship ties, treated politics as another marketplace in which particularistic self-interests could be pursued. On the other side, the middle-class Protestant, reared in a milieu that delineated man's individuality, separateness, and equality before God, understood politics to be the pursuit of "justice," the ground upon which one created a "city on the hill" that would radiate its worth to the surrounding countryside.

The opposing institutional networks created by political machines and their reform opponents reflected these value differences. Machines favored ward elections, long ballots, decentralized governing arrangements, and the close connection between government, party, neighborhood, and ethnic association. Reformers preferred citywide elections, short ballots, centralized governing institutions, and the application of universalistic norms in the provision of government services. Governmental efficiency was to be preferred over responsiveness to neighborhood, party, and ethnic particularities.

There is much to be said for this analysis. Many conflicts in New York, Chicago, Philadelphia, St. Louis, San Francisco, and other big cities divided sharply along just these lines. The ethnic compositions of machine and reform leaders stood markedly in contrast with one another. Over time, public institutions have become more centralized partly in response to reform pressures. But these cultural conflicts and structural innovations provide only weak evidence for a high level of class conflict in local politics. First, the leadership of political machines was hardly less well connected with local commerce and industry than were the reformers. Although the middle- and upper-class origins of the reformers cannot be disputed, there is no less evidence that leading machine politicians were—or at least became—prosperous businessmen, lawyers, and real estate developers.[10] Second, the incidence of reform structures in American cities has been unrelated to the class composition of cities, once regional differences are taken into account.[11] Whatever the class bias of the reformers, they must not have differed from machine politicians so decidedly that working-class supporters rushed to the defense of machine institutions wherever their numbers permitted it. Third, the public policies of machine cities have not differed from those of reform cities in ways that conform to a class model of politics. Few studies have shown any clear-cut differences; those that do are unable to show that either the working class as a whole or the unemployed and needy in particular are better treated in the machine cities.[12] Finally, and fundamentally, the political machine was an institution marvelously suited to the needs of businessmen in a rapidly industrializing society. American workers, no less than their European counterparts, experienced long hours, low wages, harsh working conditions, and great fluctuations in employment opportunities. Strikes, unionizing efforts, socialist agitation, violent confrontations between workers and police, and systematic suppression of union leaders by corporate detectives and federal judges were regular features of late-nineteenth-century politics. But these factory disputes seldom had a decisive influence in local politics. Although local political parties sometimes cooperated with union leaders, they were never beholden to them. Political machines seldom put their weight behind the most vigorous expressions of working-class protest; by and large, they stood on the side of "law and order" in the local community.[13]

Scott's comparative analysis of the functions of political corruption in emergent, industrializing societies is a most useful corrective to those applying a class model to the politics of machine and reform.[14] He shows the regularity with which corruption occurs whenever formal political equality coincides with great disparities in private wealth and social position. Where the masses are politically active, the privileged support political leaders who can manage voter discontent without challenging the socioeconomic status quo. Patronage and corruption lubricate the friction between the world of equality and the world of privilege. Nowhere did this process operate more smoothly than in industrializing nineteenth-century America. The political machine in the United States was at once at home with the ethnic immigrants and with the business entrepreneur, who was always willing to make a deal. From the capitalists' perspective, machines hardly needed replacement by silk-stockinged reformers. In many cities, Chicago being only the best known example, businessmen regularly rejected reform appeals for help.[15]

Inasmuch as conflicts between machine and reform are only poorly understood when phrased in class categories, the persistence with which social scientists and historians have resorted to this interpretation requires explanation. One factor, it seems, is the easy but mistaken equation that is made between national and local politics. For example, municipal reformers are often unfavorably compared with the New Deal reformers. In Hofstadter's terms, the former were a reactionary group protesting the disappearance of a bygone rural past, while the latter were liberals seeking to moderate the worst abuses of a capitalist system.[16] In other comparisons the municipal reformers were structural or procedural innovators who provide only for new political arrangements, while the New Deal reformers focused on substantive changes in the social and economic order.[17] In these comparisons it is assumed that substantive social innovation can be introduced as easily at the local as at the national level. There are no limits to what cities can do. As we shall see, these assumptions have little warrant. Once the limits on cities are appreciated, the conflict between machine and reform appears in another light. The cultural conflict remains, but it assumes a different social and political significance.

Comparative Analysis of Urban Public Policy

In recent years the traditional studies of community power and of machine-reform conflict have been superseded by a growing interest in urban public policy. These studies are noted for their large data banks, technical sophistication, and focus on policy outcomes as well as political processes.[18] Yet the most influential of these studies owe much to the earlier literature, for they, too, treat local public policy largely in terms of the conflict and bargaining among disparate groups, agencies, and factions internal to the local political system. For example, students of taxation and expenditure policies have interpreted their findings largely in terms of local political relationships. In one widely cited study, the authors argue that the lower correlations between demographic variables and expenditures in reform, as compared with nonreform, cities are due to the lesser "responsiveness" of reform systems.[19] When Clark found higher expenditure levels in more decentralized political systems, he concluded that decentralization allowed easier access to officials by a wider number of pluralist claimants for public benefits.[20] And even economists now include numerous "taste" variables (percent nonwhite, percent foreign stock) in regression analyses of variations in state and local expenditure patterns.[21] Without apology, these economists make the crude assumption that every resident (of whatever age) has equal influence in shaping the collective "taste" function of the local community.

Yet, with all the attempts to explain public policy in terms of political variables, the extensive findings on expenditure patterns among states and localities within the United States remain largely a muddle. Two decades after the pioneering efforts in this tradition, no internally consistent set of propositions has begun to emerge.[22] In part this is due to the internal politics model itself, which is so flexible that it can be folded and stretched to cover almost any finding. High correlations show high government responsiveness; low correlations show low government responsiveness. If one governmental characteristic has no explanatory power, then the analyst need only search for a means of quantifying another. In the end the model becomes less of a theoretical construct guiding the selection and analysis of data than a coverlet loosely resembling the society's democratic myths (a big red, white, and blue blanket, as it were) that can be tossed over almost any empirical result.

Almost, I say, because a second problem has been the difficulty of incorporating within the bargaining model the numerous instances when "environmental" variables—incomes, property values, urbanization, and so on—account for much of the variation. Indeed, Thomas Dye's work on state revenue policy, in which he concluded that variables endogenous to most bargaining models of policy-making had little impact on policy at all, has been a continuing embarrassment.[23]

Finally, the whole research tradition has been mired in a seemingly insoluble dilemma of finding comparable units of analysis. Although units of government in the United States often have the same names—states, counties, municipalities—these entities, even when they have the same name, differ in theoretically significant ways to an extent that makes it very difficult to treat them as comparable systems. Especially if one regards public policy as the outcome of a bargaining process among competing groups and interests, these differences create problems that have almost always defied solution. Every alternative is open to serious question.

Consider those studies which take expenditures by municipal governments as the dependent variable to be explained.[24] The rationale for comparing these units of government is that in each case they have primary responsibility for the governance of a community and that all decision makers are subject to some set of group pressures and competing interests. In nearly all cases formal authority is in the hands of elected officials. However, the functional responsibilities assigned to these municipal governments by the state vary enormously in different parts of the country. In some cities these governmental units not only are responsible for routine housekeeping functions such as police and fire protection but also are the managers of health, welfare, and educational systems. In other cities the state has assigned just the basic housekeeping functions to municipal governments and has reserved for itself or assigned to counties or special districts the responsibility for hospitals, schools, parks, and welfare. All sorts of combinations can be found. In other words, the same word, "municipalities," refers to political entities with vastly varying functional responsibilities; any attempt to explain overall expenditure patterns in terms of local political pressures is confounded by the fact that differing functional responsibilities are themselves the primary determinant of expenditure variation.[25]

An alternative solution that other scholars have employed is to combine all the expenditures by all the local governments servicing a particular geographic area.[26] The total of all expenditures by the entire local government system is taken to be the policy to be explained. The assumption here is that within each geographic area—a city, a metropolitan area, or a county—comparable governmental functions are being performed by the total system of local government. By looking at what is associated with the variations in expenditures by this system, one can illuminate the factors that affect the level (in terms of financial costs) at which the system performs its functions.

In some ways this is a considerable improvement on taking as the dependent variable only those expenditures by a single type of local government. One reduces substantially the variation in functional responsibilities assigned to the governmental systems being compared. Nonetheless, it remains the case that there will be variation in the degree to which the state government will have reserved to itself certain governmental functions. For example, in some states no local government plays a financially significant role in the distribution of welfare benefits; in other states some combination of local governments is responsible for nearly half of the welfare expenditures.

For those explaining policies in terms of internal political processes a second problem is even more severe. The total of local expenditures is a measure of the sum of activities by the entire local government system servicing an area. Each part of that system may have its own distinctive method of resolving political conflict. The municipal government may be elected in a partisan election, the school board may be chosen by a caucus and elected almost unanimously in a low-turnout, nonpartisan election, and the sanitation district commissioners may be appointed by a government whose boundaries do not even coincide with the geographic area in question. What set of political variables can be meaningfully related to the aggregated expenditures of these several governments? It is no wonder that most political scientists have felt uncomfortable with this solution.

These same problems of comparison have been equally troublesome at the state level. Some research has taken as its dependent variable the expenditures directly appropriated by statewide institutions.[27] But in these cases the analyst fails to take into account the great differences among the states in the governmental functions the state has reserved to itself as distinct from those it has assigned to local authorities.[28] The alternative solution is to combine all state and local expenditures within a state into one dependent variable. But if policies are the product of a state's internal politics, the inclusion of both state and local expenditures into one combined measure of governmental activity can hardly be justified. As Ira Sharkansky has observed: "When they combine the spending of state and local governments, the researchers fuse the decisions of many separate authorities. As a result, they mask real political processes and lose the opportunity to gain an understanding of financial decisions at either state or local level."[29] In other words, how can measures of statewide political activities, such as the competitiveness of the state party system, or participation in statewide elections, be expected to predict overall levels of expenditure which are the product of both state and local government decisions?

These methodological issues help account for the durability—and futility—of the debate in the expenditure literature concerning the relative importance of political and economic variables. When governmental units whose functional responsibilities are similar have been compared, it has been inappropriate to introduce political variables into the analysis. When Dye chose to do so, it was not surprising that he found political variables had little impact.[30] On the other hand, when one can obtain meaningful indicators of differences in political processes, the expenditure data do not lend themselves to easy comparison because these units do not have similar functional responsibilities. Consequently, the debate on the relative importance of political and environmental variables continues on its meaningless course.[31]

Once the limits on cities are defined, a different approach becomes possible. As will be shown in chapter 3, the political variables no longer remain relevant to the analysis, because the internal political arrangements of the city are not treated as the decisive factors affecting local policy. At the same time the environmental variables are no longer understood as nonpolitical determinants of policy. Instead, they become indicators of the factors external to the city which give precision to the limits within which city policymakers exercise their discretion. One is no longer interested in the relative importance of political versus environmental variables but in the relative importance of different environmental variables. Each social and economic factor provides information on a set of constraints which limit city choice; to discover the relative importance of these environmental variables is to learn about the way in which the structure of local government operates to limit political choice. What was once taken to be information about elements external to the political system is now understood to be information about the structure and interests of local government.

Modern Federal Theory

Modern federal theory has replaced the older concept that each level of government must pursue the functions appropriate to it with the flexible idea that the national government can and does exercise any function performed by state and local governments. Martin Grodzins's metaphor of the "marble cake" captured this new understanding of relationships in the American federal system.[32] He argued that power was both widely diffused and widely shared. The overall pattern had become marked more by cooperation and mutual assistance than by confrontations between dual sovereigns. Intergovernmental relations were characterized by endless processes of sharing and exchange. The resulting formation, like a marble cake. had no discernible structure at all.

The metaphor diffused rapidly in the literature on federalism. It fitted nicely with the current process-oriented focus of the political science discipline as a whole; and it seemed to give point and direction to descriptive studies of intergovernmental relationships. The more innovative writers added their own metaphoric variations: picket fence, upside-down cake, harlequin ice cream brick, or what have you.[33]

Although Grodzins revitalized federal theory by focusing attention away from an outdated concern with dual sovereignty and toward an understanding of contemporary intergovernmental relationships, his successors have not advanced his work much beyond the marble cake metaphor. However apt and appealing this analogy may be, comparing federalism to a structureless piece of pastry is in the end nontheory. It suggests flux, change, and complexity when one purpose of theory is to identify, to the extent possible, simplicity, pattern, and order. It directs attention toward individuals, groups, and processes when the essence of federalism is a stable relationship among structures of government.

As a result, we have yet to develop a theory of federalism. Contemporary descriptive analyses, persuasive as they sometimes are, have (1) failed to give a distinctive meaning to federalism, (2) failed to preserve any distinctions among functions appropriate to each level of government, and (3) failed to identify any pattern to cooperative and conflictual elements in the federal system. Influenced by the process-oriented behavioralism of the discipline at large, they have all but ignored the structural arrangements of the federal system. Instead, they have concentrated research energy on the activities of groups, elites, constituencies, and bureaucrats at all governmental levels.

Crucially, their definitions of federalism are so vague that it is impossible to distinguish federalism from relationships between central and field offices in a unitary government. Daniel Elazar's efforts are more careful than most, but even he defines federalism

as the mode of political organization that unites smaller polities within an overarching political system by distributing power among general and constituent governments in a manner designed to protect the existence and authority of both national and subnational political systems, enabling all to share in the overall system's decision-making and executing processes.[34]

By this all-encompassing definition, even the United States Forest Service is a federal system. Its decision-making processes are divided between central and field offices, which are united by a handbook of rules and regulations that protects the existence and authority of each layer. Yet Kaufman has judged the Forest Service to be a highly centralized agency.[35] By Elazar's definition, relations between the federal government and defense contractors are also aspects of a federal system. Indeed, a book that he has coedited devotes an entire section to such public-private relationships.[36] But, certainly, the concept of federalism, when applied in this way, begins to encompass almost all political relationships. Perhaps this is Elazar's intent, for in the same paragraph he says that federalism "is more than an arrangement of governmental structures; it is a mode of political activity that requires certain kinds of cooperative relationships through the political system it animates."[37] This free-flowing assertion is certainly in keeping with the emphasis on process characteristic of behavioral approaches, but it does little to focus the study of intergovernmental relationships. To be sure, modern interpreters of American federalism are understandably concerned not to define federalism in narrow, constitutional terms. But modern federal theorists have not supplied a sufficiently focused substitute for traditional definitions of federalism in order that a distinctive, middle-range theory of intergovernmental relations could emerge.

Furthermore, without a definition of federalism, modern writers have been unable to state the characteristic and appropriate function of each level of government. Grodzins himself was reluctant to undertake such a task. In a fascinating commentary Martin Diamond observed that Grodzins "was driven by the difficulty of defining localness towards rejecting any standard for distributing functions between state and national government. He came to argue that 'Local

Is As Local Does.'"[38] The theory degenerates into sheer description. And, once again, it becomes impossible to distinguish the federal system from a decentralized administrative structure.

Perhaps it is unkind to suggest that modern theorists are left without a standpoint from which to study intergovernmental relationships. After all, Grodzins, Elazar, and other students of Grodzins have commented extensively on the federal "partnership," and have given intelligent accounts of a cooperative sharing of power among governmental levels.[39] But even though their empirical studies are lucid and helpful, general theoretical explanations of the pattern of cooperation and conflict among governmental levels have not emerged.

A modern theory of federalism becomes possible only when cities, states, and national governments are understood to differ in their essential character. If cities are like nations, then any activity performed by nations can be performed by cities. And politics at the national level will be similar to politics at the local level. But once the particular limits on local governments are defined, one can establish a theory of government structure that assigns certain functions to the central government and others to local governments. This becomes a central concern of chapter 4.

Plan of the Book

Many studies of urban politics and of intergovernmental relations have conceptualized local governments as nearly autonomous sovereignties with almost as much discretion as national government.[40] Of course few, if any, studies explicitly make this assumption; on the contrary, in many of the studies one finds discussion of external influences, the impact of higher levels of government, and the need for understanding the community in the context of the larger society. Yet these references are never integrated into the analytical constructs employed. Instead, the repeated emphasis on internal political relations implies that it is within the city that the key determinants of public policy are to be found. Although much can be said within that framework, the study of local government can no longer ignore a city's limits.

In subsequent chapters the significance of city limits for both public policy and local politics is elaborated. In chapter 2 the theory underlying the analysis is elaborated. I find the primary interest of cities to be the maintenance and enhancement of their economic productivity. To their land area cities must attract productive labor and capital.

Part 2 is devoted to the study of urban public policy. Chapter 3

develops a typology of public policies. Those policies which enhance the city's productivity are called developmental; those which
have an adverse economic effect, even though the needy of the
community may benefit, are identified as redistributive; and those
whose economic effects are more or less neutral are labeled
allocational. Because each of these types of public policy affects the
interests of cities differently, the factors producing them vary from
one policy area to the next. I demonstrate the differences among the
three policy areas through a regression analysis of the determinants
of expenditure levels for nine different public policies. Any reader
who is reluctant to subject himself to statistical pyrotechnics can
pass over the latter half of this chapter with its accompanying tables
and still grasp my basic argument. Chapter 4 shows the distribution
of policy responsibilities among varying levels of government. The
national government bears the greatest responsibility for redistributive policies, while local governments are primarily responsible for allocational policies. Chapter 5 concludes by showing
that policies vary depending upon the structure of local government
systems. In big cities, where local governments are large and have
monopolistic control over a large land area, some degree of redistribution occurs even at the local level. Where local governments
are small, numerous, and highly competitive with one another, as in
suburbia, redistribution is kept to a minimum. This analysis is illustrated by a detailed examination of school policy, the activity which
weighs most heavily on the local taxpayer.

Part 3 examines urban political processes. Chapter 6 examines the
marginal role played by parties and groups. Chapter 7 looks at developmental policies; it concludes that in this policy arena the
findings of "power-elite" theorists are most applicable. Chapter 8
examines the pluralist nature of allocational politics. Chapter 9 explains why redistributional issues give the appearance of "another
face of power" that keeps certain topics off local agendas.

Finally, part 4 explores empirically and normatively certain efforts
to change the limits on local politics. Chapter 10 examines New
York City, a case which some may think runs counter to the thesis of
this monograph. The concluding chapter offers a set of policy recommendations that would dramatically broaden the city's limits.

Two

The Interests of the Limited City

Like all social structures, cities have interests. Just as we can speak of union interests, judicial interests, and the interests of politicians, so we can speak of the interests of that structured system of social interactions we call a city. Citizens, politicians, and academics are all quite correct in speaking freely of the interests of cities.[1]

Defining the City Interest

By a city's interest, I do not mean the sum total of the interests of those individuals living in the city. For one thing, these are seldom, if ever, known. The wants, needs, and preferences of residents continually change, and few surveys of public opinion in particular cities have ever been taken. Moreover, the residents of a city often have discordant interests. Some want more parkland and better schools; others want better police protection and lower taxes. Some want an elaborated highway system; others wish to keep cars out of their neighborhood. Some want more inexpensive, publicly subsidized housing; others wish to remove the public housing that exists. Some citizens want improved welfare assistance for the unemployed and dependent; others wish to cut drastically all such programs of public aid. Some citizens want rough-tongued ethnic politicians in public office; others wish that municipal administration were a gentleman's calling. Especially in large cities, the cacophony of competing claims by diverse class, race, ethnic, and occupational groups makes impossible the determination of any overall city interest—any public interest, if you like—by compiling all the demands and desires of individual city residents.

Some political scientists have attempted to discover the overall

17

urban public interest by summing up the wide variety of individual interests. The earlier work of Edward Banfield, still worth examination, is perhaps the most persuasive effort of this kind.[2] He argued that urban political processes—or at least those in Chicago—allowed for the expression of nearly all the particular interests within the city. Every significant interest was represented by some economic firm or voluntary association, which had a stake in trying to influence those public policies that touched its vested interests. After these various groups and firms had debated and contended, the political leader searched for a compromise that took into account the vital interests of each, and worked out a solution all could accept with some satisfaction. The leader's own interest in sustaining his political power dictated such a strategy.

Banfield's argument is intriguing, but few people would identify public policies as being in the interest of the city simply because they have been formulated according to certain procedures. The political leader might err in his judgment; the interests of important but politically impotent groups might never get expressed; or the consequences of a policy might in the long run be disastrous for the city. Moreover, most urban policies are not hammered out after great controversy, but are the quiet product of routine decision making. How does one evaluate which of these are in the public interest? Above all, this mechanism for determining the city's interest provides no standpoint for evaluating the substantive worth of urban policies. Within Banfield's framework, whatever urban governments do is said to be in the interest of their communities. But the concept of city interest is used most persuasively when there are calls for reform or innovation. It is a term used to evaluate existing programs and to discriminate between promising and undesirable new ones. To equate the interests of cities with what cities are doing is to so impoverish the term as to make it quite worthless.

The economist Charles Tiebout employs a second approach to the identification of city interests.[3] Unlike Banfield, he does not see the city's interests as a mere summation of individual interests but as something which can be ascribed to the entity, taken as a whole. As an economist, Tiebout is hardly embarrassed by such an enterprise, because in ascribing interests to cities his work parallels both those orthodox economists who state that firms have an interest in maximizing profits and those welfare economists who claim that politicians have an interest in maximizing votes. Of course, they state only that their model will assume that firms and politicians behave in such a way, but insofar as they believe their model has empirical validity, they in fact assert that those constrained by the businessman's or politician's role must pursue certain interests. And so does Tiebout when he says that communities seek to attain the optimum size for the efficient delivery of the bundle of services the local government produces. In his words, "Communities below the optimum size seek to attract new residents to lower average costs. Those above optimum size do just the opposite. Those at an optimum try to keep their populations constant."[4]

Tiebout's approach is in many ways very attractive. By asserting a strategic objective that the city is trying to maximize—optimum size—Tiebout identifies an overriding interest which can account for specific policies the city adopts. He provides a simple analytical tool that will account for the choices cities make, without requiring complex investigations into citizen preferences and political mechanisms for identifying and amalgamating the same. Moreover, he provides a criterion for determining whether a specific policy is in the interest of the city—does it help achieve optimum size? Will it help the too small city grow? Will it help the too big city contract? Will it keep the optimally sized city in equilibrium? Even though the exact determination of the optimum size cannot presently be scientifically determined in all cases, the criterion does provide a most useful guide for prudential decision making.

The difficulty with Tiebout's assumption is that he does not give very good reasons for its having any plausibility. When most economists posit a certain form of maximizing behavior, there is usually a good commonsense reason for believing the person in that role will have an interest in pursuing this strategic objective. When orthodox economists say that businessmen maximize profits, it squares with our understanding in everyday life that people engage in commercial enterprises for monetary gain. The more they make, the better they like it. The same can be said of those welfare economists who say politicians maximize votes. The assumption, though cynical, is in accord with popular belief—and therefore once again has a certain plausibility.

By contrast, Tiebout's optimum size thesis diverges from what most people think cities are trying to do. Of course, smaller communities are often seeking to expand—boosterism may be the quintessential characteristic of small-town America. Yet Tiebout takes optimum size, not growth or maximum size, as the strategic objective. And when Tiebout discusses the big city that wishes to shrink to optimum size, his cryptic language is quite unconvincing. "The case of the city that is too large and tries to get rid of residents is more difficult to imagine," he confesses. Even more, he concedes that "no alderman in his right political mind would ever admit that the city is too big." "Nevertheless," he continues, "economic forces are at work to push people out of it. Every resident who moves to the suburbs to find better schools, more parks, and so forth, is reacting, in part, against the pattern the city has´ to offer."[5] In this crucial passage Tiebout speaks neither of local officials nor of local public policies. Instead, he refers to "economic forces" that may be beyond the control of the city and of "every resident," each of whom may be pursuing his own interests, not that of the community at large.

The one reason Tiebout gives for expecting cities to pursue optimum size is to lower the average cost of public goods. If public goods can be delivered most efficiently at some optimum size, then migration of residents will occur until that size has been reached. In one respect Tiebout is quite correct: local governments must concern themselves with operating local services as efficiently as possible in order to protect the city's economic interests. But there is little evidence that there is an optimum size at which services can be delivered with greatest efficiency. And even if such an optimum did exist, it could be realized only if migration occurred among residents who paid equal amounts in local taxes. In the more likely situation, residents pay variable prices for public services (for example, the amount paid in local property taxes varies by the value of the property). Under these circumstances, increasing size to the optimum does not reduce costs to residents unless newcomers pay at least as much in taxes as the marginal increase in costs their arrival imposes on city government.[6] Conversely, if a city needs to lose population to reach the optimum, costs to residents will not decline unless the exiting population paid less in taxes than was the marginal cost of providing them government services. In most big cities losing population, exactly the opposite is occurring. Those who pay more in taxes than they receive in services are the emigrants. Tiebout's identification of city interests with optimum size, while suggestive, fails to take into account the quality as well as the quantity of the local population.

The interests of cities are neither a summation of individual interests nor the pursuit of optimum size. Instead, policies and programs can be said to be in the interest of cities whenever the policies maintain or enhance the economic position, social prestige, or political power of the city, taken as a whole.[7]

Cities have these interests because cities consist of a set of social interactions structured by their location in a particular territorial space. Any time that social interactions come to be structured into recurring patterns, the structure thus formed develops an interest in its own maintenance and enhancement. It is in that sense that we speak of the interests of an organization, the interests of the system, and the like. To be sure, within cities, as within any other structure, one can find diverse social roles, each with its own set of interests.

But these varying role interests, as divergent and competing as they may be, do not distract us from speaking of the overall interests of the larger structural entity.[8]

The point can be made less abstractly. A school system is a structured form of social action, and therefore it has an interest in maintaining and improving its material resources, its prestige, and its political power. Those policies or events which have such positive effects are said to be in the interest of the school system. An increase in state financial aid or the winning of the basketball tournament are events that, respectively, enhance the material well-being and the prestige of a school system and are therefore in its interest. In ordinary speech this is taken for granted, even when we also recognize that teachers, pupils, principals, and board members may have contrasting interests as members of differing role-groups within the school.

Although social roles performed within cities are numerous and conflicting, all are structured by the fact that they take place in a specific spatial location that falls within the jurisdiction of some local government. All members of the city thus come to share an interest in policies that affect the well-being of that territory. Policies which enhance the desirability or attractiveness of the territory are in the city's interest, because they benefit all residents—in their role as residents of the community. Of course, in any of their other social roles, residents of the city may be adversely affected by the policy. The Los Angeles dope peddler—in his role as peddler—hardly benefits from a successful drive to remove hard drugs from the city. On the other hand, as a resident of the city, he benefits from a policy that enhances the attractiveness of the city as a locale in which to live and work. In determining whether a policy is in the interest of a city, therefore, one does not consider whether it has a positive or negative effect on the total range of social interactions of each and every individual. That is an impossible task. To know whether a policy is in a city's interest, one has to consider only the impact on social relationships insofar as they are structured by their taking place within the city's boundaries.

An illustration from recent policy debates over the future of our cities reveals that it is exactly with this meaning that the notion of a city's interest is typically used. The tax deduction that homeowners take on their mortgage interest payments should be eliminated, some urbanists have argued. The deduction has not served the interests of central cities, because it has provided a public subsidy for families who purchase suburban homes. Quite clearly, elimination of this tax deduction is not in the interest of those central city residents who wish to purchase a home in the suburbs. It is not in the interest of those central city homeowners (which in some cities may even form a majority of the voting population), who would then be called upon to pay higher federal taxes. But the policy might very well improve the rental market in the central city, thereby stimulating its economy—and it is for this reason that the proposal has been defended as being in the interest of central cities.

To say that people understand what, generally, is in the interest of cities does not eliminate debate over policy alternatives in specific instances. The notion of city interest can be extremely useful, even though its precise application in specific contexts may be quite problematic. In any policy context one cannot easily assert that one "knows" what is in the interest of cities, whether or not the residents of the city agree. But city residents do know the kind of evidence that must be advanced and the kinds of reasons that must be adduced in order to build a persuasive case that a policy is in the interest of cities. And so do community leaders, mayors, and administrative elites.

Economic Interests

Cities, like all structured social systems, seek to improve their position in all three of the systems of stratification—economic, social, and political—characteristic of industrial societies. In most cases, improved standing in any one of these systems helps enhance a city's position in the other two. In the short run, to be sure, cities may have to choose among economic gains, social prestige, and political weight. And because different cities may choose alternative objectives, one cannot state any one overarching objective—such as improved property values—that is always the paramount interest of the city. But inasmuch as improved economic or market standing seems to be an objective of great importance to most cities, I shall concentrate on this interest and only discuss in passing the significance of social status and political power.

Cities constantly seek to upgrade their economic standing. Following Weber, I mean by this that cities seek to improve their market position, their attractiveness as a locale for economic activity. In the market economy that characterizes Western society, an advantageous economic position means a competitive edge in the production and distribution of desired commodities relative to other localities. When this is present, cities can *export* goods and/or services to those outside the boundaries of the community.

Some regional economists have gone so far as to suggest that the welfare of a city is identical to the welfare of its export industry.[9] As exporters expand, the city grows. As they contract, the city declines and decays. The economic reasoning supporting such a conclusion is quite straightforward. When cities produce a good that can be sold in an external market, labor and capital flow into the city to help increase the production of that good. They continue to do so until the external market is saturated—that is, until the marginal cost of production within the city exceeds the marginal value of the good external to the city. Those engaged in the production of the exported good will themselves consume a variety of other goods and services, which other businesses will provide. In addition, subsidiary industries locate in the city either because they help supply the exporting industry, because they can utilize some of its by-products, or because they benefit by some economies of scale provided by its presence. Already, the familiar multiplier is at work. With every increase in the sale of exported commodities, there may be as much as a four- or fivefold increase in local economic activity.

The impact of Boeing Aircraft's market prospects on the economy of the Seattle metropolitan area illustrates the importance of export to regional economies. In the late sixties defense and commercial aircraft contracts declined, Boeing laid off thousands of workmen, the economy of the Pacific Northwest slumped, the unemployed moved elsewhere, and Seattle land values dropped sharply. More recently, Boeing has more than recovered its former position. With rapidly expanding production at Boeing, the metropolitan area is enjoying low unemployment, rapid growth, and dramatically increasing land values.

The same multiplier effect is not at work in the case of goods and services produced for domestic consumption within the territory. What is gained by a producer within the community is expended by other community residents. Residents, in effect, are simply taking in one another's laundry. Unless productivity increases, there is no capacity for expansion.

If this economic analysis is correct, it is only a modest oversimplification to equate the interests of cities with the interests of their export industries. Whatever helps them prosper redounds to the benefit of the community as a whole—perhaps four and five times over. And it is just such an economic analysis that has influenced many local government policies. Especially the smaller towns and cities may provide free land, tax concessions, and favorable utility rates to incoming industries.

The smaller the territory and the more primitive its level of economic development, the more persuasive is this simple export thesis. But other economists have elaborated an alternative growth thesis that is in many ways more persuasive, especially as it relates to larger urban areas. In their view a sophisticated local network of

23

public and private services is the key to long-range economic growth. Since the world economy is constantly changing, the economic viability of any particular export industry is highly variable. As a result, a community dependent on any particular set of export industries will have only an episodic economic future. But with a well-developed infrastructure of services the city becomes an attractive locale for a wide variety of export industries. As older exporters fade, new exporters take their place and the community continues to prosper. It is in the city's interest, therefore, to help sustain a high-quality local infrastructure generally attractive to all commerce and industry.

I have no way of evaluating the merits of these contrasting economic arguments. What is important in this context is that both see exports as being of great importance to the well-being of a city. One view suggests a need for direct support of the export industry; the other suggests a need only for maintaining a service infrastructure, allowing the market to determine which particular export industry locates in the community. Either one could be the more correct diagnosis for a particular community, at least in the short run. Yet both recognize that the future of the city depends upon exporting local products. When a city is able to export its products, service industries prosper, labor is in greater demand, wages increase, promotional opportunities widen, land values rise, tax revenues increase, city services can be improved, donations to charitable organizations become more generous, and the social and cultural life of the city is enhanced.

To export successfully, cities must make efficient use of the three main factors of production: land, labor, and capital.[10]

Land

Land is the factor of production that cities control. Yet land is the factor to which cities are bound. It is the fact that cities are spatially defined units whose boundaries seldom change that gives permanence to their interests. City residents come and go, are born and die, and change their tastes and preferences. But the city remains wedded to the land area with which it is blessed (or cursed). And unless it can alter that land area, through annexation or consolidation, it is the long-range value of that land which the city must secure—and which gives a good approximation of how well it is achieving its interests.

Land is an economic resource. Production cannot occur except within some spatial location. And because land varies in its economic potential, so do the economic futures of cities. Historically, the most important variable affecting urban growth has been an area's relationship to land and water routes.

On the eastern coast of the United States, all the great cities had natural harbors that facilitated commercial relations with Europe and other coastal communities. Inland, the great industrial cities all were located on either the Great Lakes or the Ohio River–Mississippi River system. The cities of the West, as Elazar has shown, prospered according to their proximity to East-West trade flows.[11] Denver became the predominant city of the mountain states because it sat at the crossroads of land routes through the Rocky Mountains. Duluth, Minnesota, had only limited potential, even with its Great Lakes location, because it lay north of all major routes to the West.

Access to waterways and other trade routes is not the only way a city's life is structured by its location. Its climate determines the cost and desirability of habitation; its soil affects food production in the surrounding area; its terrain affects drainage, rates of air pollution, and scenic beauty. Of course, the qualities of landscape do not permanently fix a city's fate—it is the intersection of that land and location with the larger national and world economy that is critical. For example, cities controlling access to waterways by straddling natural harbors at one time monopolized the most valuable land in the region, and from that position they dominated their hinterland. But since land and air transport have begun to supplant, not just supplement, water transport, the dominance of these once favored cities has rapidly diminished.

Although the economic future of a city is very much influenced by external forces affecting the value of its land, the fact that a city has control over the use of its land gives it some capacity for influencing that future. Although there are constitutional limits to its authority, the discretion available to a local government in determining land use remains the greatest arena for the exercise of local autonomy. Cities can plan the use of local space; cities have the power of eminent domain; through zoning laws cities can restrict all sorts of land uses; and cities can regulate the size, content, and purpose of buildings constructed within their boundaries. Moreover, cities can provide public services in such a way as to encourage certain kinds of land use. Sewers, gas lines, roads, bridges, tunnels, playgrounds, schools, and parks all impinge on the use of land in the surrounding area. Urban politics is above all the politics of land use, and it is easy to see why. Land is the factor of production over which cities exercise the greatest control.

Labor

To its land area the city must attract not only capital but productive labor. Yet local governments in the United States are very limited in their capacities to control the flow of these factors. Lacking the more direct controls of nation-states, they are all the more constrained to pursue their economic interests in those areas where they do exercise authority.

Labor is an obvious case in point. Since nation-states control migration across their boundaries, the industrially more advanced have formally legislated that only limited numbers of outsiders—for example, relatives of citizens or those with skills needed by the host country—can enter. In a world where it is economically feasible for great masses of the population to migrate long distances, this kind of restrictive legislation seems essential for keeping the nation's social and economic integrity intact. Certainly, the wage levels and welfare assistance programs characteristic of advanced industrial societies could not be sustained were transnational migration unencumbered.

Unlike nation-states, cities cannot control movement across their boundaries. They no longer have walls, guarded and defended by their inhabitants. And as Weber correctly noted, without walls cities no longer have the independence to make significant choices in the way medieval cities once did.[12] It is true that local governments often try to keep vagrants, bums, paupers, and racial minorities out of their territory. They are harassed, arrested, thrown out of town, and generally discriminated against. But in most of these cases local governments act unconstitutionally, and even this illegal use of the police power does not control migration very efficiently.

Although limited in its powers, the city seeks to obtain an appropriately skilled labor force at wages lower than its competitors so that it can profitably export commodities. In larger cities a diverse work force is desirable. The service industry, which provides the infrastructure for exporters, recruits large numbers of unskilled workers, and many manufacturing industries need only semiskilled workers. When shortages in these skill levels appear, cities may assist industry in advertising the work and living opportunities of the region. In the nineteenth century when unskilled labor was in short supply, frontier cities made extravagant claims to gain a competitive edge in the supply of ordinary labor.

Certain sparsely populated areas, such as Alaska, occasionally advertise for unskilled labor even today. However, competition among most cities is now for highly skilled workers and especially for professional and managerial talent. In a less than full-employment economy, most communities have a surplus of semiskilled and unskilled labor. Increases in the supply of unskilled workers increase the cost of the community's social services. Since national wage laws preclude a decline in wages below a certain minimum, the increases in the cost of social services are seldom offset by lower wages for unskilled labor in those areas where the unemployed concentrate. But even with high levels of unemployment, there remains a shortage of highly skilled technicians and various types of white collar workers. Where shortages develop, the prices these workers can command in the labor market may climb to a level where local exports are no longer competitive with goods produced elsewhere. The economic health of a community is therefore importantly affected by the availability of professional and managerial talent and of highly skilled technicians.

When successfully pursuing their economic interests, cities develop a set of policies that will attract the more skilled and white collar workers without at the same time attracting unemployables. Of course, there are limits on the number of things cities can do. In contrast to nation-states they cannot simply forbid entry to all but the highly talented whose skills they desire. But through zoning laws they can ensure that adequate land is available for middle-class residences. They can provide parks, recreation areas, and good-quality schools in areas where the economically most productive live. They can keep the cost of social services, little utilized by the middle class, to a minimum, thereby keeping local taxes relatively low. In general, they can try to ensure that the benefits of public service outweigh their costs to those highly skilled workers, managers, and professionals who are vital for sustaining the community's economic growth.

Capital

Capital is the second factor of production that must be attracted to an economically productive territory. Accordingly, nation-states place powerful controls on the flow of capital across their boundaries. Many nations strictly regulate the amount of national currency that can be taken out of the country. They place quotas and tariffs on imported goods. They regulate the rate at which national currency can be exchanged with foreign currency. They regulate the money supply, increasing interest rates when growth is too rapid, lowering interest rates when growth slows down. Debt financing also allows a nation-state to undertake capital expenditures and to encourage growth in the private market. At present the powers of nation-states to control capital flow are being used more sparingly and new supranational institutions are developing in their place. Market forces now seem more powerful than official policies in establishing rates of currency exchange among major industrial societies. Tariffs and other restrictions on trade are subject to retaliation by other countries, and so they must be used sparingly. The economies of industrialized nations are becoming so interdependent that significant changes in the international political economy seem imminent, signaled by numerous international conferences to determine worldwide growth rates, rates of inflation, and levels of unemployment. If these trends continue, nation-states may come to look increasingly like local governments.

But these developments at the national level have only begun to emerge. At the local level in the United States, cities are much less able to control capital flows. In the first place, the Constitution has been interpreted to mean that states cannot hinder the free flow of goods and monies across their boundaries. And what is true of states is true of their subsidiary jurisdictions as well. In the second place, states and localities cannot regulate the money supply. If unemployment is low, they cannot stimulate the economy by increasing the monetary flow. If inflationary pressures adversely affect their competitive edge in the export market, localities can neither restrict the money supply nor directly control prices and wages. All of these powers are reserved for national governments. In the third place, local governments cannot spend more than they receive in tax revenues without damaging their credit or even running the risk of bankruptcy. Pump priming, sometimes a national disease, is certainly a national prerogative.

Local governments are left with a number of devices for enticing capital into the area. They can minimize their tax on capital and on profits from capital investment. They can reduce the costs of capital investment by providing low-cost public utilities, such as roads, sewers, lights, and police and fire protection. They can even offer public land free of charge or at greatly reduced prices to those investors they are particularly anxious to attract. They can provide a context for business operations free of undue harassment or regulation. For example, they can ignore various external costs of production, such as air pollution, water pollution, and the despoliation of trees, grass, and other features of the landscape. Finally, they can discourage labor from unionizing so as to keep industrial labor costs competitive.

This does not mean it behooves cities to allow any and all profit-maximizing action on the part of an industrial plant. Insofar as the city desires diversified economic growth, no single company can be allowed to pursue policies that seriously detract from the area's overall attractiveness to capital or productive labor. Taxes cannot be so low that government fails to supply residents with as attractive a package of services as can be found in competitive jurisdictions. Regulation of any particular industry cannot fall so far below nationwide standards that other industries must bear external costs not encountered in other places. The city's interest in attracting capital does not mean utter subservience to any particular corporation, but a sensitivity to the need for establishing an overall favorable climate.

In sum, cities, like private firms, compete with one another so as to maximize their economic position. To achieve this objective, the city must use the resources its land area provides by attracting as much capital and as high a quality labor force as is possible. Like a private firm, the city must entice labor and capital resources by offering appropriate inducements. Unlike the nation-state, the American city does not have regulatory powers to control labor and capital flows. The lack thereof sharply limits what cities can do to control their economic development, but at the same time the attempt by cities to maximize their interests within these limits shapes policy choice.

Local Government and the Interests of Cities

Local government leaders are likely to be sensitive to the economic interests of their communities. First, economic prosperity is necessary for protecting the fiscal base of a local government. In the United States, taxes on local sources and charges for local services remain important components of local government revenues. Although transfers of revenue to local units from the federal and state governments increased throughout the postwar period, as late as 1975–76 local governments still were raising almost 59 percent of their own revenue.[13] Raising revenue from one's own economic resources requires continuing local economic prosperity. Second, good government is good politics. By pursuing policies which contribute to the economic prosperity of the local community, the local politician selects policies that redound to his own political advantage. Local politicians, eager for relief from the cross-pressures of local politics, assiduously promote goals that have widespread benefits. And few policies are more popular than economic growth and prosperity. Third, and most important, local officials usually have a sense of community responsibility. They know that, unless the economic well-being of the community can be maintained, local business will suffer, workers will lose employment opportunities, cultural life will decline, and city land values will fall. To avoid such a dismal future, public officials try to develop policies that assist the prosperity of their community—or, at the very least, that do not seriously detract from it. Quite apart from any effects of economic prosperity on government revenues or local voting behavior, it is quite reasonable to posit that local governments are primarily interested in maintaining the economic vitality of the area for which they are responsible.

Accordingly, governments can be expected to attempt to maximize this particular goal—within the numerous environmental constraints with which they must contend. As policy alternatives are proposed, each is evaluated according to how well it will help to achieve this objective. Although information is imperfect and local governments cannot be expected to select the one best alternative on every occasion, policy choices over time will be limited to those few which can plausibly be shown to be conducive to the community's economic prosperity. Internal disputes and disagreements may affect policy on the margins, but the major contours of local revenue policy will be determined by this strategic objective.

Bifurcation of Economic and Status Interests

Thus far I have ignored the possibility that economic and status objectives may bifurcate. Indeed, in larger American cities status is too dependent upon economic prosperity for "balanced" community development to be sacrificed to residential exclusiveness. But in suburban areas governmental jurisdictions do not coincide with the boundaries of economic exchange, and as a result, many communities hope to externalize the negative effects of commerce and industry by zoning these productive activities outside their own jurisdiction. Where this is done successfully, residential status can be enhanced without endangering community access to the marketplace. Thus, bifurcation of community objectives is particularly likely in suburban areas, where a locality can emphasize either market or status objectives.

The possibility for bifurcation between economic and status objectives has given rise to the construction of typologies of communities according to the goals they seem to pursue. Williams and Adrian were the first to distinguish between those communities that took as their primary concern the promotion of economic growth and those concerned about providing life's amenities.[14] More recently, Eulau and Prewitt have noted the importance of two kinds of policies: those that promote economic development ("planning, zoning urban renewal, attract business, etc.") and those that extend urban amenities ("library, civic center, recreation, etc.").[15]

Since these two kinds of objectives were the only ones either study found prevailing in local communities, their findings are quite consistent with my argument that cities pursue their economic, social, and political interests. Although both studies constructed their typologies inductively while my elaboration of city interests is deduced from what is known more generally about stratification systems, their identification of community purposes is very similar to the ones I have outlined. Admittedly, neither study found communities whose major objective seemed to be the achievement of greater political power in the larger governmental system. Perhaps there are not yet enough resources in the public sector to make that a dominating objective for many cities. And it must also be conceded that Williams and Adrian identified communities which seemed not to have either economic or status objectives. Instead, they only maintained traditional services and/or arbitrated group conflict. But these activities are not substantive objectives the community can maximize; they are only the residual functions that seem to be a community objective when government is too inefficient to pursue vigorously its economic or status interests. No wonder Eulau and Prewitt found little use for these categories in their research.

Significantly, neither of the two studies found a need in their typology for communities whose goals was the enhancement of the material well-being of workers, the poor, or minorities. Neither in word nor deed were local governments so committed to this objective that it seemed to dominate policy choice in a broad range of policy sectors. On the contrary, when councilmen in the San Francisco Bay area were asked the improvements most needed for their community, the most frequent responses were parks and recreation areas, urban renewal, downtown development, and a new civic center.[16] Low-income housing and welfare assistance to the poor simply did not appear on their agenda. And even in working-class communities studied by Williams and Adrian local governments seemed interested only in providing minimum services, not in redistributing resources from the more affluent to the poor.

Also, there is evidence in both studies that economic interests, which shall be the focus of the remainder of this analysis, were more important than status interests in at least the larger cities. City size is one of the most important variables in the Eulau and Prewitt study. Using a range of indicators, they present considerable evidence that the larger the city, the more likely the city council to prefer "balanced" economic growth to exclusive concern with the residential quality of its community.[17] Williams and Adrian, moreover, report that

the rhetoric of boosterism takes up a disproportionate part of the discussions concerning city policies. The "attracting industry" and "favorable climate for business" arguments are introduced at nearly every juncture and in connection with every decision, no matter how far-fetched the connection.[18]

All in all, it seems that empirical efforts to identify community objectives do not reach conclusions that differ radically from the definition of city interests I have proposed. Although in some smaller communities the emphasis is more on status than on economic interests, it is only a modest—and, as we shall see, most useful—simplification to state that cities are above all concerned with their economic well-being.

Fiscal Policy

A city's economic well-being can be significantly affected by its taxation and expenditure policies. Although monetary policy, international trade agreements, and other crucial questions are the exclusive province of national policymakers, economists have shown that decisions taken locally can have their own economic consequences. When government increases its expenditures on desired public services, such as schools, property value is enhanced.[19] Conversely, as heavier taxes are laid on local property, land values decline by the capitalized value of the tax increase.[20] If state governments provide relatively substantial payments to welfare recipients, persons in need of such assistance will migrate into the area.[21] And if governments restrict entry of low-income residents into their communities, land values rise.[22] Although research on these questions is only beginning, a quite consistent set of findings which affirm the connectedness between the local polity and the local economy is beginning to emerge.

Tiebout provides a theoretical explanation for such a connectedness.[23] He notes that residents can migrate freely from one community to another and, as a consequence, they will calculate the impact of local government decisions in choosing their community of residence. According to Tiebout, the free migration of residents permits a Pareto-optimal distribution of public goods produced by local governments. What residents prefer will match what governments produce, because migration will continue until each resident finds the package of taxes and services he most desires. Tiebout was forced to posit highly restrictive assumptions (all residents depend on dividends for a livelihood, migration costs are nil, and so on) to derive his Pareto-optimal equilibrium, but no such restrictive assumptions are necessary to derive the simpler, if less satisfying, conclusion that individuals consider the relative costs and benefits of government services in choosing places of residence.

If migrants calculate the costs and benefits of public services, local governments, to ensure local prosperity, must anticipate the preferences of potential migrants. Governments which use their revenue policies to maximize their economic prosperity operate as efficiently as Tiebout suggests. They provide each resident with exactly that package of taxes and benefits which he most prefers. Each resident receives desired benefits in return for the taxes he pays, and (necessarily) each resident pays in taxes an amount that covers the average cost of producing the benefits received. In this ideal Tiebout world, the government achieves a revenue policy that maximizes the community's economic welfare. Because each resident is getting what he wants from government in return for the taxes he pays, government revenue policy provides the maximum inducement for living and working within the community.

Unfortunately, it is almost certain that no local government ever achieves the ideal Tiebout hypothesizes. First, government services are necessarily similar for large numbers of residents. Roads, streets, parks, schools, and police protection cannot be varied infinitely to suit each person's taste. Because many government services have the property of being at least to some degree a collective good, what is provided to one is provided to many, if not to all. Yet the bundle of public services is so varied that it is doubtful that any two households have exactly the same preferences. Even among those with identical incomes living in the same homogeneous suburb, there are significant differentials in individual needs and preferences. Households with children want higher quality schools; the elderly want more convenient public transport; the recreation-minded want more park and sports facilities; the fearful want more police and fire protection; and opinion varies on the level at which local roads need to be maintained. Not only the amount but the quality of a public good may be in dispute. Should schools provide sex education? Should they concentrate on college preparation or vocational training? Should classrooms be highly structured, or should they allow children considerable discretion in the use of their time? Homogeneity in the public service preferences of local residents can be approximated only to a greater or lesser degree; complete agreement is implausible even under the most favorable circumstances.

Second, public services cannot be provided efficiently because no pricing mechanism pinpoints misallocations of public resources. Even if all residents of a community had identical preferences, the services they received would not be provided at the lowest possible cost. Within the community the local government monopolizes the distribution of public services. To obtain a comparable bundle of services at a lower price, residents would have to bear both the search costs of finding the more efficient community and the costs of migration. Residents will tolerate inefficiencies that do not exceed these moving costs. Because potential migration from one monopolistically controlled system of public services to another provides only the roughest sort of pricing mechanism, city governments must use bureaucratic techniques of hierarchical supervision and control to limit the costs of production. As is well established by organizational theorists, these are a poor substitute for a price mechanism.[24]

Third, local governments cannot charge consumers according to the amount of a public service each consumes. Because residents of a community have differing tastes and needs, they consume public services differentially. And, in most cases, local governments are unable to allocate the costs among residents in such a way that each pays according to the benefits he receives. Constitutional limitations are probably the most severe obstacle to the strict application of this principle to local revenue policies. Taxation must be equitable. Constitutionally, taxation of equal incomes must be equal, taxation of equally valued property must be equal, and taxation of the same product at the same price must be equal. As a result, it is expected that two houses of similar size and value are to be taxed equally whether or not one contains a family of six, consuming the educational and recreational resources of the community, and the other shelters an elderly widow. Also, cities are constitutionally or practically constrained from charging tolls to limit access to their services. Schools cannot charge tuition; access to streets and sidewalks is free and open to the general public; and police and fire protection is not conditioned upon payment for the service. Since these charges cannot be related to use, some residents subsidize the benefits received by others.

Because of these constraints, it is unlikely that any local government system will closely approximate Tiebout's ideal world, where, in the aggregate, government services match citizen preferences. And it is just as unlikely that any local government ever maximizes the relative attractiveness of its land areas to potential migrants. Instead, the marginal cost of local public services is always greater than the perceived marginal benefits of the average taxpayer, whose marginal benefit/tax ratio is consequently always less than 1.0. Some portion of the marginal tax imposed on him will always be perceived as a surcharge imposed as a cost of living in that particular community.

Although this average taxpayer always receives less from the community in benefits than he contributes in taxes, at the same time he never receives from a local government all the services that he is willing to purchase. In most contexts, local governments cannot service any one person in a community without at the same time servicing others. If each taxpayer's particular demands were supplied, many others would receive the same service, even though they had little economic demand for it. The aggregate of public services supplied would far exceed the aggregate demand at that price. The benefit/tax ratio would fall precipitously. Consequently, the supply of government services to the average taxpayer is always less than his economic demand for them. His supply/demand ratio is always less than 1.0.

The overall level of government expenditures in a local community is a function of the conjoint effects of these benefit/tax and supply/demand ratios, as diagrammed in figure 2.1. Expenditures continue until the ratio of benefits to taxes for the average taxpayer equals his supply/demand ratio. In Tiebout's world these two ratios are unitary, as every taxpayer obtains the services he demands and at the same time receives benefits equivalent to the taxes paid. In a world of imperfect information and imperfect mobility, the intersection of these two ratios is at a point well below unity, but local governments nonetheless are constrained to offer a level of service at approximately the point where these two ratios meet. To depart drastically from this equilibrium point would endanger the economic well-being of the community. It is also in the interest of the community to shift the point of equilibrium to as high a level as possible. For example, if the equilibrium in figure 2.1 can be shifted upward from E_1 to E_2, then taxpayers will have more of their demands supplied at lower cost to themselves. When that is achieved, the community becomes a more desirable locale, and productive labor and capital are attracted to the area.

Certain words in this section require emphasis and elaboration. First, by average taxpayer I do not mean the ordinary property owner, much less the median voter or the person with the median

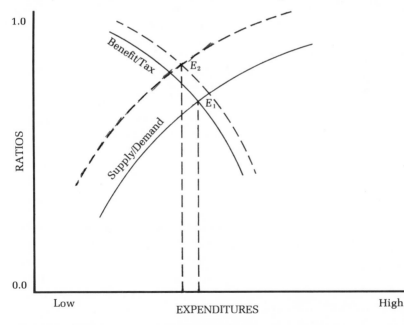

Figure 2.1. Ratios of the supply of local public goods to effective demand and of the benefits received from local public goods to taxes paid by average taxpayer at varying expenditure levels.

income in the city. By average taxpayer I mean the entity—person, business, corporation, and so on—for whom the benefit/tax ratio falls at the mean. One-half of all taxes paid receive a higher return in benefits, while another half receive less. In calculating this mean, each taxpayer is weighted in proportion to the amount in taxes that he pays. If one person or entity pays one-half of the taxes in a certain community and if his benefit/tax ratio is less than that of the other taxpayers (as it probably would be), then he is the average taxpayer. It is the contribution to the fiscal base of local government that is crucial, not the number of votes the entity casts in local elections. A city concerned about its economic interests does not consider each taxpayer's benefit/tax ratio equally but in proportion to his contribution to the local coffer.

Second, it is the *marginal* benefits of local government as related to the *marginal* tax costs whose ratio is always less than 1.0 for the average taxpayer. It might very well be that he values the sum total of all government services—both national and local—to an amount equal to what he pays in taxes. For example, most people place such a high price on public order and safety, on the preservation of basic liberties, and on defense of the country against foreign aggression that very large sums, far surpassing the cost of actually supplying these services, could probably be voluntarily secured from them by a monopolist—so long as the monopolist had the capacity to withdraw the services from those who failed to pay. But even though the police powers of local government may be highly valued, a city is not in a monopoly position where it can secure contributions from taxpayers far out of proportion to the cost of actually supplying police services. Other localities can attract productive elements away from a city by offering the same police protection for less. And where competition limits the price that a supplier of a service can charge, there is a tendency for the price to fall to a point where it simply covers the cost of production. For reasons stated above, that equilibrium point is never reached in the case of local government services, but a city can enhance its economic position by pursuing the objective nonetheless.

Finally, in considering the practical implications of this rather abstract discussion, one must recognize that local governments consider—as best they can—both the direct and indirect incidence of the taxes they levy. Although cities must be concerned that benefits received match taxes paid, their governments are sensible enough to consider the productive forces of the city that generate the earnings out of which taxes are paid. Accordingly, they take into account not only the direct sources of taxes paid but indirect contributors as well. Admittedly, economists cannot determine with precision the final incidence of taxes, and local governments have no private knowledge that enables them to consider the totality of the economic effects their decisions have. But this does not prevent practical policymakers from making reasonable inferences and estimates. Consider, for example, the industrial firm which pays nothing in local taxes (perhaps because a special agreement to this effect was signed prior to the firm's arrival in the city) but which generates a sizable proportion of the local payroll. A government concerned about maintaining its local economy will be as interested in providing services needed by the firm as it is in providing services to workers employed by the firm. In effect local government recognizes that the firm pays taxes indirectly; workers must be paid more in wages to cover the taxes they pay for local services. In short, local governments consider both the direct and indirect incidence of the taxes they levy.

Conclusions: Efficiency versus Equality

Efficiency in local government promotes city interests. By efficiency I am referring to a state in which no person can be made better off without some other person being made worse off. In Tiebout's world local governments operate with perfect efficiency such that everyone receives the services for which he has an economic demand and no one receives services unless he has such a demand. At the same time the price paid equals the lowest average cost of producing the service. No one can be made better off without someone else bearing the cost.

Although this utopia is quite beyond the capacity of local governments, the closer any locality moves toward this ideal match between taxes and services, the more attractive a setting it is for residents, and the more valuable its land becomes. It is thus in the interest of local governments to oprate as efficiently—in this Pareto-optimal sense of the word—as possible.

Operating efficiently hardly means operating so as to enhance equality. As many critics of Pareto's definition of efficiency have pointed out, an efficient distribution of resources, as Pareto defines it, is incompatible with gross inequalities. One cannot redistribute wealth without making some worse off at the same time others are made better off. If a society has great inequalities in the beginning, it does not reduce these inequalities merely by increasing its efficiency. Consequently, the pursuit of a city's economic interests, which requires an efficient provision of local services, makes no allowance for the care of the needy and unfortunate members of the society. Indeed, the competition among local communities all but precludes a concern for redistribution.

Recall the finding that the benefit/tax ratio for the average taxpayer is always less than 1.0. The person who pays the mean dollar in taxes always receives less in benefits than he pays in taxes (while at the same time having unsatisfied demands for services). Then consider the fact that this benefit/tax ratio declines as the amount of redistributive activity by local governments increases. Since the person or entity that pays the mean dollar in taxes is likely to be better off than the low-income residents of the community, increased redistribution from the richer to the poorer implies a reduction in the services the person paying the mean tax dollar receives as a proportion of the amount he pays in taxes. From the point of view of this average taxpayer, the local government service-delivery system appears highly inefficient, however ably the redistributive service-delivery system is run. If other communities provide fewer services to the needy, he will see an economic advantage in migrating. Over time, this adversely affects the economic well-being of the community with a mind to redistribute.

2

City Limits and
Public Policy

_____

Three

The Three Policy Arenas

Since cities have an interest in policies that enhance their economic well-being, local public policies are treated differentially, depending upon their impact on the economic vitality of the community. Three types of public policies can be logically deduced from this fact.[1] *Developmental* policies enhance the economic position of the city. *Redistributive* policies benefit low-income residents but at the same time negatively affect the local economy. *Allocational* policies are more or less neutral in their economic effects. These definitions are very general and require further elaboration and specification. In doing so, we shall discover that just as policies have varying economic consequences, so they are produced by different economic and political conditions. For one thing, for each policy type different factors affect the level of fiscal support state and local governments can and will provide. Also, the level of government responsible for financing a policy varies with the policy arena. Finally, the kinds of politics associated with each type of policy are highly variable. To say more would anticipate much of the remainder of my argument. In this chapter we shall be content with laying out the three policy arenas and showing how the factors that produce variation in their level of fiscal support vary from one policy arena to the next.

Developmental policies are those local programs which enhance the economic position of a community in its competition with others. They strengthen the local economy, enhance the local tax base, and generate additional resources that can be used for the community's welfare. They are praised by many and opposed only by those few whose partial interests stand in conflict with community interests.

41

Developmental policies enhance the local economy because their positive economic effects are greater than their cost to community residents. The most obvious cost is any increase in taxes the program requires. Other costs may include the opportunity costs of allocating land for the designated purpose. The creation of an industrial park or a shopping center may come at the expense of parkland or residential neighborhoods. Any air, water, or noise pollution associated with the policy is also a cost the local community must bear. But in return for these costs, the community may gain new employment opportunities, increased demand for locally provided services, increased land values, and higher local government revenues.

Developmental policies need not always entail the attraction of business and industry to a community. It may be that the creation of a wildlife preserve will so enhance the attractiveness of surrounding residential property that any opportunity costs involved in allocating land for such a purpose will be more than offset by the increased market value of the adjacent areas. Under some circumstances, improvements in local schools will make an area such an attractive place for families that the increased cost of supplying the service will be more than offset by the increased value residents will place on living in a locale with excellent schools. The same can be said for other local government services.

A convenient way of roughly calculating whether or not a policy is in the interest of a city is to consider whether its benefit/tax ratio is more or less than 1.0, that is, whether the marginal benefits exceed the marginal cost to the average taxpayer. If the average or above average taxpayers (the persons who receive no more than the mean level of marginal benefits from their marginal taxes) find their benefit/tax ratio enhanced by the policy, then they will place a higher value on remaining in the community. Those policies which can be financed out of user charges paid by community residents or taxes levied on users of the service can usually be treated as developmental policies. In these cases the people receiving the service indicate by their behavior that they value the service more than what they must pay to supply it. The fact that toll roads can be financed solely out of costs imposed on drivers indicates that road building of this sort is a developmental policy.

But although a self-financing program is usually a developmental policy, not all developmental policies must be self-financing in a narrow, cost accountant sense of the word. Tax concessions to businesses locating in a community are not literally self-financing, but the economic benefits to the area of their choosing the community as their center for economic activity may be so great that in the long run the program pays for itself. And it is the judgment by local officials that a program will cost the community little or nothing in the long run that is the best indication that a program is a developmental policy.

At the opposite end of the scale are those public policies that are not only unproductive but actually damage the city's economic position. Many kinds of economically harmful policies can be imagined, but most are not sufficiently viable to be serious contenders for the public purse. No serious participant in local politics suggests that every city employee be given a black Cadillac with a full-time chauffeur. Apart from any other consequence, these sorts of policies would bankrupt City Hall. On a smaller scale, of course, regressive policies are tolerated. Through long established political connections, a fire commissioner may be able to retire handsomely in the Caribbean on an extraordinary pension, even though such a concession is a cost to taxpayers, with no apparent compensating benefits. But except for those interested in political corruption, most economically regressive policies have little theoretical relevance.

One kind of unproductive local policy can make a plausible claim for public support, however. Because *redistributive* policies help the needy and unfortunate and because they provide reasonably equal citizen access to public services, such policies are sometimes incorporated into local government practice, even when their economic consequences are pernicious.

I wish to limit my use of the term "redistribution" in two ways. First, I speak only of redistribution from the better off to the less well off segments of the community. Although technically redistribution can refer to any transfer of money, in recent years it has been given the more specific meaning of income transfers from higher to lower income segments of the population. Second, I speak only of those redistributive policies that have negative effects on local economies. In some cases redistribution may be economically beneficial. Whenever a local community needs additional low-income residents to help staff its service industries or more unskilled workers to operate its manufacturing industries, then the city may have an interest in supplying these workers some redistributive services, such as low-cost housing or free medical care. But in the contemporary United States such shortages of unskilled workers are rare, and it must be recognized that in most cases redistributive programs have negative economic effects. While they supply benefits to those least needed by the local economy, they require taxation on those who are most needed. Such a strong claim can be made on behalf of the poor and the needy that, although local governments often shy away from these painfully regressive redistributive policies, they are the one kind of regressive policy cities sometimes undertake.

One can roughly calculate whether a policy is redistributive by estimating whether those who pay for the service in local taxes are recipients of the service. Where there is no overlap at all, a pure case of redistribution is indicated. Welfare assistance to the non-taxpayer is the purest case. More generally, any service which increases the marginal benefit/tax ratio of those above the mean ratio for all taxpayers is a redistributive service. Without the service they already are privileged recipients of local services; with the service their relatively high level of benefits (as compared with taxes paid) is enhanced still more. Because low-income residents usually pay the lowest absolute amounts in taxes (however high their tax rate as a proportion of their income), it is these low-income residents who have relatively high benefit/tax ratios and who are the most likely beneficiaries of redistributive services.

Once again, this is only a rough way of determining whether a policy is regressively redistributive. Under some circumstances the non-taxpayer may be making such significant contributions to the local economy that he indirectly supports a local government's revenue base. A private university excused from paying property taxes but which generates in its environs numerous secondary and service industries that do pay local taxes is a case in point. Yet in most cases redistributive programs which help those whose benefit/tax ratio is already relatively high only make the community a more costly locale for the more productive community members. As desirable as many redistributive programs may be in other ways, they harm the local economy.

Allocational policies are neither developmental nor redistributive. Marginal expenditures for such services have neither much of a positive nor much of a negative effect on the local economy. In a sense, the category only gives a formal classification to the midpoint of the range between the policies that help develop the local economy and those that do the most to redistribute valued things to non-taxpayers. But inasmuch as many local government services fall into this middle ground and local conflicts often focus on allocational policies, the midpoint on the continuum deserves as much consideration as the two extremes.

The housekeeping services of local government are the best example. On the whole, they are neither redistributive nor developmental in character. Instead, all members of the community benefit from the most valued aspects of police and fire protection, and from systematic, community-wide collection of garbage and refuse. These services reduce the likelihood of catastrophic conflagrations, wholesale violations of persons and property, community epidemics, and the use of public spaces as dumps and junkyards. The value each individual places on these services may vary, but all receive important benefits. Moreover, it is likely that marginal allocations for these services are appreciated more by richer taxpayers, who have more resources in need of protection.

These housekeeping services are usually performed with greater effectiveness in areas of a community where tax payments are greater. In the parts of the city where property is more valuable and owners pay more in taxes, one also characteristically finds lower crime rates, less fire damage, and cleaner streets.[2] One cannot claim that these outcomes are simply a function of the overt efforts of city departments. Indeed, police, fire, and sanitation efforts are more concentrated in lower income neighborhoods.[3] The relative peace and quiet of the more wealthy areas is a function of environmental variables influenced more by local government zoning laws than the overt efforts of specific city departments. Nonetheless, a combination of urban government policies produces city services that operate with higher levels of effectiveness in areas of the city where more valuable property is located.

Housekeeping services are thus widely and proportionately allocated. On the one hand, they do not particularly benefit a needy segment of the community at the expense of the average taxpayer. On the other hand, these programs do not pay for themselves in the same way that developmental policies do. Housekeeping policies, administered by local monopolists, operate with less than perfect efficiency, and user charges are seldom levied in ways that rationalize use. As a result, the distribution of benefits is different from the distribution of costs and, above a bare minimum of service, there is little likelihood that the marginal benefits to the average taxpayer are greater than 1.0.

Many of the employment policies of local government are another type of allocational politics. Apart from the levels of wages and benefits, which must be kept competitive with other cities, local governments can pursue a range of policies in the recruitment of personnel without endangering the local economy. One city may prefer to hire in accord with specified professional qualifications, such as length of schooling, scores on civil service examinations, and the like. Other cities prefer to hire political cronies of elected leaders. Some cities prefer strict adherence to merit criteria, while others balance their employment opportunities among the city's racial and ethnic groups. Since these approaches probably have equal chances of finding willing and able recruits, any of them can be followed without having much effect on local efficiency.

Formally, allocational policies are those which provide the average taxpayer with an average ratio of benefits to taxes. Increased expenditures on allocational policies neither increase nor decrease the attractiveness of the city to this average taxpayer (who, of course, is probably well above the average citizen in wealth). This means that the marginal benefit from allocational policies is less than the marginal cost in local taxes. For example, even though the average taxpayer wants police services, he would prefer that the marginal dollar spent on such services be saved. At the same time there is some other allocational policy for which the average taxpayer would be willing to pay an increased tax in order to receive it. But were he provided that service, his benefit/tax ratio would increase and some other individual who did not want that increment would become the average taxpayer, still suffering from a modest benefit/tax ratio. Thus, to the average taxpayer allocational policies always provide too little service at too great a cost.

Variation in the Level of
Public Services Provided

The level of developmental, redistributive, and allocational policies provided by local governments varies from one community to the next. The factors producing this variation differ among policy arenas. To give a formal explanation for these differences, I shall rely on the language of benefit/tax ratios to which the reader has already been introduced. This is necessary to give precision to the presentation of the argument. But the reader should always recognize that local governments are not run by narrow-minded, pettifogging cost accountants who calculate the balance between direct taxes paid and direct services received. It is the more general impact on the local economy which in the end is their greatest concern.

Three factors affect the supply of developmental, redistributive, and allocational policies: fiscal capacity, the cost of supplying the service, and the demand for the service. First, other things being equal, the fiscal capacity of a community affects its level of expenditure. *This is due to the relatively small amount of variation among localities in the rate of taxation of their economic resources.* Because the benefit/tax ratio to the average taxpayer for most government expenditures is less than 1.0, relatively higher local tax rates make a community relatively less attractive. To protect a community's economic resources from net outward flow, tax rates must not be significantly greater in any one community than they are in competing areas. At the same time, communities will spend up to the tax rate levied by communities in competing areas, because the demand for services by the average taxpayer will always be less than the supply (see figure 2.1). Where greater fiscal capacity exists, a higher percentage of these demands can be supplied without imposing a relatively high tax rate. The local community has every incentive to meet service demands until the benefit/tax ratio drops below that of its competitors.

Although numerous exceptions can be found, rates of taxation of economic resources thus tend to become similar among jurisdictions competing in similar markets. For example, if one looks at the total per capita general expenditures by state and local governments, one finds considerable differences among the fifty states. In 1973, the state by state standard deviation in expenditures varied by $229 around a mean of $637, producing a coefficient of variation of 0.36. As can be seen in table 3.1, grants from the federal government reduced these interstate differences only marginally. However, the amount of revenue raised by state and local governments per $1,000 of personal income varied within one standard deviation by only $19 around a mean of $162, yielding a coefficient of variation of only 0.12. In other words, states differed considerably in their expenditures for public services while the rate at which they taxed personal income for these services was fairly similar. Moreover, similarities in rates of taxation cannot be attributed to differential revenue support from the federal government.

As these data show, similarity in rates of taxation produces substantial variation in the level of local government expenditures. At the same tax rate, communities with greater per capita economic resources have greater revenues per capita available for public expenditure. It can thus be hypothesized that differentials in local government expenditure are positively correlated with indicators of a community's fiscal resources, whether these be median family income, per capita income, median property value, sales and gross receipts, or some combination thereof.

Table 3.1: State and Local Finances, 1973

	Mean	Standard Deviation	Coefficient of Variation
General expenditure per capita excluding federal aid	$637	$229	.36
General expenditure per capita including federal aid	$860	$276	.32
General revenue from own resources per $1000 personal income	$162	$19	.12

Source. Maxwell and Aronson 1977, tables A-7 and A-9.
Note. Data are for the fifty states.

Second, the cost of supplying public services affects levels of expenditures among state and local governments. If the labor and materials governments must purchase to supply a good are in relatively short supply, their costs increase and so do levels of public expenditure. At least, this is true for those government services for which the price elasticity of demand is less than 1.0. Although the number of units that will be purchased declines as costs increase, the total expenditure for the service increases.

Third, government expenditures are a function of the economic demand for public services. As demand increases, governments purchase more services and expenditures increase. These relationships seem obvious and straightforward, but it is to be remembered that the concept of demand is used in the sense employed in a market analysis. Unlike most studies of public policy, demand here is not equated with the preferences of the median voter. It is the demands of the potentially migratory taxpayer which are critical. Preferences become demands only to the extent that the individual is willing and able to pay for the service desired. Resident preferences are considered demands only in proportion to the level of taxes they pay (or, more generally, the amount they contribute to the economic vitality of the community). One does not therefore expect to find local government responsiveness to each and every resident or voter in the community. It is the concerns of the above average taxpayer that are given the greatest weight.

How these three factors—fiscal capacity, supply, and demand— vary with the level of expenditures depends on the type of public policy in question (see table 3.2). In the case of redistributive policies, the relationship between fiscal capacity and expenditure levels is strong. Because the beneficiaries of the policy are different from the taxpayers, any increase in the tax rate for redistributive services is likely to have particularly harmful economic consequences. Consequently, tax rates financing redistributive policies must be much the same from one community to another, and variations in fiscal capacity will determine much of the variation in expenditure. Measures of the "need" for redistributive policies, on the other hand,

Table 3.2: Hypothesized Determinants of
Local Government Expenditure

| Type of Policy | Determinants of Expenditure | | | |
	Fiscal Capacity	Demand	Supply	Need
Redistributive	High	. . .	Low	Low or negative
Allocational	Moderate	Moderate	Moderate	. . .
Developmental	Low	High	Moderate	. . .

will be weakly correlated with expenditures. Because the need for redistributive policies is unlikely to be felt by taxpaying residents of the community, there is no way for the need to become translated into effective demand. Similarly, one does not hypothesize a strong relationship between the cost of supplying a service and expenditure levels. Because the benefit/tax ratio is low, redistributive policies are the one type of local government service for which demand elasticity is probably equal to 1.0. As costs of the service increase, the supply of the service will decrease by a comparable amount so that overall expenditures will remain the same.

Exactly opposite patterns of correlation are expected in the case of developmental policies. Because the marginal benefit/tax ratio for these services is high and the perceived benefits may even exceed costs, fiscal capacity is not likely to have a significant effect on expenditure levels. Even those communities with relatively low fiscal capacities will find it in their interest to spend money on programs that help develop that fiscal base. Measures of demand, on the other hand, will be strongly correlated with expenditures. A community that benefits from the tourist trade will spend more on parks and recreational programs because there is a demand for the service. The costs incurred by the local government are offset by the increase in the tourist trade. Supply variables can also be expected to affect expenditures, as the demand elasticity for such policies is likely to be less than 1.0. To take the tourist trade example once again, communities will probably provide fewer recreational services as their costs increase, but the service decline will probably be less than the cost increase, thereby producing higher overall expenditure levels.

Allocational policies fall somewhere in between these polar extremes. Because the benefit/tax ratio is less than 1.0, fiscal capacity will affect the level at which services are provided. Communities with weak fiscal capacities cannot afford to levy much heavier taxes simply to provide higher levels of allocational services. On the other hand, economic demand and the cost of supplying the service will also affect expenditure levels. Not only will service provision be greater where taxpayers perceive greater needs, but since demand is less price elastic than in the redistributive arena, increases in the cost of supplying the service are not fully offset by decreases in the amount of service provided. As policemen cost more, fewer policemen are hired; nevertheless, overall expenditure levels still increase.

In sum, different policies have different effects on a city's economic interests, and therefore the level at which they are provided is determined by different economic factors. The amount of financial support for developmental policies, which promote a city's economic growth, is determined by the economic demand for such policies. Cities that need more industry will give tax concessions to in-migrating businesses. Cities that need more tourists will spend more on recreational services. Cities that are more geographically dispersed will spend more on streets and highways. These needs are satisfied because they are the equivalent of economic demands in the private market. Satisfaction of the needs by local government enhances the economic welfare of the community and the revenue base of City Hall.

Redistributive policies that weaken the local economy are only provided at a level which the city can afford. A community with a weak fiscal base does not provide a high level of redistributive services, even if many are poor and needy. To do so would require a higher rate of taxation, which would make the community less attractive to commerce, industry, and productive labor, all of which are needed to sustain the local economy. Note that these relationships are exactly the opposite from what one would expect were local policies determined by the politics internal to the city. Where poor people are present in abundance, one would expect to find higher levels of redistribution. But insofar as the presence of the poor weakens a local fiscal base, one must expect to find instead an inverse relationship between poverty and redistributive expenditures.

Allocational policies are neither fish nor fowl. They have little effect on a city's economic growth. The level at which they are provided is a function not just of fiscal capacity but also of economic demand and the cost of supplying the service.

Empirical Differentiation of the Policy Arenas

The connection between the three types of policies and the environmental conditions in which a city finds itself is simple and straightforward. Yet it is not easy to find a way of showing these connections with readily available information about city governments. There are two major types of problems. The most troublesome is finding comparable units of analysis. The word "city" does not mean the same thing in every place. Some "cities" operate a host of public services; other "cities" direct little more than the police and fire departments. Some "cities" raise most of their own revenues; other "cities" get large grants from their state governments. We discussed in chapter 1 the difficulties others have encountered in resolving this problem.

For reasons given in chapter 1, I have concluded that one cannot examine "city" expenditures by themselves. Because state-local relationships are so intertwined, it is necessary to examine the combined expenditures of state and local governments. The comparable units of analysis thus become the fifty state-local government systems in the United States. I treat the combined activities of each state-local system as theoretically comparable to the combined activities of each of the others.[4] Any differences in their expenditure patterns can thus be meaningfully related to the varying economic environments in which they find themselves. Not only does this procedure solve the unit-of-analysis problem, but it has the added advantage of providing a "hard" case against which to test the propositions that have been developed. What has been said about local governments applies with somewhat less force to state governments, which are responsible for a larger land area and therefore somewhat less sensitive to external economic forces than are cities. If the propositions are supported by data collected on the combined expenditures of state and local governments, they almost surely hold for the activities of cities and other local government jurisdictions.

The second problem is that state and local governments do not nicely classify their policies as developmental, redistributive, and allocational. Any attempt to apply this system of classification to those used by governments will necessarily be less precise than one would like. However, the categories by which governmental expenditures are classified in the United States census provide a breakdown which permits some reasonable approximations of the pure distinctions I have outlined. State and local expenditures for welfare and for health and hospitals seem fairly obvious examples of relatively redistributive policies. In general, there is at best only a loose correpondence between the individuals who pay for these services and the individuals who receive them. There may be some question as to the degree to which these policies redistribute benefits across class lines, whether these services really benefit the people they are supposed to help, and whether the primary beneficiaries are the recipients or the employees providing the services. But at the very least, few claim that in these policy areas there is a close correspondence between taxes paid and services received. Additional measures of welfare policy are provided by the average payments made by state and local governments in old age assistance, aid to dependent children, and unemployment benefits. These amounts, which are subject to state and local discretion, give particularly good evidence of a state-local system's commitment to redistributive objectives.

In the United States, developmental policies on which high levels of expenditure are made are more difficult to discern. Most types of services whose beneficiaries can be readily identified and charged accordingly are handled by the private market. But for some government policies there is at least a rough correspondence between taxpayer and beneficiary. The most obvious examples are governmental efforts to improve the transportation and communication systems of the society. In many of these cases the direct consumers of these services pay charges covering their costs. Gasoline taxes and automobile and truck licenses cover the costs of highway building. More generally, states and localities benefit economically from being better connected with the transportation of the larger society. Thus, in the analysis that follows, expenditures for highways constitute the one example of a developmental policy for which data were readily available.

The best examples of allocational policies are expenditures for police and fire services. As stated earlier, these are designed to benefit the community as a whole and have little redistributive impact, and yet their marginal benefit to the average taxpayer is probably substantially less than their marginal cost.

I have classified education separately in the following tables, because the classification of this governmental function is particularly difficult. The problem is a central concern of chapter 5, which documents the significantly greater redistributive impact of education in central cities than in suburban areas. In general, one must conclude that educational services are slightly redistributive—more so than police and fire services, but less so than expenditures on welfare and health. However, educational services are heavily financed at the local level, and they are the single most costly item to the local taxpayer (see chapter 4). Since it is the most expensive of the redistributive programs local governments finance, expenditure levels for even this modestly redistributive program may still be sensitive to a community's fiscal capacity.

Eight independent variables were selected to identify the relative importance of fiscal capacity, demand-supply factors, and non-economic "need." The two indicators of the fiscal capacity of state and local governments were median family income and per capita property value. Three measures of urbanization—the percentage living in metropolitan areas, population density, and the percent employed in nonagricultural occupations—provided indicators of variation in the economic demand for and the cost of supplying several of the dependent variables. Because urbanization is correlated with wage rates and the price of many materials, it may be accepted as a proxy for variations in the cost of supplying government services. At the same time, urbanization provides an indicator of increased demand for allocative policies, such as police and fire protection. Urbanization is also negatively associated with the economic demand for roads and highways. Besides these three measures of urbanization, a more direct indicator of the cost of supplying government services was included—the average wage paid in the manufacturing sector. Finally, two indicators of need for redistribution unable to reflect themselves in economic demand were included—the percent with low incomes and the percent of blacks. A full description of all the independent and dependent variables is given elsewhere.[5]

In the tables that follow I analyze the ways in which these eight factors affect redistributive, allocational, and developmental expenditures. To show that the relationships are robust, I analyze the data in a variety of different ways, introducing different combinations of variables in each table. Some readers may find the presentation, which demands some familiarity with statistical techniques, too technical to warrant detailed scrutiny. The reader who is willing to accept my claim that the information presented generally supports the hypotheses I have offered may move to the conclusions of this chapter. The reader who wishes to peruse the tables that follow should keep in mind the distinction between low and negative correlations. If a coefficient of correlation is low, that means that the two variables are apparently unrelated. In Table 3.3, for example, the low .06 coefficient of correlation between property values and highway expenditures means that highway expenditures were no higher in states with high property values than those with low ones. A negative coefficient, if strong, shows that two variables are inversely related. For example, in the same table, the −.58 between metropolitan population and highway expenditures indicates that per capita expenditures on highways are less in those states where a higher percentage of people live in metropolitan areas. From this inverse, negative correlation, one may infer that more expenditures per capita are provided in rural areas to accommodate the needs of a low-density population.

The simple correlations between these eight independent variables and each of the nine public policies are presented in table 3.3. In general, the pattern of correlation is consistent with the hypotheses. The two indicators of fiscal capacity, median family income and property value, were the variables most strongly associated with expenditures for redistributive and educational purposes. Factors associated with variations in the cost of living for low-income people, including population density and urbanness, were positively but less strongly related to the level of redistribution. Significantly, percent black and percent low income, presumably measures of need and of the political power of needy groups, were *negatively* related to expenditures for redistribution.

Table 3.3: Simple Correlations between Public Policy and Fiscal Capacity, Demand-Supply, and Need

| | Determinants of Expenditure | | | | | | | |
| | Fiscal Capacity | | Demand-Supply | | | | Need but No Demand | |
Type of Policy	Income	Property Values	Density	Metropolitan Population	Nonagri-cultural Employment	Average Wage	% Poor	% Black
Redistributive								
Old age assistance	.50	.44	.12	.20	.32	.26	-.41	-.25
Aid to dependent children	.71	.59	.45	.26	.45	.37	-.76	-.57
Unemployment benefits	.81	.74	.46	.53	.58	.47	-.70	-.33
Welfare expenditures	.59	.58	.53	.47	.56	.22	-.50	-.28
Health and hospitals	.33	.47	.16	.33	.42	.17	-.14	.19
Educational	.74	.54	.11	.22	.35	.70	-.66	-.46
Allocational								
Police	.70	.73	.37	.60	.65	.39	-.50	-.11
Fire	.69	.73	.55	.64	.71	.28	-.56	-.20
Developmental								
Highways	.12	.06	-.35	-.58	-.25	.38	-.15	-.44

Source. Peterson 1979a.

The determinants of expenditure levels for developmental policies differed significantly from those in the redistributive arena. Highway expenditures were not significantly affected by the fiscal capacity of the state-local government system. Instead, they were most strongly affected by indicators of the demand for the service and the cost of supplying it. The density of the population, the percent living in metropolitan areas, and the percent employed in nonagricultural employment were negatively related to highway expenditures, because the economic demand for highways is greater in less densely populated rural parts of the country. Expenditures were also greater where wage levels were higher. Determinants of allocational policies took still a different form. For these policies the fiscal capacity variables and the demand-supply variables were about equally important for explaining expenditure levels.

The simple correlations presented in table 3.3 can be misleading. Apparently strong relationships may turn out to be spurious when controls are introduced; apparently weak relationships may become stronger once variables that impede identification of the relationships are removed. At the same time, the problem of multicollinearity when several highly correlated independent variables are included together in a regression analysis creates other problems of interpretation. After numerous analyses, in which we sought to minimize these contrasting but uniformly exasperating problems, it was discovered that almost as much of the variance in the public policies could be explained by just three variables—income, metropolitan population, and percent black—as by regressions including twice that number. Since the three variables provided one indicator of each of the three theoretically significant concepts that had been elaborated, the simple regression presented in table 3.4 proved to be the best test of the hypotheses.

In this table it becomes even more apparent how important fiscal capacity is for determining redistributive policies. The level of old age assistance, the amount of aid to dependent children, and the level of unemployment benefits are all heavily dependent on the fiscal resources of state and local governments. To a lesser extent, overall expenditures on welfare and on health and hospitals are also dependent on the fiscal resources of the jurisdiction. Educational policies, too, are a function of the state's income level. Even though education is a less redistributive policy than the others, it is heavily financed by local governments and therefore seems especially sensitive to fiscal factors.

It is equally important to note the variable with which redistributive policies are unrelated. Although blacks are one of the

Table 3.4: Income, Metropolitan Population, and Percent Black as Determinants of Public Policy

| | Determinants of Expenditure | | | |
Type of Policy	Fiscal Capacity: Income	Demand-Supply: Metropolitan Population	Need but No Demand: % Black	Multiple R
Redistributive				
Old age assistance	.58**	−.14	−.01	.51
Aid to dependent children	.63**	−.07	−.32**	.78
Unemployment benefits	.71**	.12	−.07	.81
Welfare expenditures	.35*	.29*	−.18	.63
Health and hospitals	.48**	.00	.38**	.48
Educational	.88**	−.29*	−.09	.79
Allocational				
Police	.59**	.24*	.08	.74
Fire	.42**	.40**	−.10	.75
Developmental				
Highways	.67**	−.97**	−.06	.81

Source. Peterson 1979a.
Note. Table gives standardized beta coefficients. Single asterisk (*) indicates T statistic significant at .05 level. Double asterisk (**) indicates T statistic significant at .01 level.

most needy groups in the American population, for most redistributive policies there is but a weak relationship between their percentage of a state's population and the level of benefits received. Indeed, the negative sign in the table indicates that the larger the percentage of blacks, the *less* the redistributive expenditure. Nor does the result change when the percent of low-income people living in the state is substituted for the percent black. As can be seen in table 3.3, both the presence of blacks and the presence of poor people have only negative effects on redistributive expenditures. The only exception to the pattern is the case of health care and hospitals, where the percent black is positively related to redistributive expenditures. In this single case there is a hint that black need for health care actually increases expenditures for the service. The peculiar mechanisms by which this need becomes an effective determinant of locally financed public health care seem worthy of special attention. But if the presence of blacks increases state and local expenditures for health care, it has the opposite effect on welfare policy. Even when controls are introduced for a state's fiscal resources (as in table 3.4), the presence of blacks dampens the amount of support for dependent children.

Allocative policies were, as predicted, responsive to both fiscal capacity and demand-supply factors. In the case of fire expenditures the two seemed roughly equal in importance. On the other hand, police expenditures seemed somewhat more responsive to fiscal capacity than to demand-supply factors. Perhaps by 1970, the year for which these data were compiled, local authorities were beginning to believe that marginal increments in police expenditures yield relatively small marginal benefits to average taxpayers, and therefore more is paid for these services only if fiscal capacity is ample.

Developmental policies proved to be very strongly related to demand-supply factors in just the way that had been anticipated: the more rural the state, the more it spends on highways. Given the greater importance of highways for the economy of the rural state, such policies are certainly sensible. Yet the strong responsiveness of this developmental policy to the demands of the rural economy contrasts sharply with the impotence of the needs of blacks and low-income groups as determinants of redistributive policy. On the other hand, my hypotheses had not anticipated the smaller but nonetheless strong relationship between fiscal capacity and highway expenditure. Apparently, capital must be available before even economically prudent investments can be made.

Skeptics may raise three objections to these findings: (1) the effects of economic demand for services and the cost of supplying them have not been separated; (2) the relationships among the variables may change once the impact of federal assistance is taken into account; and (3) the findings may be heavily influenced by the presence of the southern states in the sample of fifty states. All three possible criticisms gain little support from additional data analysis.

First, consider table 3.5, which makes an attempt at separating out the effects of the economic demand for services and the cost of supplying them. Income remains the indicator of fiscal capacity, and in this table metropolitan population is treated as an indicator of positive demand for allocational services and of negative (because rural areas have greater per capita needs) demand for highway expenditures. I also include the average hourly earnings in manufacturing as a plausible indicator of the cost of supplying public services. The findings confirm the initial propositions in almost all details. Redistributive policies are strictly a function of fiscal capacity; the other variables have little effect. As might be expected, educational policies are influenced both by fiscal capacity and by the cost of supplying this labor-intensive service. Relationships for allocational policies are also much as hypothesized. They are influenced by both fiscal capacity and demand, though the cost of supplying the service is not positively related to expenditure levels. Finally, highway expenditures, the one example of a developmental policy, are most heavily influenced by the higher demand for the

Table 3.5: Income, Metropolitan Population, and Average Wages as Determinants of Public Policy

| Type of Policy | Determinants of Expenditure[a] | | | |
	Fiscal Capacity: Income	Demand: Metropolitan Population	Cost of Supply: Average Wages	Multiple R
Redistributive				
Old age assistance	.71**	−.18	−.16	.52
Aid to dependent children	1.04**	−.30**	−.24*	.76
Unemployment benefits	.82	.06	−.08	.81
Welfare expenditures	.69**	.13	−.27*	.64
Health and hospitals	.25	.20	−.04	.37
Educational	.71**	−.28**	.30**	.82
Allocational				
Police	.57**	.28*	−.05	.74
Fire	.67**	.30**	−.23*	.77
Developmental				
Highways	.47**	−.93**	.31**	.84

Source. Peterson 1979a.
[a]See note to table 3.4.

services in rural areas, but it is quite consistent with our expectations that they are also influenced by cost factors. The one unanticipated finding is that highway expenditures are also a function of fiscal capacity.

Next, consider the impact of federal aid on locally financed expenditures. In doing so, remember that the dependent variable includes only those expenditures not directly financed by federal grants-in-aid. Table 3.6 nonetheless shows that federal aid is strongly associated with welfare and highway expenditures locally. The causal direction of this relationship is not easily discerned. On the one hand, the availability of federal assistance may encourage local spending on these programs. On the other hand, matching formulae produce increased federal commitments whenever local contributions increase. In any case these correlations are not my primary consideration; what is relevant to the argument presented in this chapter is whether federal aid changes the relationships between expenditures and the fiscal capacity, demand, and supply factors. Table 3.6 reveals that the federal impact on these relationships is minimal. Fiscal capacity remains the primary determinant of redistributive expenditures; demand-supply variables remain the most important determinant of developmental expenditures; and allocational policies remain affected by both fiscal capac-

Table 3.6: Federal Aid and Local Expenditure

			Determinants of Expenditure[a]		
Type of Policy	Federal Aid	Fiscal Capacity: Income	Demand-Supply: Metropolitan Population	Need but No Demand: % Black	Multiple R
Redistributive					
Welfare expenditures	.67**	.62**	.02	−.08	.89
Health and hospitals	−.06	.47**	.03	.38**	.49
Educational	.19*	.88**	−.37**	−.14	.81
Allocational					
Police	.15	.54**	.33*	.08	.76
Fire	.12	.38**	.47**	−.10	.76
Developmental					
Highways	.65**	.34**	−.47**	.02	.94

Source. Peterson 1979a.
[a]See note to table 3.4.

ity and demand-supply factors. Except for health policy the needs of minorities have no significant effect on expenditure levels.

Finally, the pattern of relationships changes only slightly when the southern (Confederate) states are deleted from the analysis. We do not know any particularly good reason for deleting the South from the analysis; it is part of the market economy of the United States and is subject to the same external pressures as any other region. Cultural differences are not so great that entirely different patterns of interaction among variables are to be expected. But for those who insist that interstate comparisons take into account the distinctiveness of the South, table 3.7 reports the findings for the thirty-nine nonsouthern states only. When the table is compared with table 3.5, it will be noticed that the beta coefficients in the two tables are very similar. Redistributive policies continue to be mostly a function of a state's fiscal capacity, the developmental policy (highways) remains more a function of the nonmetropolitan character of the state than of any other factor, and allocational policies are still influenced by both fiscal capacity and demand-supply factors.

Review of Related Studies

Although this typology has not previously been used to analyze state and local finance, my findings are consistent with a good deal of previous, largely atheoretical research. Although different statistical techniques are applied and different samples are used for testing the data, and even though methodological problems abound, the results

Table 3.7: Determinants of Public Policy in Non-Southern States

Type of Policy	Determinants of Expenditure[a]				
		Demand-Supply			
	Fiscal Capacity: Income	Metropolitan Population	Nonagricultural Employment	Need but No Demand: % Black	Multiple R
Redistributive					
Old age assistance	.54**	−.17	.09	−.14	.52
Aid to dependent children	.58**	−.01	.01	−.25	.59
Unemployment benefits	.61**	.29	−.07	−.08	.76
Welfare expenditures	.13	.28	.32	−.21	.62
Health and hospitals	.27	−.18	.39*	.18	.55
Educational	.98**	−.28	−.32*	.04	.70
Allocational					
Police	.39*	.13	.24	.09	.72
Fire	.17	.31*	.42**	−.17	.76
Developmental					
Highways	.72**	−1.04**	−.10	−.01	.84

Source. Peterson 1979*a*.
[a]See note to table 3.4.

are surprisingly consistent with mine.[6] Consider first Fisher's study of state and local government expenditures in 1960, which reports beta coefficients for seven independent variables that account for expenditures in a number of policy areas.[7] In table 3.8, I present the specific findings from his analysis which best test the hypotheses we have presented. First, note the moderate correlations between indicators of fiscal capacity and expenditures for redistributive government functions, and then note the weak relationships between expenditures and population density, a measure of the cost of supplying these goods. From an egalitarian perspective, it might be said that education and health care are most badly needed in those states where adult educational attainments are low. Yet since this need is unlikely to be translated into an effective demand for the product, these services are least provided where they are most needed. Second, expenditures for two types of allocational policies—police and fire—are moderately correlated with measures both of fiscal capacity and of demand and supply. Only sanitation expenditures are considerably more a function of fiscal capacity than of demand-supply variables. With this exception, the pattern of allocational expenditures is quite consistent with what I found in my own analysis. Finally, the relationship between economic demand and level of expenditure is particularly strong for the one example of a developmental policy included in the Fisher study. For the most

Table 3.8: Determinants of State and Local Expenditure—the Fisher Study

| | Determinants of Expenditure | | | | |
| | Fiscal Capacity | | Demand-Supply | | Need but No Demand: |
Type of Policy	Income	Tax Yield[a]	Density	Urbanization	Education
Redistributive Health and hospitals	.38	.41	.22	. . .	. . .
Educational Schools	.56	.29	. . .	. . .	. . .
Allocational Police	.40	. . .	.36	.25	.35
Fire	.47	. . .	.34	.36	. . .
Sanitation	.98	. . .	. . .	. . .	.50
Developmental Highways	.30	.31	−.62	−.22	. . .

Source. Fisher 1964, table 2.
Note. Table gives beta coefficients generated by a seven-variable regression analysis. Correlation coefficient not given, if statistically insignificant.
[a]The expected tax yield from a standard pattern of taxation applied to all states.

relevant measure of economic demand—density—the correlation coefficient attains a high negative value of .62. Although some relationship between fiscal capacity and expenditure also exists, it is comparatively modest.

Consider next the relevant findings from Dye's massive study of state and local expenditures given in table 3.9.[8] Dye presents data for only redistributive and developmental policies, and only simple correlation coefficients were reported, making it difficult to identify the separate effects of fiscal capacity and demand-supply variables. But within these limitations the contrasts between redistributive and developmental policies are dramatic. Whereas his indicator of fiscal capacity is always strongly associated with redistributive expenditures, it is not at all correlated with expenditures for highways. Also, it is quite apparent that education, welfare, and health expenditures are not concentrated in states where, from an egalitarian perspective, there might seem to be the greatest need. In fact, the opposite pattern obtains. On the other hand, for the developmental policy arena, there is a strong relationship between need for a policy and the level of expenditures. The less densely populated, less urban areas spend more monies per capita on roads and highways. In this case need becomes translated into effective demand. Dye himself noticed these differences between the redistributive and developmental policy arenas. "The states which spend more on highways," he says, "do so

Table 3.9: Determinants of State and Local Expenditure—the Dye Study

Type of Policy	Determinants of Expenditure: Fiscal Capacity: Income	Demand-Supply: Industrialization	Demand-Supply: Urbanization	Need but No Demand: Education
Redistributive				
Unemployment compensation	.80	.30	.55	.67
Aid to dependent children	.74	.26	.51	.55
General assistance	.76	.39	.58	.43
Health expenditure	.56	.39	.45	.42
Educational	.83	.36	.51	.59
Developmental				
Highways	.02	−.51	−.37	.04

Source. Dye 1966, tables IV-2, V-5, and VI-2.
Note. Table gives simple coefficients of correlation.

by digging deeper into state treasuries and into personal incomes. This is in contrast to the states which spend more on education and welfare; we have found that these states are wealthier and able to spend more on these functions without using a larger share of personal income to do so."[9]

Dye's research has spawned a considerable body of statistically more sophisticated studies on the determinants of state and local expenditures. For the most part, these studies have concentrated on the relative importance of environmental as opposed to political variables, a matter discussed in chapter 1. But the studies do document, if only in passing, the differential characteristics of redistributive and developmental policies. The most extensive documentation exists on redistributive policies, which tend to attract the interest of political scientists. Here the studies convincingly demonstrate (by a variety of statistical techniques) the continuing significance of a state's fiscal base for its commitments to redistribution. Cnudde and McCrone, for example, demonstrate that with but one exception the inclusion of income in a regression analysis significantly reduces the causal power of apparently important political variables.[10] On the other hand, they show that the two demand and supply indicators—urbanization and percentage not employed in agricultural occupations—do not have the same effect on these redistributive policies.[11]

More recently, Tompkins has included both economic and political variables in a complex analysis that attempts to show the political path by which economic variables explain welfare policy.[12] Once again, the one economic variable whose explanatory power persisted throughout his analysis of this redistributive program was the best indicator of the fiscal capacity of the state—its per capita income.

It is a factor analysis by Sharkansky and Hofferbert that produces the most suggestive set of findings.[13] In an attempt to differentiate among different kinds of public policies, they empirically distinguished two factors: "welfare and education" and "highways and natural resources." Without much distortion, the two factors could be just as easily relabeled "redistributive" and "developmental," for the first was heavily loaded with indicators of a state's commitment to high welfare payments to its poor, and the second with indicators of a state's commitment to build roads and develop its natural resources. Of greatest interest in this context are the simple correlations between two environmental factors that the analysts labeled "affluence" and "industrialization."[14] The first is an excellent measure of a state's fiscal capacity, and the second a good inverse measure of the demand for roads and other assets disproportionately utilized in rural areas. The simple correlations among the four items are given in table 3.10. Here we can see that both affluence and industrialization are correlated with both redistributive and developmental policies. However, fiscal capacity is by far the more important correlate of redistributive policies, and the demand factor the more crucial determinant of expenditures for highways and natural resources.

Besides these statewide analyses, examinations of local government finance contain numerous findings that bear upon the distinctions among the three policy arenas that I have drawn. In the appendix many of these studies are reported and discussed. In general the findings are quite consistent with those that have been reported in the text.

Table 3.10: Determinants of State and Local Expenditure—the Sharkansky-Hofferbert study

	Determinants of Expenditure	
Type of Policy	Fiscal Capacity (affluence)	Demand (industrialization)
Redistributive Welfare, education	.69	.37
Productive Highways, natural resources	.43	−.69

Source. Sharkansky and Hofferbert 1969, table 8.
Note. Table gives simple coefficients of correlation (Pearson's R).

Conclusions

Redistributive policies differ from developmental policies, while allocational policies share some of the characteristics of each. Redistributive policies are not easily implemented by local governments. To the extent that they are promulgated, they are located in areas where there appears to be the least need for them. Only where the fiscal base of a community is relatively substantial can policies of benefit to minorities and the poor be implemented. Because the greater tax base in the prosperous communities allows greater fiscal resources to local governments at no greater a rate of taxation, these communities can provide for some degree of redistribution. But in less advantaged communities, where low-income people are probably found in greater abundance, the level of redistributive programs must be held to a bare minimum. The great irony of redistribution at the local level is that it occurs most where the poor are relatively scarce, and vice versa.

Developmental policies are relatively free from these fiscal constraints. Where there is a need for the policy, that need can be met by the less as well as the more prosperous communities. In fulfilling the need, the community enhances its own economic prosperity, thereby strengthening its capacity to provide other services. To some extent the same can be said of allocational policies, and as we shall see in chapter 4 it is in these two arenas that local governments are particularly active.

For all three policy arenas the level of fiscal support is strongly influenced by factors which in the short run are quite beyond the realm of local politics. The strong relationships between expenditures, fiscal capacity, economic demand, and the cost of supplying services are fully apparent even when no attention is paid to the internal political processes of the city. A great deal can be said about local public policy without considering any variations in the recruitment of elected officials, the strength of political parties, the degree of organized group activity, or the level of turnout in local elections. Powerful forces external to the city carry great weight in local policymaking.

I thus find myself in some agreement with Thomas Dye, whose work on public policy has emphasized the environmental rather than the political determinants of public policy.[15] Yet the debate which Dye's work has spawned is artificial, drawing a false dichotomy between the economic and the political, as if events in the complex political economies of our cities and states can be neatly inserted into the arbitrary pigeonholes that divide the social sciences. The decisions taken by local governments in the developmental, redistributive, and allocational arenas are political decisions taken by local government officials. Yet these men and women operate within certain constraints. Uppermost in their minds must be the long-term economic welfare of their community. Although exceptions can be found, in the aggregate they are sane, reasonable, prudent individuals with a sense of the limits on what is possible. To say that environments constrain what these officials do hardly means that politics is absent. Indeed, in part 3 I shall show how politics varies among the developmental, redistributive, and allocational arenas. But first I shall examine the way in which these policy arenas intersect with the structure of American federalism.

Four

Toward a New Theory of Federalism

We no longer have a theory of federalism. The word has become at once so encompassing and so vacuous that any multitiered decision-making system can be entitled a federation. Even relations between central governments and private business firms are now considered to be an element of federalism.[1] And once the concept of federalism is stripped of any distinctive meaning, we no longer have criteria for the appropriate division of governmental responsibilities among layers of government. Federalism is what federalism does. Even more, we have no orienting concepts which can assist us in explaining the patterns of conflict and cooperation among governmental levels.

Traditional theories of federalism took as their point of departure the presence of two sovereigns within a single domain. Each had sovereign power over its citizens with respect to the functions for which it was responsible. Neither had power to interfere with the proper role of the other sovereign. A constitution defined the distribution of powers between the dual sovereigns.

Sovereignty was divided between central state and local republic in order to avoid both internal and external threats to liberty. Small republics limited the possibility of internal despotism, because the citizen knew and understood affairs of state that touched him closely. He could readily be called upon to participate in the defense of his freedoms. The small republic, however, could be easily overcome by external enemies. Only through joining together in a federation with other republics could a common defense be maintained. It was the permeability of the small republic to external forces that justified its relinquishing certain powers to a higher sovereign.[2]

This dual-sovereignty theory of federalism linked governmental structure to political processes and policy outcomes. It provided a rationale for the proper division of powers between the central state and the local republics within the federation. It gave federalism a core definition: the presence of a contractual arrangement—a constitution—that divided powers among the sovereigns. Although changing circumstances would require continuous interpretation of that constitution, the theory provided the necessary conceptual apparatus for doing so.

In the United States, constitutional interpretations after the Civil War expanded the powers allocated to the central government so that the concept of dual sovereignty, somewhat forced even in 1789, became increasingly difficult to sustain. At the close of the Civil War, the "civil rights" amendment to the Constitution decisively asserted the preeminence of the federal prerogative. By 1937 the Supreme Court recognized the interstate effects of almost all commerce, thereby greatly broadening the federal power to regulate business and commercial activities (NLRB v. Jones & Laughlin Corp.). Also, the Court legitimated almost all forms of federal grants-in-aid to states and localities (Steward Machine Co. v. Davis). However valid the dual-sovereignty theory remained in principle, it had little applicability to a country that came to believe that its liberties were as safe, if not safer, in the hands of the central government.

There can be no return to a theory of dual sovereignty; the work by Grodzins and others discussed in chapter 1 has surely laid that notion to rest.[3] But any new theory, like the traditional theory of dual sovereignty, needs to do at least three things. First, it must provide a definition which clarifies the way in which a federal system is distinguished from a decentralized administrative structure. Second, it must use its definition to specify characteristic and appropriate activities of the central and local governments within the federal arrangement. Finally, the theory must account for persistent patterns of conflict and cooperation among levels of government.

Federalism Defined

Federalism is a system of government in which powers are divided between higher and lower levels of government in such a way that both levels have a significant amount of separate and autonomous responsibility for the social and economic welfare of those living within their respective jurisdictions. Within the federation the central government assumes responsibility for relations with foreign countries and determines the exchange relationships among the component units of the federation. The central government may exercise numerous additional powers, but for the system to remain a federation, lower levels of government must have at least two crucial powers.

First, they must have a significant amount of control over the recruitment of their own political and administrative leadership. A local government whose leaders are selected by officials of the central government, or whose recruitment processes are governed by such stringent, centrally determined criteria that the local community has no effective choice, is a local government without power to take responsibility for the well-being of its inhabitants. Second, local governments must have the power to tax their citizens in order to provide the necessary range of government services. A local government totally dependent upon centrally determined grants has very limited responsibility for the determination of the well-being of the local community. It will always be dependent on external sources of funds and, consequently, will always feel a need for more such funds. Because the funds do not come directly from its own resources, the local authority will have to be subjected to strict central-government supervision to ensure that expenditures are directed toward objectives the central government deems necessary and proper. Without independence from central resources, local government loses the capacity to act responsibly on its own behalf, and thus becomes simply an agent of the central government.

Federalism is thus to be distinguished from simple decentralization, which can occur without the granting of either the recruitment or the financial power to lower decision-making levels. For example, although the United States Forest Service grants considerable decision-making autonomy to its field offices, these lower administrative units do not gather their revenues from local sources or act independently in the recruitment of personnel. If the central administrators of the Forest Service or any other department or agency were to lose these two powers to their district offices, the organization could no longer be considered a single government unit. Indeed, these are precisely the circumstances for which the term "federalism" is appropriately reserved and which at one time might have been characterized as dual sovereignty.

Within a federal system the objectives of central and local governments stand in contrast to one another. Local governments are more concerned about operating efficiently in order to protect their economic base, while the domestic policy structure of the national government is more concerned about achieving a balance between developmental and redistributive objectives. These national-local differences are not a function of any particular political movement or any political party or group that happens to be in power at a specific time. Although partisanship and group pressures may aggravate or alleviate the tension between the objectives of national and local governments, the local emphasis on economic productivity and the relatively greater national emphasis on equality are functions of the structural relationship of the two levels within the federal system.

Contrasts between National and Local Governments

The interests of local government require that it emphasize the economic productivity of the community for which it is responsible. Because they are open systems, local governments are particularly sensitive to external changes. To maintain their local economic health, they must maintain a local efficiency that leaves little scope for egalitarian concerns. These limits on local government, which have already been elaborated at length, require that local governments concentrate on developmental as against redistributive objectives.

By comparison, central governments are concerned with more than simply developmental objectives. This is not to say that central governments are uninterested in the economic capacities of their societies. For one thing, they have assumed responsibility for managing the domestic economy through manipulation of fiscal and monetary policies. They also promote economic growth through large-scale capital investments in transportation systems, research and development, and, now more than ever, the management of energy and other natural resources. As a result, many federal programs are as concerned with developmental objectives as are programs carried out by states and localities. But these developmental concerns are often coupled with a continuing concern for achieving some degree of equity in social relationships. Tax, welfare, housing, health, and educational policies of the central government are formulated with questions of equality and redistribution often carrying as much weight as questions of economic stability and growth. The commitment to redistributive objectives is due in part to the availability of powers that curb the impact of the external world environment on the nation's economy. The most important of these powers is the capacity to issue passports and visas. Through the exercise of these powers, almost all highly industrialized countries have in recent years carefully restricted immigration. As ethically disturbing as these laws often are, without them many residents of less advantaged countries would move to the industrialized areas, overwhelming their high-wage economies and swamping their social-welfare systems. The case of the Vietnamese "boat people" provides a particularly poignant example of the dilemma liberal-minded citizens in wealthy countries face.

If control over human migration is vital, national governments also protect their economies from worldwide forces through a host of controls over the movement of capital, goods, and services. Tariffs, quotas, a national currency, control over exchange rates, and the capacity to fund its own indebtedness are among the powers a national government uses to increase its autonomy from external forces. Not all countries can use these devices with equal effectiveness. The United States is particularly fortunate in that foreign exchange amounts to less than 10 percent of its total economic activity. Smaller countries with less self-contained economies have much less scope for autonomous action. But all except the smallest and most dependent—perhaps Hong Kong is the limiting case—have economies less permeable than those for which local governments are responsible.[4]

Where governments in relatively open, pluralist polities have the capacity to redistribute, competition for popular support will provide political parties with an important incentive to advocate the redistribution of income from smaller numbers of high-income groups to the larger numbers having less income. Although the surge for redistribution may be episodic and in response to external impacts such as the major depression of the 1930s and the mobilization of black discontent in the 1960s, competitive politics in industrial societies periodically brings such redistributive pressures to bear on the policies of central governments.

Once a policy has been promulgated, an agency is founded and the administrative staff responsible for implementing the policy develops a loyalty to the substantive mission of the program.[5] As part of the government, the agency has a legitimate claim on a continuing—perhaps slightly increasing—portion of the national budget. To perpetuate its program, the staff solicits the backing of organized elements serviced by its program, which campaign on its behalf in Congress, in other parts of the executive, in the news media, and among the public at large.

National policies are thus loaded with a variable mix of developmental and redistributive objectives. Programs promulgated at a time when the nation is primarily concerned with economic growth are apt to take an almost exclusively developmental turn. Other programs are passed when the political forces favoring redistribution have gained unusual strength. Other governmental policies, formulated under more ambiguous circumstances, may have a more mixed set of orientations. But, on balance, the redistributive orientation is greater at the national than at the local level.

Differences in National and Local Politics

Because the interests of local and national governments diverge, the patterns of public policies promulgated by the two levels of government are different. Most clearly, national and local governments tend to rely on contrasting principles for raising revenue.[6] The national government depends largely on the *ability-to-pay* principle, which legitimates redistribution. It raises most of its general revenues through a progressive income tax, taxes on corporate earnings, and an excise tax on luxury commodities. Local governments, in contrast, rely more on the *benefits-received* principle, which legitimates developmental policies. It specifies that individuals should be taxed in accordance with the level of services they receive. In this way, each individual consumes no more services than he pays for at the price necessary to recover the costs of producing the service. Demands for government services are controlled by a pricing mechanism. If the ability-to-pay principle is defended in the name of equality, the benefits-received principle provides an equally compelling efficiency criterion.

The emphasis local governments place on efficiency at the expense of equality is due not to any antiegalitarian commitments of local policymakers but to the constraints under which local governments operate. In order to protect the economic well-being of the community, the government must maximize the benefit/tax ratio for the above average taxpayer. Indeed, it is especially important that the benefit/tax ratio of those taxpayers who contribute disproportionately to the local economy be comparable to that in competing local areas. If residents are taxed according to their ability to pay, the benefit/tax ratio for higher income residents will be particularly low. On the other hand, if residents are taxed according to the level of services received, the ratio of benefits to taxes for the average taxpayer will increase.

Although constitutional and statutory limitations prevent them from applying the benefits-received principle rigorously, local governments are allowed to levy user charges, which are a close approximation of the benefits-received principle. However, local governments face many obstacles in levying user charges. In many cases, the beneficiaries of government services are difficult to ascertain precisely. In other situations, benefits cannot easily be supplied to some residents without providing them to all. Indeed, these are among the reasons the services became governmental functions in the first place. And even where user charges are practicable, other constraints exist. Courts have ruled that, where charges are levied, the charge must be no more than the amount necessary for providing the service. And what service is being provided is often defined narrowly by the judiciary. Finally, user charges are not deductible against federal income taxes in the same way that property, income, and sales taxes are. Consequently, this particular form of raising local revenues is not subsidized by the federal government in the way local taxes are.

But even though local governments are constrained from applying the benefits-received principle to all revenue raising, they seem to rely on this principle much more than does either the state or the federal government. As can be seen in table 4.1, over the past two decades local governments have relied on user charges to raise over one-fourth of their locally generated total revenues, whereas state governments rely on them for only 12 percent of their revenue and the federal government for only 6 percent. To be sure, many localities fail to exploit user charges fully, and therefore they do not achieve as close an approximation of the benefits-received principle as legal requirements allow. For example, Oakland officials set user charges at levels determined by precedent or by the practice in neighboring communities, and not necessarily at a level which fully recovers costs.[7] And the United States Advisory Commission on Intergovernmental Relations, even while noting that "[t]here has been a steady growth in the fiscal importance of local user charges," has urged their more widespread use as a mechanism "for diversifying local revenue structures when specific beneficiaries of particular government services can be . . . identified."[8] But even if the potential for user charges has not been fully tapped, disproportionate and continuing dependence on such charges by local governments is nonetheless noteworthy.

Even if exploited fully, user charges have only a limited capacity for generating revenues. As a result, most local revenues are not generated by user charges but by a tax. The tax that has become the distinctive prerogative of local governments is the property tax, as can be seen in table 4.1. Admittedly, the increasing dependence of local governments on intergovernmental transfers from the state and federal authorities reduces their dependence on any form of local taxation. And it is true that states no longer depend on the property tax for their revenues. However, as a source of locally generated revenue, the significance of the property tax has abated hardly at all. From 1957 to 1972, the percentage of local revenue raised by the property tax declined by only 4 percent (from 58 to 54 percent).

Table 4.1: Local, State, and Federal Sources of Revenue, Excluding Intergovernmental Transfers (percentage distributions)

Revenue Source	Local				State				Federal			
	1957	1962	1967	1973	1957	1962	1967	1973	1957	1962	1967	1973
User charges[a]	28.3	26.4	26.3	26.1	16.5	12.8	13.9	12.4	7.9	7.0	6.6	5.8
Property tax	58.0	58.3	56.7	54.1	2.3	2.1	1.8	1.4	...	...	...	...
Income tax	.9	1.0	2.1	3.0	7.5	9.1	10.5	16.1	40.9	42.8	38.1	41.7
Corporation tax	...	...	...	...	4.8	4.3	4.8	5.6	24.3	19.3	21.0	14.6
Sales, gross receipts[a]	5.5	5.1	4.8	6.4	45.8	43.7	42.8	40.3	12.8	12.6	9.8	8.0
Death, gift, other	.5	2.0	2.0	1.8	4.3	7.2	6.5	5.4	2.1	2.6	2.4	2.6
Miscellaneous (general revenue)	4.9	5.2	6.0	6.4	3.3	3.1	3.6	3.9	2.0	2.2	3.2	3.1
Insurance	2.0	2.0	2.1	2.2	15.5	17.6	16.1	15.1	10.0	13.6	18.9	24.3
Total (%)	100.0	100.0	100.0	100.0	100.0	100.0	100.0	100.0	100.0	100.0	100.0	100.0
Total ($m)	21,357	31,598	44,419	81,216	20,728	30,117	46,794	97,108	87,066	106,441	161,351	247,849

[a]Sources and other notes to this and subsequent tables in this chapter are given in Peterson 1979a.

Significantly, 82 percent of all revenue raised in 1972 from local tax sources still came from the property tax.[9]

This dependence of local governments on the property tax has been a matter of some debate among economists. Critics have claimed that (1) it is income inelastic, (2) it is a surcharge on one particular type of economic good, and (3) it taxes low-income groups disproportionately. However, recent analyses have countered each of these criticisms. To the argument that the property tax does not expand with inflation or economic growth, defenders reply that revenues from this tax grew rapidly in the postwar period.[10] To the claim that the tax is an excise tax on housing that discourages consumption of this particular good, defenders respond that differentials in property tax among local governments are borne by property owners, not necessarily by those consuming the property, and that moreover there are reasons for regarding the tax as more a tax on capital than an excise tax.[11] The claim that the property tax is a regressive tax is dependent on the conclusion that it is largely an excise tax borne by the consumer. Since many of the assumptions on which this conclusion rests have been called into question, it is now safer to assert that the property tax is levied roughly in proportion to income and has neither positive nor negative redistributional effects.

These arguments among economists are relevant for those interested in developing any normative theory of tax policy. However, they do not provide satisfactory explanations for the persisting dependence on the tax by local governments. Whatever the objections to the property tax, local governments continue to prefer it over the income or sales tax, simply because it is a tax on those products least equipped to escape its application. Consider the difficulties posed by the major alternatives. Taxes on sales encourage residents to purchase products outside the jurisdiction. Taxes on profits earned within a territory provoke businesses into carrying on their most profitable activities elsewhere. Taxes on locally earned income give residents an incentive to seek employment externally. By comparison, the property levy taxes immobile land and structures attached thereto; the things taxed cannot be readily transported to a new locale. And their users must undergo the substantial costs of permanent physical migration to avoid the tax's application to them. Of course, the tax remains a disincentive for new investments in the community, but from the point of view of local governments much is to be said for a tax whose adverse consequences are delayed as long as possible. Consequently, the traditional property tax remains an integral part of local fiscal policy, and the faddish new sales and income taxes have made but modest headway as sources for local revenue.

Local governments directly tax the profits of local businesses hardly at all. Indeed, the United States census does not even have a separate classification for a direct local tax on business. The reasons are not difficult to discover. According to traditional economic theory, the corporation tax is an excise tax paid by the consumer when he buys a product upon which a surcharge in an amount equivalent to the tax has been placed. But this assignment of the corporation tax burden is applicable only if the tax is applied uniformly throughout a self-contained economic system. If such taxes were levied differentially by local governments and were passed on to the consumer via price increases, the products affected would no longer be competitive with products sold by businesses located in low-tax areas. Businesses in high-tax areas would be driven from the marketplace. Few local governments are eager to kill their golden geese by such a tax.

Fourth, the remaining taxes that local governments utilize are seldom progressive and at times downright regressive. Unlike the federal excise tax, which is reserved for luxury items, the state sales tax is levied on items for which lower income residents spend a relatively high proportion of their budget. Those who save portions of their income (presumably the wealthier save more) are not taxed on that aspect of their earnings at all. And it is the sales tax, not the more progressive income tax, that state and local governments favor as a source of revenue. Not only did states depend on the sales tax for 40 percent of their revenues in 1973, but local governments turned to this tax for 6.4 percent. By comparison, the income tax, which raises 42 percent of federal revenue, accounted for only 16 percent of state revenue and a puny 3 percent of local revenue. Moreover, the few local income taxes that are levied do not usually have the same progressive features characteristic of the federal income tax. Instead, it is the "general practice" with respect to state and local taxes "to follow the flat rate approach."[12]

One need not posit any local business elite to account for this propensity of local governments to favor more regressive taxes. The economic interests of cities which officials must safeguard are of themselves a sufficient explanation. The more starkly the ability-to-pay principle governs local tax policy, the greater the disjunction between taxes levied and benefits received, and the greater the negative impact revenue policy has on the economic well-being of the community. On the other hand, a proportional or (even more) a regressive tax structure comes closer to approximating the benefits-received principle, the principle which, if applied, best strengthens the local economy.

Finally, it is evident that localities have become increasingly dependent on intergovernmental transfers from the state and federal governments. As can be seen in table 4.2, the percentage of local revenues coming in intergovernmental transfers increased from 26.1 percent in 1957 to 37.1 percent in 1973. Of course, it is to the economic interest of localities that their activities be subsidized by grants coming from sources external to the community. And as a result, local governments compete with one another for as many state and federal resources as they can obtain. But the increasing shift in support for local services from locally generated revenues to revenues generated at the state and national levels cannot be attributed simply to the local interest in getting others to foot the bill. That has always been present. Instead, the increasing role of intergovernmental transfers is a concomitant of the redistributive role that local governments are increasingly expected to play.

Federal tax policies are so well known that their difference from the local emphasis on the benefit principle needs only brief mention. First, as can be seen in table 4.1, income tax accounts for over 40 percent of national government revenue, as compared with 16 percent of state and 3 percent of local revenue. The federal income tax is also much more progressive than any of the state and local income taxes. Second, the federal government is the only government that raises a substantial proportion of its revenue through a direct tax on corporate profits. Significantly, the amount collected by this tax has declined steadily from 24 percent in 1957 to 14 percent in 1973. It may be that the potential of capital flight to overseas locations is now putting constraints on national tax policy that hardly existed twenty years ago, when the United States more effectively dominated the world economy. But the federal government is still the one level of government capable of taxing corporate profits directly. Third, excise taxes on luxury items are responsible for a modest amount of federal income—quite in contrast to the heavy dependence of states on the sales tax. The one federal tax which is collected on the benefit principle is the social security tax, which is accounting for an increasing percentage of federal revenue. If the world economy becomes more unified and the national government becomes in-

Table 4.2 Local and Intergovernmental Components of Local Revenues (percentage distributions)

	1957	1962	1967	1973
Local resources	73.9	73.0	68.8	62.9
Intergovernmental transfers	26.1	27.0	31.3	37.1
Total (%)	100.0	100.0	100.1	100.0
Total ($m)	28,896	43,278	64,608	129,082

creasingly unable to control capital flows, one might anticipate an increasing dependence on this comparatively regressive tax. But at the present time there is little doubt that the federal tax system is far more redistributive than that of states and localities.

In sum, the tax structure of a federal system is highly differentiated. One does not find a marble cake of revenue-generating strategies such that any and all forms of taxation are preferred equally by all levels of government. Although some overlap is obvious, direct intergovernmental comparisons reveal different emphases in the tax policies of the various levels of government. The greatest emphasis on the benefits-received principle seems to lie at the local level, where user charges and other regressive forms of taxation are strongly preferred. The national government is most likely to collect taxes according to the ability-to-pay principle. Although states fall somewhere in between, they share many of the characteristics of the bottom tier.

The Three Policy Arenas

There are structured differences in the expenditure policies of the three levels of government as well. Allocation is the function that local governments can perform more effectively than central governments, because decentralization allows for a closer match between the supply of public services and their variable demand. Citizens migrate to those communities where the allocation best matches their demand curve. Redistribution, on the other hand, is a national function. The more a local community engages in redistribution, the more the marginal benefit/tax ratio for the average taxpayer declines, and the more the local economy suffers. The state can be expected to have policy responsibilities midway between. Finally, developmental policies will be the shared responsibility of all levels of government. For example, stabilization of the economy through fiscal and monetary policies, a most important developmental activity, is a national prerogative. Should a local community attempt to perform this activity, any positive effects its actions have will be quickly dispersed into the larger environment, while the interest on debts incurred will remain a burden the community itself must carry. But other developmental policies may have more specifically local consequences, and in these cases local governments are able to commit their own resources. Building highways and distributing utility services are obvious examples. The level of government that assumes responsibility for a particular type of developmental policy depends on the extent of its ripple effects.

The pattern of financial responsibility for government policies, as presented in table 4.3, is generally consistent with these hypotheses. Redistributive policies have been the fiscal responsibility of the federal government. Forty-seven percent of its domestic budget was allocated for redistributive purposes even at the beginning of the 1960s and, after the Great Society programs, this increased to over 55 percent. By contrast, the percentage of local revenues used for redistribution was only 12.9 percent in 1962. Significantly, even a decade after the civil rights movement and its supposed impact on local service-delivery systems,[13] this percentage had increased by less than 1 percent. In 1973 the state was contributing somewhat less than 35 percent of its budget to redistributive programs, more than the local but less than the national contribution in this area.

Table 4.4 provides an alternative way of analyzing the division of fiscal responsibility among the various levels of government. Here the data are percentages across the rows rather than down the columns. Instead of obtaining the percentage of each level of government's total resources devoted to a governmental activity, this table provides the percentage of all expenditures devoted to a particular activity contributed by each level of government. Presented this way, the figures are even more dramatic. Not only was the local contribution to redistribution scarcely more than 10 percent in 1962, but it has declined since that time. On the other hand, the federal role is once again shown to be increasingly significant. If the political pressures for federalizing welfare policy and health care are any sign, this pattern is likely to persist. As the United States continues to become an increasingly integrated political economy, the redistributive function may very well become an almost exclusively federal prerogative.

The allocational function is just as clearly the domain of local governments. The housekeeping services that all members of the community depend upon are both delivered *and financed* locally. As can be seen in table 4.3, over 28 percent of local government revenues were devoted to this purpose in 1973. The state plays a supporting role, but the proportion of its revenues devoted to this purpose is less than half that of the local governments. Meanwhile, the federal government is involved hardly at all.[14]

The developmental function is the more or less equal concern of the three levels of government, all of whom have allocated about 20 percent of their revenues for these activities. The role of the federal government in promoting economic productivity is larger than these figures suggest, once its interest payments on the national debt are taken into account. Since these are in large measure due to the federal government's responsibility for managing the national economy through its fiscal policies, they may be considered to be a cost of

Table 4.3: Governmental Expenditures from Own Fiscal Resources (percentage distributions among functions)

Function	Local			State			Federal[a]		
	1962	1967	1973	1962	1967	1973	1962	1967	1973
Redistributive									
Welfare	2.5	2.5	2.0	6.2	6.4	11.2	12.2	11.9	12.6
Health and hospitals	6.1	6.7	8.4	7.4	7.2	6.2	3.3	3.7	3.5
Housing	2.4	1.5	.9	.2	.2	.4	1.5	1.9	3.4
Social insurance	1.9	2.2	2.3	14.4	9.4	17.0	29.7	34.0	35.6
Subtotal	12.9	12.9	13.8	28.2	23.2	34.8	46.7	51.5	55.1
Allocational									
Housekeeping	26.8	26.4	28.5	12.4	12.9	8.4	4.6	4.5	3.8
Developmental									
Utilities	13.2	13.1	11.1	...	...	...	...	...	...
Postal	...	...	...	...	...	...	7.0	7.2	5.1
Transportation	8.1	6.6	5.7	17.8	16.0	11.3	6.2	5.8	4.2
Natural resources	1.1	1.1	.7	2.9	3.5	2.3	19.3	9.9	7.8
Subtotal	22.4	20.8	17.5	20.7	19.5	13.6	32.5	22.9	17.1
Interest	4.1	4.4	5.6	2.2	2.3	2.7	12.3	12.1	9.9
Education	33.4	35.2	34.2	33.6	39.5	38.4	3.2	7.2	8.2
Other	.4	.3	.4	3.0	2.6	2.2	.8	1.8	5.8
Total (%)	100.0	100.0	100.0	100.0	100.0	100.0	100.0	100.0	99.9
Total ($m)	33,591	45,853	77,886	29,356	45,288	89,504	58,960	86,852	186,172

[a]Domestic only.

Table 4.4: Governmental Expenditures from Own Fiscal Resources (percentage distributions among governments)

Function	Local			State			Federal			Total		
	1962	1967	1973	1962	1967	1973	1962	1967	1973	1962	1967	1973
Redistributive												
Welfare	8.5	7.8	4.3	18.4	20.1	28.7	73.1	72.1	67.2	100.0	100.0	100.0
Health and hospitals	33.2	32.2	35.4	35.2	34.0	29.6	31.6	33.8	35.0	100.0	100.0	100.0
Housing	46.7	29.3	9.7	2.5	3.8	4.5	50.7	66.9	85.8	100.0	100.0	100.0
Social insurance	2.9	2.9	2.2	18.9	12.3	18.2	78.1	84.8	79.6	100.0	100.0	100.0
Subtotal	10.8	9.7	7.4	20.6	17.2	21.5	68.6	73.2	71.1	100.0	100.0	100.0
Allocational												
Housekeeping	58.7	55.4	60.2	23.7	26.6	20.4	17.5	17.8	19.4	100.0	100.0	100.0
Developmental												
Postal	...	...	...	...	...	...	100.0	100.0	100.0	100.0	100.0	100.0
Utilities	100.0	100.0	100.0	...	...	...	...	...	...	100.0	100.0	100.0
Transportation	23.3	19.7	20.1	45.1	47.3	45.0	31.6	33.0	34.9	100.0	100.0	100.0
Natural resources	3.0	4.7	3.3	6.7	14.9	12.0	90.3	80.4	84.7	100.0	100.0	100.0
Subtotal	23.0	24.9	23.8	18.5	23.1	21.0	58.5	52.0	55.2	100.0	100.0	100.0
Interest	14.9	14.8	17.2	6.9	7.6	9.6	78.2	77.6	73.2	100.0	100.0	100.0
Education	48.9	40.0	34.9	43.0	44.4	45.0	8.1	15.6	20.0	100.0	100.0	100.0
Other	8.6	5.4	2.2	60.1	41.1	15.3	31.3	53.5	82.5	100.0	100.0	100.0

carrying out its developmental function.[15] The bulk of local expenditures for developmental purposes is used to operate municipal utilities. Since customers pay for services received, costs and benefits are largely internalized. It is this type of developmental function that a local government can most easily perform.

I have again listed education separately in tables 4.3 and 4.4, because classification of this governmental function is particularly difficult. In chapter 5, I show that the probable impact of government educational policies is slightly redistributive, but the redistributive impact seems to be much less than in the welfare, housing, or health policy arenas.[16] Accordingly, the fiscal responsibility for education is shared among the three governmental tiers. Local governments contribute substantial portions of their resources to the financing of local schools. In 1973, 34 percent of all local government expenditures were for educational purposes, a level of local commitment unlikely to prove feasible if education were a highly redistributive public policy (see table 4.3). Yet there have been long-term pressures for increased state and federal support for schooling and, indeed, the percentage of the federal domestic budget devoted to education increased from 3.2 percent to 8.2 percent in the decade between 1962 and 1973. When one examines the data percentaged across the rows in table 4.4, the increasing federal role is all the more apparent. Whereas local governments paid for nearly one-half of the public cost of education in 1962, their contribution declined to little more than a third by 1973. In the meantime, the federal share increased from 8 to 20 percent. It is worth noting that this change in the financing of education occurred precisely at the time when redistributive pressures in the educational sector were most intense.

The increasing role of the federal government in education has been exercised largely by means of a system of intergovernmental transfers. And it is not only in the field of education that intergovernmental transfers have been a concomitant of redistributive policymaking. In table 4.5, the budgetary distribution among policies of intergovernmental revenues from the federal and state governments to lower governmental levels is reported. The states allocate most of their intergovernmental monies for educational purposes. But the primary role of the federal government has been to finance the redistributive expenditures of states and localities. Even in 1973, after the establishment of a revenue-sharing program by the Nixon administration, 40 percent of intergovernmental revenues received by states and localities were specifically designated for redistributive functions. The increase in undesignated revenues in that year came largely at the expense of funds for developmental and educational purposes, not as a substitute for redistributive activities.

Table 4.5: Intergovernmental Expenditures by State and Federal
Governments (percentage distributions)

Function	State			Federal		
	1962	1967	1973	1962	1967	1973
Redistributive						
Welfare	16.3	15.2	18.4	31.6	28.2	29.0
Health and hospitals	1.8	1.6	2.1	2.2	2.7	4.2
Housing	.3	.4	.4	4.1	4.5	5.1
Social insurance	...	...	...	6.0	3.8	1.9
Subtotal	18.4	17.1	20.9	43.9	39.2	40.2
Allocational						
Housekeeping	...	...	...	.9	.9	2.1
Developmental						
Transportation	12.2	9.9	7.4	36.3	27.4	13.2
Natural resources	.2	.2	.2	1.8	1.6	1.6
Subtotal	12.4	10.1	7.6	38.1	29.0	14.8
Education	59.4	62.2	57.1	15.1	26.1	20.1
Other and undesignated	9.7	10.6	14.4	2.0	4.9	22.0
Total (%)	100.0	100.0	100.0	100.0	100.0	100.0
Total ($m)	10,906	19,056	40,822	7,735	15,027	41,666

The responsibility for financing public policies in the American
federal system is not distributed casually among all levels of government. Instead, central and local governments characteristically
assume different functional responsibilities. Local governments
allocate services in accord with community needs and, where spill-
over effects are modest, engage in developmental activities to promote the local economy. In addition to its responsibilities for overall
economic growth and for developmental policies that have widespread repercussions, the national government bears the primary
responsibilities for redistribution.

Intergovernmental Cooperation and Conflict

Given the structural differences between federal and local governments, intergovernmental programs that require mutual action will
have different experiences, as they are implemented in the federal
system, depending on whether they are developmental or redistributive in character. Where the national policy is developmental,
local and national goals will overlap and the policy will be executed
with a good deal of cooperation and mutual accommodation. But
where the central government is pursuing a more redistributive objective, its goals are likely to conflict with those of local governments. The national interest in equity will conflict with the local
interest in efficiently developing its local economy. As a result, the

processes of implementing the national program will be considerably more complicated.

These differences between developmental and redistributive programs are exemplified by the objectives and administrative arrangements for the National Defense Education Act (NDEA) Title III and the Elementary and Secondary Education Act (ESEA) Title I. Conceived shortly after Sputnik was launched in 1958, NDEA Title III was a developmental policy that probably had nothing other than positive effects on local economies but at the same time contributed little to educational equity. Federal funds under NDEA Title III were expended for the purpose of enhancing instruction in mathematics, science, and foreign languages, the very programs of greatest interest to the academically oriented, university-bound, middle-class segment of local communities. With higher quality local school services, the community had additional resources for persuading higher income families and new industries to move into and remain in the community. Moreover, since states and localities had to match every federal dollar with a state or local dollar, the communities with the greatest fiscal resources were the best placed to take advantage of the program.

Title I of ESEA, passed in 1965, at the height of the civil rights movement, has quite an opposite focus. As enacted by Congress and implemented by the Office of Education, the monies were to be for learning-deficient children from low-income families. In many ways the program has greatly increased the possibility of achieving improved equity in education, but its effect on local economies has been far more problematic. Except insofar as it may in the long run decrease social unrest in the community, the program provides no particular resources to prosperous middle-class families whose contributions to local commercial activity and to the community tax base are so important. And if in any particular locale the program succeeds in providing quality services to low-income people, it only makes the community more attractive to low-income families elsewhere, who will be tempted to move into the community. The very achievement of national goals by a local community only increases its economic disabilities.

Just as these two programs differed in their objectives, so they differed in the manner of their implementation. In the case of the developmental policy, NDEA Title III, the federal "partnership" operated as a model of cooperation and mutual reinforcement. Even though the law required that states match each federal dollar with a state dollar for the same program, within one year every state except Arizona had voted to participate in the program.[17] The Office of Education chose to distribute the monies among the forty-nine states with hardly any guidance about the purposes of the Act. In drawing up its plan, the state had only "to list its priorities for reimbursing local projects and to describe the kinds of local projects and the standards for equipment it would help pay for."[18] Since national standards and priorities were not clearly defined, the states "in their plans mostly stuck to bland and general descriptions . . . some said that in effect standards would be as high as the programs called for."[19] Indeed, it was left to a private publishing house to produce a catalog that listed the equipment it felt was sure to qualify for state and federal reimbursement. In short, "federal aid was [not only] unencumbered by federal control [but] it was also innocent of scientific guidance and advice from Washington."[20]

After NDEA Title III expenditures were allocated and programs implemented, the Office of Education did little to monitor the way in which its resources were being utilized. States reported their Title III science activities only in terms of dollars and projects; they were not called upon to demonstrate the ways in which these dollars had improved science education.[21] Evaluation of program impact was virtually nonexistent. Yet these program "inadequacies" had few political repercussions. Popular at both the national and local levels, the program expanded as part of the growing role of the federal government in education.

Implementation of the redistributive program, Title I of ESEA, has taken a dramatically different course.[22] Although all states have been eager to participate in the program from the beginning, this might be attributed to the lack of any matching requirement in the legislation. In the first six months of operation, the Office of Education followed its past practice of giving very little guidance about the way in which funds were to be allocated. But before the end of the first year, the Office of Education became increasingly concerned about the substantial divergence of state programs from the objectives stated in the Title I legislation. In order to better achieve the redistributive goals of the Act, the Office began to limit the amount of expenditures on structural renovation, new equipment, and other "hardware"; required that the money be concentrated in schools with large numbers of children from low-income families; and specified that within these schools the monies be spent on children with learning deficiencies. It also required that local educational authorities establish parent advisory councils that could participate in program development. Above all, it insisted that monies for educational services be denied to segregated school districts in the rural South.

The success that the Office of Education has had in securing state and local compliance with these and numerous other administrative regulations governing the distribution of Title I funds has been mixed. During the first few years, the Office of Education had a small staff, poor-quality data on the performance of local districts, only limited experience in the supervisory role that Title I seemed to require, and a history of cordial relations with fellow school professionals at state and local levels that it was hesitant to disrupt. It therefore found it difficult to preclude local modification of Title I priorities. In many parts of the country, Title I funds were distributed throughout the system rather than concentrated on schools with high proportions of needy children; elsewhere, they were used to preserve segregated schooling rather than to enhance integrated educational experiences. Moreover, parent advisory councils seldom became effective parts of the Title I policymaking process.

As the Office of Education, and, more recently, the Department of Education, has become more experienced in administering the program, it has become better able to ensure that funds are used in schools attended primarily by low-income children.[23] However, the Office has had continuing difficulties in ensuring that Title I funds are supplemental funds rather than substitutes for what otherwise would have been spent by state and local sources. Moreover, school districts seem reluctant to concentrate funds in a few specific schools, thereby maximizing their impact. Most recently, local school administrators have begun to campaign for the replacement of ESEA with an unencumbered block-grant funding arrangement.

Federalism and the Great Society

The structural difference between central and local governments also helps account for many of the difficulties encountered in the implementation of other Great Society programs. These policies, with their emphasis on special assistance to the poor and the needy, demonstrated a stronger commitment to redistribution by the central government than evident at any other time save, perhaps, for the New Deal. Unfortunately, the zeal for reform was uninhibited by any satisfactory structural understanding of the American federal system. Instead, it was felt that one could make federalism "creative" by lubricating it with federal dollars. Enthusiastic supporters of President Lyndon Johnson's reforms drew upon the language of the marble-cake theorists of American federalism to justify and rationalize the mechanisms for redistribution they adopted. In the words of one:

> Federalism means a relation, co-operative and competitive, between a limited central power and other powers that are essentially independent of it. In the long American dialogue

over states' rights, it has been tacitly assumed that the total amount of power was constant and, therefore, any increase in federal power diminished the power of the states and/or "the people." Creative federalism starts from the contrary belief that total power—private and public, individual and organizational—is expanding very rapidly. As the range of conscious choice widens, it is possible to think of vast increases of federal government power that do not encroach upon or diminish any other power. Simultaneously, the power of states and local governments will increase.[24]

Johnson's great zeal for reform in American domestic social policy was accompanied by an equally intense commitment to the execution of these policies through state and local governments. In 1965 Congress enacted twenty-one health programs, seventeen educational programs, fifteen economic development programs, twelve programs to meet city problems, four programs for manpower training, and seventeen resource development programs. All were implemented through joint action between the federal and one or more of the lower levels of government.[25] Federal intergovernmental transfers to state and local governments increased from $7.7 billion in 1962 to $41.7 billion in 1973. In 1962 intergovernmental transfers constituted 27 percent of the budget of local governments; by 1973 these transfers constituted 37.1 percent.[26] Great Society programs were federal programs, formulated and financed by central departments, but administered and executed by state and local governments.[27]

Time has not treated "creative federalism" generously. Many of the Great Society programs proved to be disappointments in practice, and instead of the cooperative partnership that had been envisaged, conflict, confusion, and simple abandonment of original objectives occurred in most of the more visible programs. In the absence of a federal theory to guide them, political analysts have advanced three rival hypotheses in their search to explain the limited success of the Great Society Programs: (1) the power of local ruling elites, (2) the complexity of intergovernmental relationships, and (3) the differential constituencies of central and local governments. Each offers a plausible but, in the end, inadequate explanation for the regularity with which national programs have been frustrated at local levels.

Local Ruling Elites

In both popular and academic literature, the favored explanation for the difficulties faced by Great Society programs is the power of local ruling elites. Local politics, it is said, has been dominated by power structures consisting of bankers and businessmen who, together with a few conservative labor leaders and politicians beholden to them, dictate the major contours of local policy.[28] More sophisticated versions of this explanation do not claim that the ruling elite makes each and every local decision but only that its presence precludes redistributive issues from reaching the agenda of local politics. Its power is used to keep policies that are of interest to low-income groups and racial minorities from ever reaching a threshold of public awareness in the local community.[29]

A study of Baltimore's community action program provided Bachrach and Baratz with an opportunity to apply this perspective directly to the implementation of the most visible of the antipoverty programs.[30] In this study, they contend that the politics of community action in Baltimore was marked by "non-decision-making." They concluded that the efforts by black leaders

> to transform the covert grievances of the black population into issues was . . . abortive, in part because they lacked arenas where they could practice the politics of conflict as distinct from the politics of confrontation, and in part because they had no access to key centers of decision-making. In short, the prevailing mobilization of bias blocked black leaders' attempts to arouse their would-be constituents to political action and thereby assured that blacks would remain "locked-out" of the political system.[31]

To support this conclusion, they note that Baltimore lacked an open-occupancy ordinance, discriminated against blacks in public and private employment, and funded the antipoverty program only frugally.[32]

About some matters Bachrach and Baratz are certainly correct. If Baltimore resembled other local governments, and insofar as the socioeconomic well-being of disadvantaged groups was concerned, the civil rights movement and the war on poverty did not dramatically change the course of local public policy. The evidence presented earlier showing only minute increases in local-level expenditures for redistribution seems conclusive. But the mechanisms precluding achievement of this objective do not seem to square with the "non-decision-making" model. Indeed, the empirical materials in the study testify to the earnestness and persistence with which redistributive issues came to the regular attention of Baltimore's leaders. As the authors point out, "by the end of 1967 the CAA (Community Action Agency), with its black director in the forefront, was operating at full tilt and practically in the open to organize the black poor for political action."[33] Unless one is prepared to accept Bachrach and Baratz's penchant for stretching the concept of "non-decision" so that it coincides with its opposite—the mayor's decision to establish a series of biracial task forces, for example, is labeled "an extremely effective non-decision"[34]—one can hardly claim that a ruling elite excluded issues of race and poverty from the agenda of local politics.

Fundamentally, the ruling-elite hypothesis is unable to cope with the signal accomplishment of antipoverty programs—the opening up of local political systems to previously excluded groups. Although the socioeconomic impact of the programs was limited, they did improve the opportunities for political participation by blacks and other racial minorities. Led by the "maximum feasible participation" focus of the community action program, most of the Great Society service-delivery programs contained features that required the active involvement of representatives of low-income groups and racial minorities in the deliberative process. Although these policies varied by locale and program, the overall impact was greatly to increase both the involvement of minorities as organized supporters of antipoverty programs and their recruitment to positions of administrative responsibility. The war on poverty was most successful in changing the agenda of local politics. Matters of concern to minority groups became regular, if not pervasive, issues in city politics. Even more significant, black leaders and groups representing minority interests became permanent elements in the institutionalized bargaining process through which local policy was formulated.[35]

Unfortunately, improved access to local politics did not thereby radically alter the socioeconomic well-being of racial minorities and low-income groups.[36] But to attribute this to the power of a ruling elite once again misguides poverty research. If the issue were simply to place on the agenda of local politics the problems of poor minorities, then the programs of the Great Society would certainly have ended poverty and racism in America. But if there are limits inherent in the functions that local governments can perform, even "maximum feasible" political participation by minorities and the poor does not alter these limits.

Organizational Complexity

Quite another interpretation of the Johnson antipoverty programs derives from an understanding of the variety, the complexity, and the changeability of political and organizational relationships in a pluralist system. From this perspective, intergovernmental relationships do not consist simply of encounters between federal officials and local elites; on the contrary, at all levels of government (federal, regional, state, and local) are numerous public and private agencies, with overlapping jurisdictions and competing clientele, that must be consulted in the course of implementing government policy. Any of these entities can act as a "veto group" to frustrate the execution of policy—or at least to delay its implementation until the original purposes are substantially modified.

As familiar as this pluralist view of American politics has become,[37] Pressman and Wildavsky's imaginative utilization of these ideas in their analysis of the innovative programs of the Economic Development Administration (EDA) is worthy of special consideration.[38] The study is a detailed analysis of the problems that beset the EDA when it sought to improve minority employment opportunities in Oakland, California, by funding a number of public improvement projects in that city. After beginning with high hopes, large projected budgetary outlays, and the appearance of cooperation on the part of both federal and local officials, EDA was frustrated by numerous delays; almost no detectable progress toward the original objective was made. Although the specific problems encountered are discussed in fascinating detail, Pressman and Wildavsky also reach for a more general explanation for the failure of this and other Great Society programs:

> What seemed to be a simple program turned out to be a very complex one, involving numerous participants, a host of differing perspectives, and a long and tortuous path of decision points that had to be cleared. Given these characteristics, the chances of completing the program with the haste its designers had hoped for—and even the chances of completing it at all—were sharply reduced.[39]

The problems of the Great Society were thus the problems encountered by any government program in a pluralist political system in which many participants influence policy. Differences must be negotiated, plans must be delayed, and policies must be modified. The solution is to either develop more simple programs, abandon federal efforts to intervene in socioeconomic relationships, or accept that long delays and major revisions are inevitable.

Although the case study is written with incisiveness and energy, in the end the argument cuts too deeply. Inasmuch as it applies to all government programs, it does not provide an adequate explanation for the particular problems encountered by the redistributive programs of the Great Society. In the first place, complexity was not a feature unique to the antipoverty programs of the Johnson administration. Many programs that have become a routinized feature of the federal system—for example, those for highways, rivers and harbors, land reclamation, and airport construction—are equally complex but have nonetheless been incorporated into the ongoing political processes of the federal system. National and local objectives have in these cases been similar enough that, whatever problems they may have encountered in particular cases, few can make the claim that the programs have failed. Indeed, local governments avidly compete for resources for these programs. Complexity is not a sufficient explanation for the diffidence with which localities participated in anti-poverty programs.

Second, Pressman and Wildavsky's assertion that programs failed because participants had diverse views with respect to complex phenomena is at best a very low level theoretical statement.[40] In this respect, Pressman and Wildavsky resemble the students of marble-cake federalism, who find relationships too complicated to identify critical elements patterning the complexity. For example, even though the empirical material in the Oakland study makes it quite clear that the "feds" were concerned primarily with redistribution (for example, employing minorities) and the "locals" were concerned primarily with obtaining aid for economic development, Pressman and Wildavsky provide no general explanation for this patterning of the differences between the two levels of government.

Differential Constituencies

Constituency theory offers the promise of identifying patterns to conflicts between central and local governments. In its most general formulation, constituency theory argues that political leaders pursue objectives desired by those who select them for office. Regarding the differences between central and local governments, McConnell has argued that the central government, with a larger constituency, can be expected to serve broader and more diffuse interests.[41] In local government, which has a smaller constituency, it is easier for dominant economic interests to control policy to the exclusion of weaker, less well organized interests. In government with a larger constituency, the mutual checking of powerful interests and the need to build coalitions of diverse interests permit consideration of weaker, broader, more diffuse concerns, perhaps including even those of the poor.

One of the best case studies of the failure of a Great Society program is quite convincingly interpreted within the tradition of constituency analysis. In her study of the "New Towns in Town" program initiated in late 1967, Derthick documents in detail the processes by which a program, originally planned to provide low-income housing through low-cost distribution of surplus federal land, failed to build any new homes for the poor at all.[42] In a thoughtful concluding chapter, Derthick emphasizes the differences in the value commitments of national and local governments and then relates them to their differing constituencies:

> In shared programs, both the federal government and local governments have a political function: both play a part in defining the objectives of public action and in responding to differences of value, interest, and opinion. The federal government, being removed from particular and parochial conflicts, is better able to express idealistic and progressive objectives. Local governments, more deeply engaged in these conflicts, are better able to respond to the actual preferences of active political interest.[43]

Although Derthick correctly identifies differing value commitments on the part of national and local institutions, she leaves unstated the exact mechanisms by which local constituencies generate demands that differ from national policies. In Derthick's case study, for example, interest groups and constituency pressures, far from constraining policy choice, are notable for their absence. Although some local officials may have anticipated opposition to a low-income housing program, even that hypothetical opposition does not account for the position of big-city mayors, who could also have anticipated support from sizable low-income and minority constituencies.

The constituency thesis is most helpful in accounting for differential local responses to national policy. But what Derthick, Pressman and Wildavsky, Bachrach and Baratz, and other researchers have documented is the consistency of conflict between national and local objectives, including those urban locales where local constituencies have every reason to be most supportive of redistributive programs.[44] Even where the poor constitute the bulk of a local electorate, local governments often frustrated the policy objectives of the Johnson administration.

Toward a New Theory of Federalism

The power of local ruling elites, the complexity of intergovernmental relationships, and the differential constituencies at the national and local levels have all been evoked as explanations for the difficulties that Great Society programs faced when being implemented within a federal system. Although all three hypotheses identify local resistance to redistribution, none provides an adequate explanation for the phenomenon. The problem with all of them is that they are theories concerning the relationships among individuals, groups, and organizations. Influenced by behavioral theories of politics and the marble-cake metaphor of federalism, all three approaches try to find explanations for structural differences in government institutions in terms of relationships among elements at the national, state, and local levels. I have offered instead an approach to the study of federalism that identifies the structural features differentiating central from local institutions and that then links these structural features to the processes of intergovernmental policy formation.

Only the simple elements of a theory of federalism have been provided thus far. To highlight fundamental features, contrasts have been drawn starkly. The sharp differences between redistributive and developmental policies have been etched, and I have emphasized the basic differentials in the orientations of national and local governments. A more complete analysis must take into account at least some of the many shadings in between. A beginning is made in this direction in chapter 5. Some of the differences between local governments are taken into account when the contrasts between central cities and their suburban hinterland are explored. At the same time I consider a policy that is particularly difficult to characterize in general. At different times and in different places it may be either redistributive, developmental, or allocative. Its effects vary with the governmental context in which the policy is executed. It is no wonder that few policy questions have received as much research attention as the effects of schooling.

Five

Cities, Suburbs, and Their Schools

Local governments are not all of a piece. Some local governments are well equipped to pursue their economic interests; other local governments operate under constraints that limit the efficiency with which they can develop their economic base. These differences among local governments can be found in every area of substantive government policy, but it is in the operation of local schools that they are most easily discerned. Schooling is the most costly of all local government activities, and its operations touch directly on the lives of many, if not most, of the families living within the community. City school operation can significantly affect community prosperity. At the same time, the structure of the schooling system affects the equality of educational opportunity in the society.

The two objectives run at cross-purposes with one another. As previously stressed, the local interest in economic growth all but precludes a commitment to redistribution. The consequences are particularly significant for education. In the first place, Americans have placed a particularly high premium on equality of educational opportunity. Much earlier than European societies, the United States expanded its educational system at elementary, secondary, and higher education levels. Although in the United States provisions for social security and health insurance have lagged behind other industrial societies, state-provided educational services have until very recently been more ample and better endowed in the United States than anywhere else in the world.[1] Americans, it is said, are committed to equality of opportunity, if not to equality of result. Second, Americans have stressed the importance of local financing and local control of the educational system. Whereas in most European countries schools are financed heavily by the national government, in the United States 80 percent of educational financing is by state and local governments, as shown in table 4.4. Indeed, these figures, which include expenditures for higher education, overstate the amount of federal assistance to elementary and secondary education; the early years of schooling are the particular prerogative of local government. Ironically, schooling, the service-delivery system said to best exemplify America's commitment to equality, is largely provided by the level of government least able to engage in redistribution.

As has been indicated previously, schooling is not necessarily a redistributive policy. Indeed, one can imagine a school system distributing educational services in a fashion so consistent with the city's economic interests that one would properly classify it as a developmental policy. Consider a system of schooling such that services are provided to those families who exchange for them a sum of equal market value. Because the family is willing to pay for the schooling and because those providing the schooling are willing to do so in return for this payment, the exchange increases the net utility of the community. Everyone is better off than he would have been without the exchange—the very definition of a developmental policy. Following Pareto, one might also label such a system an efficient system of education. Within this efficient system, those paying the most for school services receive the most in benefits.[2]

A redistributive school system, on the other hand, treats all children (except, perhaps, the handicapped) in any given age cohort as equals. Each child receives the same educational benefits, regardless of his family's income, social position, or contribution to local tax coffers.

In short, schooling services can be classified as more of a developmental policy or more of a redistributive policy depending on the degree to which the benefits of schooling are distributed either in proportion to the amount paid for the services or to all members of the community equally.

Emergence of a Dual System of Education

There is now some evidence that a dual system of education may have emerged in metropolitan areas. The part located in central cities may be a modestly successful agency of redistribution. The other, located in a vast array of small suburbs, is organized in such a way as to facilitate developmental objectives. The imbalance between the social objectives pursued by this dual system may contribute to the contemporary urban crisis and preclude further contributions to equality by central-city school systems.

Developmental Policies in Suburbia

In American suburbs competing school districts provide a range of educational services of varying quality, emphasis, and price. Consumers with the wherewithal to make their interest in, or demand for, high-quality (high-cost) education effective find living quarters in communities that have reputations for excellent schools. Those with less effective demand (that is, with less interest in high-cost education or with lower incomes) choose homes in less exclusive parts of the metropolitan area. At the bottom are the "problem" suburbs, where both schooling benefits and the cost of purchasing or renting living space are much less. Tax rates also vary from area to area, depending on per capita taxable wealth and the effective demand for schooling. Altogether, the system, though far from Tiebout's ideal of perfect efficiency,[3] dispenses benefits roughly in accord with the amount of taxes paid for them.

Two separate research traditions have generated evidence that lends some credence to the belief that suburban educational benefits are distributed roughly in accord with economic demand for them. The first tradition has emphasized the great variation in expenditures among locally financed school districts. For example, Miner found in a national sample a coefficient of variability of .72 among school districts in expenditures from state and local resources.[4] Moreover, both Miner and other researchers discovered that these differences were strongly related to the fiscal capacity of the state and locality.[5] More recently, Grubb and Michelson have demonstrated that interstate inequalities remained relatively constant from 1955 to 1968.[6] Even the increased federal role in educational finance had done little to reduce interstate differentials. In addition, substantial intrastate inequalities among school districts were evident in all fifteen of the states they investigated.[7]

Variations in interdistrict expenditures are also related to variations in the fiscal capacity of families. Those with more income tend to live in districts where expenditures are greater, and as a result those who have more effective demand for education receive more educational benefits (as measured by expenditure data). The results of a 1960 survey of families showed that just as property taxes paid increased with income, so did educational benefits received.[8] These data did not provide information on the exact sums spent on the individual children of the families surveyed; instead, it was assumed that these children received a resource allocation identical to that of the average child in the district they attended. The data therefore are probably a conservative statement of the extent to which family income and educational benefits are related. However, they provide a clear demonstration that the great variability in expenditures among school districts contributes to differentials in educational expenditures across income groups.

These data were collected on a nationwide basis. Evidence on patterns specific to suburbia are available only for particular metropolitan areas. In an early study, Hirsch found that variations in local property values were the most important determinant of school expenditures in the metropolitan area surrounding St. Louis.[9] Sacks and Hellmuth found a positive relationship between the personal wealth of a community and its expenditures in an investigation of suburban districts near Cleveland.[10] Studies of suburban areas in Chicago and Santa Clara, California, also found per capita income and property values to be important determinants of expenditure.[11] In general, those suburban communities with greater economic resources provided a financially more luxurious educational experience for district children. Those who paid more in taxes received more in educational benefits, as measured by per pupil expenditures.

A second tradition of research on educational services provides information on the degree to which suburban families value the products local school systems are providing. This research has shown, first of all, that educational benefits, as measured by tests of verbal ability, have a value in the marketplace. Two separate studies, one of New Jersey suburbs, the other in the Los Angeles area, demonstrate that as performance on verbal ability tests improves, community property values climb.[12] In both studies many other factors affecting property values, such as the size and age of the home, the accessibility of the community to centers of employment, the community tax rate, and (most important) median family income, were controlled in a multiple regression analysis. Given the control for family income, one cannot explain away the finding on the grounds that communities with high property values produce children who perform well on tests. Apparently, consumers of educational services believe that schools do affect the performance level of children, and they place a high value on those schools where children learn more.

There is a second finding in this research tradition which suggests even more clearly that suburban school systems are reasonably efficient at promoting local economies. When educational benefits are measured by expenditure levels and not by test scores, school services continue to have a positive effect on property values. Significant positive effects of educational expenditures on property values have been identified in suburban communities in New Jersey, Illinois, Massachusetts, and California.[13] In all these studies, the findings held, even after controls for median family income, tax rates, and home age and size had been introduced.

Educational expenditures have a positive effect on property values because consumers perceive some relationship between dollar inputs into education and the outcomes of schooling. Admittedly, the utilization of resources seems to be less than perfectly efficient for promoting economic growth. In most studies the positive effect of increased educational expenditures merely offset the negative effect on property values of increased local taxes. Moreover, educational expenditures generally do not have as significant an effect on property values as do verbal ability test scores, suggesting some slippage between educational input and output. But even with these qualifications there is a reasonable amount of evidence that suburban educational systems promote local economies. Suburbia may not yet approximate Tiebout's ideal world of the perfectly efficient system for distributing public goods, but at the very least market forces respond as if consumers value the school services suburban governments provide.

Redistributive Policies in Central Cities

If suburban schools have developmental policies, central-city schools in the dual system of metropolitan education lean more in a redistributive direction. Big-city school systems fall within a single large school district governed by a central board of education which has delegated most of its power to a highly centralized administrative staff. These administrators, often in the name of efficiency, have rigorously applied principles of equality and fairness to the distribution of resources among neighborhood schools within the central city.

Partly to reform education and partly to enhance their own power, big-city school superintendents developed universalistic rules for the distribution of scarce school resources.[14] All schools were allocated similar teacher/pupil ratios, similar classroom sizes, similar textbook/pupil ratios, similar extracurricular facilities and supplies, and so forth. Variation and diversity encouraged political pressures by principals, community groups, politicians, and board members. Generalized principles for the distribution of school resources protected administrators against pressure, enabling them to claim that every pupil was being treated equally and fairly. These principles also provided for a certain kind of efficiency that the accountant could appreciate, though the superintendent's brand of efficiency had little in common with the Pareto-optimal efficiency about which economists write. On the contrary, it helped to ensure a far greater equality in educational provision within the central cities than almost any theory of community power might have anticipated.

Only a few systematic studies of the distributional policies of big-city school systems have been published, but the findings are surprisingly consistent. Burkhead found both in Atlanta and supposedly "machine-ridden" Chicago that resources were distributed even-handedly to schools serving all income categories so that expenditures per pupil, teacher/pupil ratios, expenditures for supplies, and most other items of resource distribution were approximately equal.[15]

When Katzman compared his results in Boston with those of Burkhead, he concluded, "The three cities [Boston, Atlanta, and Chicago] are strikingly similar in the relatively equal distribution of expenditures per student."[16] Levy, Meltsner, and Wildavsky found a rough equality in the distribution of resources in Oakland, California.[17] In this case, however, there was a tendency to allocate extra resources to schools in both the poorest and the richest neighborhoods. If these four cities from four different regions of the country are at all representative, then Katzman is surely correct in concluding that "big cities more effectively narrow the gap in educational opportunity than do the multitude of autonomous suburbs."[18]

The one exception to this pattern is the differential in teacher salaries among central-city neighborhood schools. Burkhead, Owen, and Grubb and Michelson all find differentials in expenditures among neighborhoods that are the product of "allowing experienced teachers to choose in which school they wish to teach, resulting in the experienced (and highest paid) teachers being concentrated in white, middle-class schools."[19] Yet there is little evidence that experience beyond the first four or five years of teaching correlates positively with pupil performance.[20] If this is the primary mechanism by which central cities bias school resources in favor of higher taxpaying neighborhoods, they have chosen a most inefficient mechanism for calibrating service delivery to tax contributions. By comparison, salary differentials in suburbs enable the more prosperous suburbs to recruit the more talented teacher from the very beginning of his career in the community. But even taking into account differentials in teacher salaries among central-city neighborhoods, within-city differences do not match intercity differences. In Owen's words, the "income elasticity of salary expenditures [within central cities] is about half of some estimates of intercity elasticities of educational expenditures."[21] This provides a "rough measure of the extent to which centralized administration of large-city educational systems has reduced inequality based on income differences."[22]

To the extent that central cities provide equality of educational resources, this comes at the expense of the development of the big-city economy. Those who pay more in taxes for schooling in central cities may not receive much more in benefits. Instead, the more prosperous families living in the central city are subsidizing the education of their poor neighbors.

Suburban–Central-City Differences:
The Evidence from Data on Verbal Ability

If these differences between central-city and suburban school systems are significant, they can be expected to affect the determinants of a child's performance on verbal ability tests. Indeed, one of the ways one can estimate the extent to which a system of schooling is pursuing developmental policies is by identifying the strength of the relationship between a child's performance on a verbal ability test and the amount a family pays for the child's schooling. If the system has a developmental orientation, there is a correlation between a child's performance and family payments for educational services. Moreover, differentials in performance between children from families who pay more for educational services and children from families who pay less increase steadily with amount of time in school. If the system is redistributive, performance on verbal ability tests is only weakly associated with family background, and whatever variation in verbal ability is initially associated with family background characteristics steadily declines over time.

The Coleman Study

When analyzed with care, the data collected by the United States Office of Education under the direction of James Coleman (hereinafter referred to as the Coleman study) reveal a system of schooling in the United States which was in northern states only marginally redistributive in 1965.[23] Table 5.1, which is taken from the Coleman study, presents data only for northern blacks and whites in grades 6, 9, and 12, because data collected for the South, other minorities, and younger children are of a more dubious quality.[24] This table reports the central findings from the Coleman study: (1) family background characteristics have a strong impact on verbal ability at all grade levels, and (2) school and teacher characteristics make the most minimal "unique" contribution; that is, they have little effect apart from the conjoint effects they share with the child's family background.

Table 5.1: Percent of Variance in Verbal Achievement Accounted for by Family Background and School Characteristics

	Grade 6	Grade 9	Grade 12
Family background (includes unique effects as well as those effects produced conjointly with school variables)			
Blacks (North)	9.51	7.68	7.53
Whites (North)	14.10	16.49	14.28
Teacher and school characteristics (variance uniquely accounted for, once family background characteristics are controlled)			
Blacks (North)	2.66	3.32	6.68
Whites (North)	2.02	2.06	3.16

Source. Coleman et al. 1966, tables 3.221.3 and 3.25.3.

The interpretation frequently given this table is that schools make little difference. But this reading of table 5.1 has several difficulties. For one thing it is insensitive to the precise meaning of the statistical techniques employed. In interpreting tables such as this one, it is important to keep in mind that, in a multivariate regression analysis, explained variance in the dependent variable (in this case, verbal ability) consists of three things: (1) the variance uniquely attributable to independent variable a (family background); (2) the variance uniquely attributable to independent variable b (teacher and school characteristics); and (3) the variance that can be attributed only to their conjoint or overlapping effects. In table 5.1, as in all of the tables in the Coleman report, the data are divided into only two, not three, of these analytical parts. Rows 1 and 2 contain combined information about (1) and (3) above; they combine the unique effects of family background with the conjoint effects of family background and school. Rows 3 and 4 provide information about (2)—the effects uniquely attributable to teacher and school characteristics.

When the analysis is conducted in this way, the amount of variance "uniquely" explained by school characteristics is a poor measure of the impact of schooling on a child's verbal ability. Any effects of schooling that overlap effects of family background are attributed entirely to the family and not at all to the school. Such overlapping effects may be considerable.[25] For example, teachers may very well work more intimately with middle-class children; the nature of the interactions with such children can be more rewarding for both teacher and pupil; and these interactions are apt to become increasingly positive and reinforcing. The opposite pattern is likely with working-class children.

Although such contrasting patterns are likely in middle- and working-class contexts, they do not appear as school effects in Coleman's own analysis. On the contrary, these school effects only increase the size of the reported correlation between family background and verbal ability. Because all overlapping effects are treated as family effects, probable school impacts are erroneously considered to be the result of entirely nonschool influences.

Although the Coleman data reported in table 5.1 tell us little about the overall impact that schools have on children's verbal ability, they nonetheless contain valuable information. First, the relationship between family background and verbal ability tells us something about the extent to which educational benefits are being distributed roughly in accord with the amount families pay for schooling. Although Coleman does not directly provide information on the amount parents pay in taxes for their children's education, the family background variables (which are fairly accurate indicators of the family's social status) correspond roughly to the amount the family pays in taxes for schooling.[26] Second, the "unique" amount of variance attributable to schools provides another indicator of the redistributive impact of schooling. Any effects of schooling that do not overlap family background are likely to be redistributive. If a school system is shifting resources from above average taxpayers to the children of less well endowed families, this is likely to appear in the form of significant school effects that are uncorrelated with family background characteristics. Table 5.1 shows that these "unique" effects of teacher and other school characteristics accounted for less than 4 percent of the variance in verbal ability in five of the six samples. From these results, one may conclude that schools make only a small contribution to equality of educational opportunity. Any redistributive impact of schooling seems very limited.

Reconsideration of Black-White Differences
in the Coleman Study

If central-city schools emphasize redistribution and suburban schools emphasize development, then differences between these two types of educational systems should be evident in Coleman's study of the effects of families and schools on verbal ability. In the published literature on the Coleman study there is no direct examination of the differential effects of central-city and suburban school systems, and it was not possible to obtain Coleman study data for reanalysis.[27] However, comparisons between blacks and whites are available. Since in the Coleman sample only 32 percent of the white children in the North attended central-city schools whereas 79 percent of the black children did, it may be possible to make some inferences about differences between cities and suburbs on the basis of differential findings between blacks and whites. If there are differences between central city and suburbia, these should be reflected in differential patterns of correlation among blacks as compared with whites.

First, one hypothesizes that generally weaker relationships between home background variables and educational achievement will be found among blacks than among whites. Since whites attend suburban schools, where developmental objectives seem well served, schools can be expected to reinforce existing social class differences. Since blacks attend a more egalitarian educational system, the impact of social class on educational performance will be weaker. Consistent with these expectations, table 5.1 in fact shows that family background differences account for less of the variation among blacks than among whites. Second, one hypothesizes that the amount of variance explained by school factors will be greater for blacks than for whites. Where school system politics are more redistributive, the observed "unique" effects of schooling will be greater. This second hypothesis is also supported by the findings in table 5.1; the "unique" effects of schooling are greater for blacks than whites at all three grade levels. This hypothesis is further supported by table 5.2, which provides unstandardized regression coefficients for each of the four family background characteristics that are the best measure of socioeconomic class. I present the unstandardized regression coefficients because they permit direct comparisons across racial groups and grade levels for each of the family background variables.[28] When these comparisons are made, it is clear that for every grade level family background characteristics

Table 5.2: Regression Coefficients for Four Family Background Variables, Controlling for Four Sets of Schoolwide Variables

Family Background Characteristic	Blacks			Whites		
	Grade 6	Grade 9	Grade 12	Grade 6	Grade 9	Grade 12
Reading material	1.4[a]	1.6[a]	1.0	2.7[a]	3.2[a]	5.0[a]
Economic well-being	2.2[a]	1.0	0.6	2.8[a]	1.6	−0.1
Structural integrity	0.6	1.1[a]	0.7	1.2[a]	1.9[a]	0.7
Education	1.0[a]	1.3[a]	2.4[a]	2.4[a]	3.7[a]	3.2[a]

Source. Smith 1972, table 12.
[a]Statistically significant at .05 level.

have a more powerful effect on the performance of whites than blacks.

There is still another finding which supports the argument that the system of schooling in suburbia is less redistributive than the system of schooling in central cities. In a school system pursuing a developmental policy, family background characteristics become increasingly powerful explanatory variables over time, while in a redistributive system the relationships between family and educational performance steadily decrease. Examine table 5.1 once again, this time noticing the changes over the time a child remains in school. For blacks, home variables, relatively weak even in grade 6, decline even further in grades 9 and 12. At the same time, the "unique" contributions of school and teacher variables increase over time. For whites, family background factors remain powerful, and in fact they even increase slightly in importance. The data in table 5.2 reveal the same pattern. By grade 12 only one of the home background variables remains statistically significant for blacks, while for whites two of the family variables were more important for the oldest students than they were for the youngest.

In the data presented thus far, the dependent variable has been the *total* amount of variation in pupil achievement. This total can be analytically separated into two parts: the amount of variation in pupil achievement that occurs *within* any single school, and the amount of variation that occurs *among* schools. It is this second aspect—the variation that occurs among schools, or what Coleman calls the between-school variance—that is most relevant to this analysis of the differences among schools in suburbs and among schools in central cities. The best test of the hypothesis, therefore, is an examination of the extent to which family background factors account for the between-school variation in pupil achievement.

Fortunately, published data are available on black-white differences in the between-school variation accounted for by family background characteristics.[29] As can be seen in table 5.3, the data strongly confirm the hypothesis. For whites, between-school variation is largely explained by family background characteristics, and

Table 5.3: Percent of Between-School Variance Accounted for by Family Background Characteristics of Northern Whites and Blacks

	Grade 6	Grade 9	Grade 12
Whites	54.2	65.9	64.1
Blacks	37.1	31.3	30.2

Source. Smith 1972, table 7.

the amount of variation explained increases over time. Since they attend suburban schools operating in accord with developmental policies, class differentials increase. For blacks the amount of between-school variation is much lower, and it declines as the child progresses through the educational system. Since they attend central-city schools with redistributive policies, class differentials, never great in the beginning, ebb away.

Conclusions

Suburban towns are small enough that they often can do much to maximize the value of their community property. Because of their limited size, they can modulate their local policies to suit the particular preferences of a relatively small number of residents. Through zoning laws they may even be able to achieve roughly equal contributions in taxes from all residents, thereby minimizing interresident variability in the benefit/tax ratio. The most favorably placed of these suburbs can, if they wish, attract the most productive elements in the metropolitan area. Communities can even zone out unpleasant, though productive, commercial activities in favor of quiet, residential gardens that become the most socially exclusive preserves in the metropolitan area. High-quality public services can be provided to all residents without any resident suffering a particular adverse benefit/tax ratio, because all residents pay roughly the same amounts for the services. Redistribution is kept to a minimum.

The central city cannot afford such an exclusive zoning policy; maintaining its economic base is far too pressing a concern. Yet it services such a large and diverse set of residents that it cannot escape from engaging in a considerable degree of redistribution. To some extent, service provision can be differentially provided among neighborhoods, so that the well-to-do, who pay more, receive more in services. But the central city is limited in its capacity to allocate resources differentially. In the first place, constitutional stipulations require that governments treat citizens in similar circumstances in much the same way. Great differentials in public service provision that corresponded to the great differentials in taxes paid could probably not stand a constitutional test. In surburbia, however, the separation of government into many small, competing parts allows for varying levels of service that have not been successfully challenged on constitutional grounds. Second, standardization characterizes the delivery of big-city services on a large scale. Partly because bureaucracies are committed to universalistic norms, partly because bureaucracies want to protect themselves from political pressures, and partly because administrative efficiency requires the implementation of standard operating routines throughout the organization's geographical reach, central cities tend to provide similar services throughout their jurisdictions. With uniformity comes redistribution, and with redistribution comes damage to the city's economic interests. By comparison, one finds in suburbia many administrative jurisdictions, each with its own policies, servicing divergent populations at a multiplicity of different levels. Redistribution in service delivery is once again kept to a much reduced level.

In this chapter these points have been exemplified with reference to educational policy, the largest and most costly of local government services and the one for which the highest quality (though still imperfect) set of data on policy consequences is available. Yet the findings seem generalizable to a wide range of policy areas. What is characteristic of central-city schools is probably also characteristic of central-city fire departments, sanitation departments, recreation programs, park districts, and street maintenance programs. There will of course be some inequality in the benefits received from these services. The higher income groups who pay more in taxes probably receive more of the benefits. Their streets are probably cleaner, their parks are probably more conveniently located and better maintained, and their garbage may be collected more efficiently and frequently. But even though services are not equal in central cities, at least some redistribution seems to occur. The tendency to uniformity in service provision precludes a careful calibration that relates benefits received to taxes paid along the lines that seem quite feasible in suburbia. Consequently, in the daily operation of routine services cities are less well equipped to pursue their economic interests than are their suburban neighbors.

At one time these differentials between cities and suburbs were a minor nuisance. Because cities were located at the nodal points of fixed water and rail transportation networks, they monopolized the most valuable land in the region. Whatever differences existed in local taxes and expenditure policies, these weighed lightly on a scale where the physical location of cities sat so heavily. The largest and most powerful of cities could exploit the great wealth their location generated to provide a level of public services that far outstripped the outlying communities. As was shown in chapter 3, redistributive policies are the prerogative of those local governments that command comparatively great economic resources. At the turn of the century and even up to World War II, the comparative advantage lay so one-sidedly with central cities that they could ignore the impact of a suburbia that had found a way of escaping the costs of redistribution.

The changed transportation and communication systems of the postwar period have challenged the dominance of central cities. Transportation systems are no longer fixed, streets and highways now connect almost all spaces in a metropolitan area in a more or less evenhanded way, and no community has a monopoly on critical land in the way central cities once did. The level of intercommunity competition both within metropolitan areas and among them has greatly increased. What governments do to enhance the economic well-being of their communities has become much more critical.

Central cities have been slow to recognize these changes in their economic and physical environment. Their policies, a reflection of a more prosperous era, are now only slowly adapting to the more competitive circumstances of today. The luxury of redistribution which was once possible is becoming increasingly difficult to sustain. Cities are beginning to cut back the most ostentatious features and are asking the federal government to assist them with others. In the meantime, the process of migration from central cities continues, as residents search for a locale where they can receive the most for what they pay in taxes. As a doctor friend of mine said recently of the small Wisconsin town to which he had moved, "I don't mind paying taxes here because you see your tax dollars working for you."

3

City Limits and
Urban Politics

Six

Parties and Groups in Local Politics

According to conventional understandings of local politics, party competition and group pressures are as much a hallmark of local as of national politics. Within this explanatory framework, it would seem difficult for cities to appraise their long-term economic interests with reasonable care and then proceed to enact policies consistent with those interests. Especially in central cities, where economic interests would seem to require policies contrary to the redistributive demands of large numbers of workers, minorities, and the poor, it might seem that internal political pressures would preclude due attention to the city's economic growth. But this view accords a too generous role to political parties and interest groups. Many cities, like Oakland, are "characterized by a lack of interest in the electoral process and an absence of political parties and groups."[1] Although there are exceptions to these patterns, a comparative analysis of national and local politics reveals significant differences. By contrast to national patterns, local politics do not typically fit the pressure group model. Instead, they are generally a quiet arena of decision making where political leaders can give reasoned attention to the longer range interests of the city, taken as a whole. Just as local policy is limited by the interests of cities, so political processes at the local level are limited.

Parties and Nonparties in the Limited City
Political Parties in National Politics

In the national politics of most industrialized societies political parties have provided the critical link connecting voters to those in authority. As a by-product of the interparty competition for power, parties formulate policy proposals, search for public support, promote or modify their schemes as proves necessary, and amass the power essential for promulgating the most popular aspects of their programs. Where two or more parties compete for voter support, they must attend to public opinion. They may attempt to change the public's mind, or they may make only the minimal policy concessions they believe are necessary, but they cannot ignore the voter altogether. To do so is to give partisan opponents an opportunity to capture public favor and eventually assume the reins of government.

The competition among parties does not ensure a perfect representation of public opinion in the counsels of government. That exists only in a utopian world of perfect information and complete certainty.[2] In the real world, voters attend to political questions in such a slipshod and haphazard manner that political leaders are allowed great discretion in the formulation of policy. Even the policymaker who wishes to choose the most popular alternatives may often be at a loss to know what the public wants. Yet it is in the world of imperfect information and uncertain futures that political parties provide their most valuable function. By offering similar sets of candidates under the same labels year after year, they greatly simplify the choices the voter has to make. As V. O. Key understood so clearly, it is because the same political parties, with roughly the same ideals, ideologies, and bases of support, regularly compete with one another that the voter does not need all that much information to know which contestant best reflects his interests and opinions.[3] If a worker knows that the Democrats have been more concerned about unemployment than inflation and if a businessman knows that Republicans are more inclined to reduce the costs of social services, neither needs to follow every twist and turn in Congressional debates to make a plausible choice on election day.[4] In this way, regular competition among the same political parties, one election after another, structures and stabilizes political relationships, facilitating voter impact on public policy.

It would be wrong to exaggerate the control over public policy that party competition gives to the voter. Many public policies are formulated by small groups of civil servants and interested group leaders in quiet discussions that attract the interest of only highly specialized publications.[5] Other policies are concocted in moments of national crisis when leaders, desperate to find some feasible solution, pay attention to electoral opinion only when giving explanations for their choices.[6] Yet it would be equally foolhardy to dismiss party politics as totally insignificant. Certainly, the great extension of the welfare state in the 1930s and thereafter, including the provision of housing, welfare, and educational services to the working population, transformed the Democratic party into the majority party. And both Republicans and Democrats have been sensitive to public pressures on race-related issues.

While party competition functions to give voters some influence over national policy, one cannot accept any eufunctional theory that assumes that party competition automatically springs into existence. National political parties are great institutions founded in moments of national crisis and conflict. However much parties may routinize the connections between citizens and their governments, the birth of parties is always traumatic. Parties are made and unmade by great issues involving war and peace, depression and recovery, race and religion, economic growth and social equality. In France and Germany the party system has been restructured each time wars or depressions have forced a constitutional crisis. In Great Britain the Liberal party was supplanted by Labour only when the Liberals were torn asunder by the Irish question and by the increasing class consciousness of trade unionists and workers at the end of World War I. Even in the relatively placid United States the contemporary party structure was shaped by great historical crises: the Civil War, which established Republicanism; the sectional conflict over industrialization coupled with the depression of 1893, which crippled the Democratic party for another third of a century; the Great Depression of the 1930s, which, together with Democratic embracement of trade unions and the welfare state, revived Democratic fortunes; and recent racial and international conflicts that not only restored competitive national elections but threatened to restructure the social base for the party system once again.[7]

Political Parties and Local Politics

If great issues have made great national parties, local politics is too limited for the same to have happened there. Local parties cannot be punished for military losses abroad or economic disasters at home, because they cannot direct armies or control—or even appear to control—the winds of economic change. Less obviously, local parties cannot permanently redress racial grievances, soften religious controversy, or incorporate trade unions into the political economy. Although some political leaders in certain local political jurisdictions may experiment with solutions to these issues, lasting settlements are always forged at the national level—and national political leaders take both the credit and the blame for the choices made. The celebrated case of John Lindsay, mayor of the nation's largest city from 1966 to 1973, illustrates the limited impact local issues have on partisan relationships. Elected on the Republican ticket, he sought to cast aside the traditional base of that party's support in

New York and build an electoral alliance that depended heavily on black and Puerto Rican support. He supported civilian review of the police department, gave minority elites discretion over federal poverty and Model Cities funds, decentralized the city's school system, and campaigned for improved minority opportunities in the housing market. In so doing, his government was torn with crises of the sort that could conceivably have restructured the city's party system. Yet his efforts had almost no effect on the national or local orientations of the two major political parties—and even less effect on voter perceptions of the same. In the end, Lindsay had no choice but to change his own party affiliation.[8]

The case is instructive because the context for the creation of a new party system at the local level could hardly have been better. Numerous combustible elements were present: a large metropolis; a highly visible political leader; issues of race and religion; strikes, boycotts, and bitter confrontations that directly affected the lives of every citizen; and exceedingly fluid electoral behavior in the short run. Yet after Lindsay the party system in New York scarcely looked any different than it had before. Ordinarily, local politics are much less interesting than these events in New York; usually they are very dull indeed. Because cities have so few policy options open to them, partisan political life becomes one-dimensional, a pale reflection of national political debates, a thin veneer that has none of the solidity of partisanship as it is usually understood.

There are several consequences for local political processes. First, national parties dominate local political systems. In most localities the parties which capture local office are parties that have gained their standing with the voter by virtue of their role in national politics. In Great Britain the vast bulk of councillors elected to local office are the candidates of the Labour, Conservative, and Liberal parties; although ratepayers groups have won a few contests and nationalist parties have had some success in recent years, these remain peripheral elements in almost all communities.[9] The dominance in local affairs of the national political parties on the European continent is even more complete.[10] And in those cities of the United States where partisan labels are allowed on local ballots, winning candidates are almost always Republicans or Democrats.

In order for a local party to gain sufficient prestige to challenge one of the national parties, it must act in some local crisis in a way that stirs deep loyalties among some significant part of the community. Under some circumstances local politics can be sufficiently meaningful that national loyalties are set to one side. Robert Dahl reported, for example, that in New Haven the Italians voted Republican because their ethnic archenemies, the Irish, dominated the local Democratic party.[11] Significantly, this Italian Republicanism persisted in New Haven when Italians elsewhere were backing the party of Al Smith and Franklin Roosevelt, the party considered to be friendly to the "wet" immigrant Catholic. More recently, voters have ignored party identification in municipal campaigns in Gary (Indiana) and Detroit, where candidates came from different racial backgrounds. Yet even these examples of a distinctive local politics demonstrate the ease with which national currents penetrate the local arena. It has proved most difficult for Republicans in New Haven to maintain themselves as a potent political force with Italians finding their interests and culture affirmed more clearly by the national Democratic party. Had not Roosevelt stabbed Mussolini "in the back" on the eve of United States entry into World War II, the Republican position in New Haven probably would have decayed much earlier. And the links between black voters and the Democratic party now seem more inseparable than ever. In general, local government does not handle the burning issues of war and peace, depression and recovery, foreign alliances, and immigration controls that can shake fundamental partisan loyalties. As a consequence, local parties are almost always derivative of national identifications.

Second, because national parties dominate local politics, one finds a strong tendency toward local one-partyism wherever geographical boundaries contain less than a rough cross section of the national population. The "solid South" has been the most notable historical case. More recently, the division between the Democratic central city and Republican suburbia has become a stable component of postwar local politics in the East and Midwest.[12] Because the national Democratic party depends heavily on the political loyalties of racial and religious minorities, Democrats dominate the local political scene wherever these minorities are found in concentration. In rural and suburban areas the white Protestant majority is overwhelming—and Republicans generally enjoy continuous control.

Third, outcomes of local elections are largely determined by public opinion toward the national political parties. One can find the best evidence for this pattern in Great Britain, where a party's success at the national level is almost always mirrored at the local level. Voters support local candidates in local British elections on the basis of the candidate's affiliation with one or another of the national political parties. In some communities a burning local issue, such as comprehensive education or an increase in local rates, or the selling of local council houses, will affect a party's margin of victory. A particularly well liked local notable will gather additional votes because of the care with which he serves the local ward or because of his well-known concern for the welfare of the community. But these are minor variations on the dominant theme of nationally conditioned local partisanship.[13]

Fletcher has shown just how difficult it is for local politicians to hold their own against a national tide in Great Britain. From 1962 to 1964 over one-half of all individual constituency swings in the fourteen boroughs he analyzed were within 2.5 percent of the median swing for all boroughs combined, and three-fourths of all boroughs fell within 5 percent of the median. The average swing in the local elections Fletcher investigated, moreover, was within 1 percent of the national swing in attitudes toward the national parties, as measured by the Gallup Poll at the time of the election.[14] In other words, as the party does in the country, so the party does in city and ward. The local politicians have little personal control over their destiny.

In the United States, national party influences at local levels have ebbed in the past few decades. But when parties were as strong in this country as they remain in Great Britain, the same impact of national preferences on local elections was evident. As James Bryce observed nearly a century ago:

> Every trial of strength in a State election is assumed to presage a similar result in a national election . . . . In fact the whole machinery is worked exactly as if the State were merely a subdivision of the Union for electoral purposes. Yet nearly all the questions which come before State legislatures have nothing whatsoever to do with the tenets of the national parties . . . . The average American voter troubles himself little about the conduct of State business. He votes the party ticket at elections as a good party man, and is pleased when his party wins . . . . The politics which he reads by preference are national politics, and especially whatever touches the next presidential election.[15]

In some cases Bryce's analysis has continuing pertinence. In those cities where municipal elections are partisan, there is a noticeable convergence of national and local electoral trends.[16] And in Congressional elections, which are always partisan contests, national influences have become increasingly more important than local constituency influences throughout the twentieth century.[17] Had local politics remained as partisan as have these Congressional elections, Bryce's assessment of municipal politics might today be more compelling than ever.

Partly because local parties have been so dependent upon national divisions, partisan politics at the local level has lost much of the legitimacy it once had. Using arguments once voiced by Bryce, reformers have driven parties from the ballot in over 70 percent of American cities with a population of 25,000 or more.[18] Local politics is in most places the politics of nonpartisanship.

In these nonpartisan cities the connections between local voters and local public officials are further weakened. In the first place, nonpartisan elections have a lower rate of voter turnout than do partisan elections.[19] Evidently, where parties do not compete for local office, voters are less interested in campaigns and less easily mobilized to participate. Moreover, the drop in voter turnout is not uniform throughout the city but is especially concentrated in working-class neighborhoods.[20] Apparently, nonpartisan institutions of political mobilization—the press, interest groups, friends and neighbors, campaign organizations—are most effective in mobilizing the higher income, better educated electorate. As a result, Republicans probably do much better in nonpartisan elections than they would if elections were held on a partisan basis.[21] Without the party label many voters who choose Democratic candidates in national elections vote for candidates whose actual though not publicly identifiable party affiliation is in fact Republican. The reverse happens less often, and, as a result, the more conservative party has a political advantage. Also, there is some evidence that the Chamber of Commerce, other businessmen's associations, middle-class interest groups, and a business-oriented, conservative press have considerable influence in the policymaking processes of nonpartisan cities.[22]

Nonpartisanship is not just conservative; it often becomes issueless politics as well. For one thing incumbents are even less likely to be defeated than they are in partisan contests.[23] Where party labels are absent, the one difference among candidates readily apparent to voters is the incumbency of one and the challenging stance of the other. With no other guide, voters value experience. To offset the advantage of incumbency, opposition campaigns are issueless efforts to secure name recognition. In Seattle one challenger who succeeded in upsetting an incumbent used an attractive advertisement showing the candidate running to catch (and just making) a bus, with the caption "Randy Ravelle is running for Council." In such elections, control of substantial financial resources and the backing of prestige groups, such as the municipal league or the citywide newspaper, is the surest path to electoral success. There is no substitute for competitive political parties, if one wishes to achieve some semblance of public influence over the workings of government.

In short, local politics is limited politics. Its issues are not great enough to generate its own partisan political life. As a result, national political parties easily eliminate any ratepayers' associations, good government leagues, or other independent groups seeking only local power. The national parties, whose voter loyalties were secured amid great national triumphs or tragedies, can amass overwhelming support in local contests on that basis alone. But these local political parties are one-dimensional, just a reflection of the national debate. Nearly a century ago, reformers saw as the answer to this problem the establishment of nonpartisan systems of electoral politics. If local issues were not powerful enough to allow for the generation of local parties independent of the national party system, all political parties should be banned. Voters would then be able to focus on local political issues and choose candidates who would best serve local community interests. The solution is appealing, until one discovers that without parties voters lose a critical mechanism for voicing their needs and wants.

Local Politics Is Groupless Politics

Since de Tocqueville, many have thought local politics to be the wellspring of democracy. It is at the grass roots level that people can most readily gather together to act directly on matters of immediate social relevance. The issues are focused, the contexts are clear, leaders are known by their constituents, and formats for mutual exchange can be easily arranged. Local government is close to the people and easily subject to their influence.

These and other claims for local government conjure up images of the New England town meeting, where citizens gather together and decide what is in their mutual interest. But the contemporary local community is usually much too large and its citizens much too distracted by nonpolitical matters to realize public decisions through such an unmediated form of citizen participation. The local governments of large central cities embrace a population that is larger than many nation-states, and even small suburban communities have populations that number in the tens of thousands, a size far too large for patterns of political participation that can involve meaningfully the whole adult community. Even in local politics, citizen participation must be organized by political groups, and these groups must act as representatives for their constituents. Otherwise, the bulk of the population is not likely to participate in local decision making at all. And if this is the case, then the public does not have quite the impact on local policy as enthusiasts for grass roots democracy imply.

Groups and National Politics

Most sophisticated statements of democratic theory recognize the importance of formally organized political groups as channels connecting public opinion to public policy.[24] And for that reason the group component of contemporary democratic theory locates an interstitial role for groups that is second only to the primary role reserved for political parties. In the context of democratic theory, political parties are especially concerned about electoral victory and the pursuit of power; their representative function is thus limited to aggregating or compromising or responding to citizen demands. It is the political group that has the flexibility and specificity to articulate these demands in the first place, forcing parties and politicians to deal with problems that citizens share.

The empirical basis for group theory is once again derived largely from the national political arena. In the United States the great influence of formally organized political groups has been handsomely documented. Formally registered lobbyists in Washington number in the thousands; political groups contribute large sums to electoral campaigns; their spokesmen constantly testify before Congress; groups issue public statements on almost all policy questions under discussion; congressmen seem to pay attention at least to those groups with whom they have formed an alliance; groups are well represented on advisory councils within the executive branch; their leaders often assume important positions on authoritative boards and commissions; and they are often credited with major modifications or outright rejections of vital Presidential policy proposals. Except for those few who believe a small elite of power holders concocts important national policy, the debate among academics has seldom disputed the influence of political groups. Instead, the debate has turned on whether these groups represent or subvert the interests of the larger public.[25]

Groups and Local Politics

At the local level, formally organized groups play a much less prominent role in policy formation. Although many instances of group influence in local policy undoubtedly occur, their overall impact is much less than implied by the group theory literature. In David Caputo's words, "It is rare for a group to have significant and sustained impact on the [local] policy-making process."[26] A decade earlier Banfield and Wilson said much the same thing about local controversies: "Civic associations are rarely effective in terms of their stated ends."[27] Summarizing the results of an earlier study, they report that civic associations took ambiguous positions; they could not influence politicians because the politicians did not know what the associations actually wanted. On other issues the associations took no stands at all; they withdrew. In still other issues, when they did take positions they used ineffective tactics.[28]

Studies of routine policymaking also affirm the marginal impact of organized groups. For example, there is little evidence that groups play much of a role in local budgetary processes. According to one study, policymakers rarely encountered much group pressure, and when they did, those in authority concluded that "the city simply does not have the resources necessary to satisfy these requests."[29] In another study a local official reports that when confronted by group demands in public hearings he and his colleagues

> either know the positions ahead of time or agree to no changes regardless of what the public says or does .... Just about anything can be turned down by citing the lack of funds or the feeling that this is special legislation and not really beneficial to the entire city.[30]

Wood's study of nonpartisan suburbia also identifies little in the way of organized group influence. Instead, decisions are taken by city managers and professionalized bureaucrats. "The conflicts and relationships among political groups are necessarily subterranean."[31]

In particular policy areas research reveals similar patterns. Gardiner's study of the traffic control policies of local police departments explains policy variation primarily in terms of the policy preferences of police commissioners. Public or group influence seems to have little effect. The efforts of safety councils, the police chiefs reported, had "little influence on drivers and none on them."[32] Similarly, Derthick reports that variations in local welfare policy cannot be "traced to differences in politically expressed community values" but are a function of administrative discretion.[33] Dahl does claim to have found significant group influences in New Haven, but his evidence of grass roots influence is largely limited to one case study in which white home owners were able to keep blacks out of their community.[34] In retrospect the case probably says more about the state of race relations in New Haven than the state of group influence across a range of policy issues. Wolfinger's study of New Haven's urban renewal program is a far more detailed, exact, and meticulous study of decision-making processes. He concluded that "the mayor played the leading role in policy formation, activating and manipulating interest groups. More than anything else, urban renewal policy resulted from his ambitions, not those of private groups."[35]

Studies of mass participation in local politics confirm reports of low group influence. For one thing, there is little doubt that voter participation is less in local than in national elections. Of course, there is a great deal of variation from one election to the next and the exact percentages depend on whether registered voters or the entire adult population are taken as the base. But the drop-off from the national to the local levels is significant, no matter what the measuring device. Whereas in Presidential elections voter turnout of the population can reach a high of 60 percent, in nonconcurrent local elections just over 30 percent of the adult population cast a ballot in an average election.[36] In seventeen cities turnout in mayoral elections averaged 58 percent of the registered voters during the period 1972–74, significantly less than the 72.2 percent voting in the 1972 Presidential election in these same cities.[37] Respondents are notorious for overreporting their voting behaviors to interviewers, but only 47 percent of a national sample claimed they always voted in local elections while 72 percent made this claim with respect to national elections.[38] Other indicators of citizen involvement at the local level yield similar results. Wildavsky once asked residents of Oberlin, Ohio, if they cared a great deal about what goes on in national, state, and local politics. Eighty-seven percent cared about national politics but only 61 and 65 percent cared about state and local politics, respectively.[39] National surveys also report that citizens follow national and international politics more closely than local politics.[40]

Conditions Affecting Citizen Participation

At one time group theorists assumed that citizens entered the political fray and formed groups spontaneously whenever policies of importance to them were under consideration. But the work of Mancur Olson and James Wilson has demonstrated that group formation is an uncertain, highly problematic political process bedeviled by the problem known as the "free rider."[41] One might think that citizens would form groups rather naturally out of simple self-interest. If government took an action adversely affecting the welfare of some segment of the population or if a segment hoped to see benefits for themselves arising out of some governmental innovation, it would seem only natural for citizens to combine politically. But it turns out that individual self-interests work in quite the opposite direction. Where government action is concerned, there is usually only a small probability that any change in the benefits one receives can be effected by one's own political activities. Either the change would have occurred even if one had done nothing at all, or else the change does not occur even after vigorous personal effort. Most people intuitively understand this. "You can't fight City Hall," goes one old saying. Another observes that "there is no sense getting involved in something you can't do anything about."[42]

A hypothetical example will clarify this point. Citizens may feel that sanitation services in their neighborhood are hopelessly inadequate. Streets are not cleaned very often, and when they are cleaned, the work is done poorly. Moreover, the garbage is collected irregularly and infrequently. Not knowing when the refuse will be collected, citizens cannot prepare for the truck's arrival. The residents of the neighborhood have a serious grievance and a common stake in taking action. One might expect that a political group would form rather easily. But there may be problems. Street cleaning and garbage collection may be provided by two different governmental bureaucracies. Each may have a strong record of resisting political pressures from politicians or neighborhood groups; and workers in each department may have their own union, which must be consulted on matters affecting conditions of employment. Most neighbors doubt that anything would be done if they did form a political group. On the other hand, things might improve without their action. The new mayor might appoint more vigorous heads of these departments, or newspaper complaints might slowly bring some improvement. Or maybe others in the neighborhood will make the effort to complain to City Hall; if they do and City Hall does respond to their demands, then even those who make no complaints at all will still benefit. Given all these considerations, most people usually wait. Unless some event galvanizes the community or some public-spirited citizen provides strong leadership, the problem can continue indefinitely.

In sum, two basic factors affect the probability that groups will form to influence governmental action. First, the greater the effect of the policy on group interests, the more likely that group activity will occur. This proposition is standard in group theory literature. Second, and equally important, the greater the probability that group action will modify public policy, the more likely that group formation will occur. Until the work of Olson and others, this latter proposition had not been given sufficient weight.[43] As we shall see, neither the first nor the second factor contributes as much to the mobilization of groups in local as in national politics.

Importance of Public Policy

The most important public policies are determined by the national government. First, the nation-state determines whether the country will be at peace or war, the cost and extent of its military preparedness, and the countries which will be its allies. As a result, peace groups, defense contractors, unions employed by them, veterans groups, and patriotic associations will all be interested primarily in national policy. Second, the nation-state determines overall fiscal and monetary policy, which influences levels of economic growth, inflation rates, and rates of unemployment. It also determines trading policies with other nations, including tariffs on imports, controls on extension of credit outside the country, currency exchange rates, the conditions under which domestic currency can be exchanged for foreign currency, subsidies for exports, conditions under which foreign workers may immigrate, and methods of taxing profits made overseas. All these policies vitally influence the broadest interests of both the business community and the trade union movement. At the same time these policies affect the special interests of particular industries and specific firms. As a result, Washington is crowded not only with broadly based groups like the Chamber of Commerce and AFL–CIO but also with the more specialized groups representing petroleum, textiles, steel, sugar, and so on.

The stakes at the local level are by comparison of only secondary importance. But even aside from the substantive importance of any particular policy question to any group, one basic element in the structure of local government diminishes the significance of local public policy: any individual or group injured by it can "exit" to another jurisdiction.[44] In local politics, as distinct from national politics, the individual always has the choice between "fighting" or "switching." And it is probably no accident that a number of instances of community conflict end with the losers leaving town.[45] Undoubtedly, the availability of "exit" locally but not nationally contributes to differentials between patterns of citizen participation at national and local government levels.

Restrictions on the Exercise of Group Influence

Some might think that the secondary importance of local issues is more than compensated for by the greater opportunities for citizen influence within the small space of local politics.[46] One finds democracy at the grass roots because people feel their efforts can make a difference. As sensible as this argument seems, it does not hold up under close scrutiny. In the first place, local governments in urban settings are not responsible for so small a population that where two or three are gathered together they can have great influence. Moreover, local political processes are so structured as to discourage group formation. Already, it has been shown that political parties do not provide the same access of citizens to leaders at the local as at the national level. In addition, citizen participation and group influence is hindered by (1) the closed procedures by which local governments conduct their business; (2) the more restricted role of the news media in local politics; (3) the lesser ambitions of local politicians; and (4) the lesser use of polling techniques in local politics.

Closed Decision-making Processes

In national politics the processes of policy formation involve many participants and are often subjected to considerable public scrutiny. Before legislation is recommended by a President, his federal department or White House staff members consult informed outsiders and affected group interests. Even within the executive branch, agencies assume responsibility for representing specific groups. Once announced, the President's recommendations are publicly broadcast, and both popular and specialized news media analyze their strengths and limitations. And this is only the beginning of a complex, prolonged policymaking process for most legislative proposals. Bills must pass through the complex subcommittees and committee structures of the two houses of Congress, and any appropriations that might be involved must be made in a quite separate legislative effort. Committees hold public hearings, Congressional debates are recorded in the *Congressional Record*, most groups with interests at stake have time to communicate to their constituents, and the resulting clash of interests is recorded in roll call votes that may be examined by groups and constituents alike.

Specialists on the national legislative process may suspect that the above paragraph is taken from a high school civics text. They are only too familiar with the propensity of Presidents to camouflage their choice making behind the anonymity of the White House staff, with the capacity of subcommittee chairmen to bury undesired legislation, with the way in which parliamentary maneuvers can obscure substantive issues in procedural votes, and with the ease with which conference committees—in secret session—can reconstruct legislation so that it no longer reflects the will of either the House or the Senate. Secrecy, surprise, and misrepresentation are integral to policymaking at all levels of government, and much can be made of the slip between the form and substance of public access to the national policymaking scene.

But when all these gaps have been duly considered, the disjunction between procedural democratic forms at national and local levels still deserves emphasis. In Washington, meetings of Congress, its committees, regulatory hearings, and even many meetings within the executive branch are open to the public, formally announced, and often quite well attended. In local politics, meetings of boards and commissions are held in secret or at times unannounced to the general public. City councils and school boards often call for executive sessions when discussing particularly significant topics, such as those affecting personnel or land use. When held in public, these meetings are often devoted only to routine topics, decisions are taken unanimously, and formal approval is given to questions previously resolved behind closed doors. Moreover, the meetings of public agencies are seldom transcribed, and when they are, the transcripts are generally not available to the public. The few times public agencies do hold public hearings, any records thereof are reserved for official eyes. There is nothing like the *Congressional Record* or the official volume of testimony presented before Congressional committees. Agendas for meetings are seldom announced, and the official documents under deliberation are not circulated to outsiders prior to passage. Decision-making bodies are unicameral, and requirements for second and third readings of legislation are unusual. The complex processes of decision making, which in Washington provide groups numerous opportunities to gather information on the state of proposed legislation and a host of points at which its shape can be altered, are noteworthy for their absence at the local level.[47]

The Press in Local Politics

The disjunction between national and local politics is never so evident as in the differing role the news media play. Hundreds of reporters daily cover the activities of the White House, both Houses of Congress, and numerous committees; the workings of the departments and regulatory agencies; and important judicial events. Important policy initiatives are at least covered in more specialized news media, and they may attract the attention of the more sophisticated publications, such as the *Washington Post* and the *New York Times*. In addition to their daily news programs, television and radio are developing their own in-depth reporting capability. Quite clearly, investigative reporting has become more fashionable in the aftermath of Watergate. Some critics say that the press has grown so powerful that earnest, capable individuals are being deterred from accepting offers to perform public service. Other critics say that the press is too submissive in the face of authority, takes only safe, middle-of-the-road positions, and withholds criticism for fear of jeopardizing contacts. But there is little doubt that in Washington we find the elite of the press corps competitively searching for the big story. If we are to believe newspaper editorials, a free press is our guarantee of liberty. But even if we view more skeptically the capacity of the news media to provide the citizenry with useful information, we can hardly imagine much public control over public policy without the vigorous watchdog that the presence of the national news media at their best provides.

By comparison to the pervasive coverage of national politics, the role of the press locally seems especially subdued. First, the news media do not have the same incentives to scrutinize local public policy. There is, for example, less competition among local than among national newspapers. In many smaller communities there may be only a weekly newspaper or a daily heavily dependent upon the wire services and local publicity handouts. Even the larger cities most often have only one newspaper, without a competitor whose efforts to get the "inside story" reporters feel they must beat. Second, it is usually the national news stories that grab the headlines and sell papers, and therefore local papers know that astute utilization of the national wire services is more important than the more expensive legwork necessary to generate good local stories. Others have observed that "the cost of really covering local government and civic affairs is high, and the return in readership, and ultimately in advertising, is usually low."[48] Third, newspapers boost their hometown, knowing that its prosperity and expansion aid their own. Harping at local faults, investigating dirty politics, revealing unsavory scandals, and stressing governmental inefficiencies only provide readily available documentary material to competing cities, which might find such information useful in campaigns to attract workers and industry. Although in larger cities the news media will seek to sell papers and exert influence by discovering a local "scandal," in moderately sized cities newspapers seem to concentrate more on local successes: scholarships local students have won, athletic victories won in the city's name, the unveiling of new public facilities, and any hint of economic expansion. City newspapers know that building confidence is necessary for local prosperity, and therefore they "must present a favorable image to outsiders,"[49] using sparingly their issue-raising capacities.[50]

Quite apart from their incentives to cover local politics gently, the local news media simply do not have the resources of national wire services, broadcasting companies, or major newspapers and magazines with a national audience. The news media have high fixed costs. The resources necessary to gather and interpret a complex news story are as great for a newspaper in a medium-sized city as for a national wire service, yet the former has neither the same audience nor the advertising revenue to cover these costs. As a result, all but the largest metropolitan newspapers must do without a large, specialized staff of news reporters. The few reporters most papers can afford to hire must acquire expertise that ranges from crime stories to schools, from finance to housing. Understandably, these reporters come to depend on the official releases of government agencies and the comments of well-known participants in the policymaking process. Even more certainly, there is little time for investigative reporting. Given their limited resources, local papers are unable to keep their best reporters from using the local beat as a mere stepping-stone to a career covering national and international stories.[51]

Ambitions of Politicians

The bifurcation of national and local political careers affects the opportunities for citizen participation and group formation. In national politics many politicians eagerly seek reelection. The competition for the presidency is keen, and few can resist the temptations of remaining in that office for as many terms as the Constitution allows. Kennedy, Johnson, Humphrey, Nixon, Carter, Ford, Reagan, and even Goldwater and McGovern all were ambitious enough to tailor their programs to what they thought would win elections. Congressmen, too, are becoming ever more professional and increasingly sophisticated in their techniques for sustaining themselves in office.[52]

Local politicians are much less politically ambitious—either to remain in their present office or to advance to higher office. In Kenneth Prewitt's words, they are "volunteers" for office, who are often initially appointed, are reelected time and again with little opposition, and finally retire from office voluntarily.[53] Several structural features discourage the more ambitious people from seeking office. First, the strictly pecuniary rewards are comparatively limited. In Washington one can become a modestly wealthy individual by serving one's Congressional district. Salaries are competitive with all but the highest paid professional positions, and the perquisites of office are handsome, including a large staff, extensive office space, inexpensive privileged services on Capitol Hill, free postage and travel, and a variety of opportunities to supplement one's income through speaking and writing. The local politician often serves without pay or with a small, partial salary that must be supplemented with a privately earned income. City council members have hardly any staff or office space, and few other side benefits of much pecuniary value.

Second, Washington politicians are forced to make a full-time career out of politics, and to continue that career, they must be constantly concerned about reelection. The physical fact of moving from one's home to Washington emphasizes the impact the office has on those holding it. The local politician more often regards his public office as occupying a position secondary to the activity that provides for most of his livelihood. Since he does not need to move from his home and community to perform his political functions, his previous friends and acquaintances continue to structure much of his social life—and they do so whether or not he remains in office. The local politician thus can leave public life without the personal and social disruption a congressman experiences.

Third, the psychological satisfactions that come from public service at the local level may for many people be less than those that come from national service. There are not the same opportunities for socializing with famous people, for travel to distant countries on official business, for seeing oneself discussed in widely distributed media, or for feeling that one has played a part in important decisions. To be sure, local dignitaries may participate in ceremonies honoring guests from foreign countries, and they may find their own opinions discussed on local news programs. For some, the sense of being a big frog, no matter how small the pond, may be quite enough. But the psychic rewards from political office—and therefore the psychic costs of removal from the same—are usually less for the local than the national political figure.

Fourth, the opportunities for political advancement are necessarily limited for even the most ambitious of local politicians. Although local offices in city government may, for a few, be a staircase to higher office, this option is not available for most local officials. Even big-city mayors have generally not been able to expand their constituency statewide by capturing gubernatorial or senatorial office. Some who have tried have, significantly enough, become more responsive to groups within the local community. The best known cases are John Lindsay and Richard Lee. Lindsay's senatorial and Presidential ambitions may have made him more accessible to group pressures in New York. And Raymond Wolfinger's fascinating account of New Haven politics reveals how significantly New Haven politics was shaped by Lee's ambitions for higher office.[54] Other instances of mayoral ambition include Cavanagh of Detroit, Clark and Dilworth of Philadelphia, Humphrey and Naftalin of Minneapolis, White of Boston, Ullman of Seattle, Yorty of Los Angeles, and Alioto of San Francisco. But except for Clark and Humphrey, none of these very astute politicians were able to break loose from the constraints big-city politics place on elected officials. After an extensive review, Wolfinger finds that "municipal government is the least useful pathway to higher office."[55] In the face of these facts most mayors accept the limits that are placed on their ambitions. No wonder Prewitt concluded that volunteerism was "undoubtedly more prevalent at the local than the state and at the state than the national level."[56]

Since local politicians are not as ambitious as national politicians, they do not have the same incentive to establish mechanisms of communication with voters and groups. At the same time, groups attempting to influence local decisions will be frustrated because politicians may not care what they want. Moreover, when these barriers to communication between groups and officials arise, the likelihood that groups will organize in the first place is reduced.

Polls and Letters

Scientific polling and less formalized sampling of constituent opinion have increasingly become the means by which Washington monitors public opinion. On the national scene, polling has established itself as a major political business. Not only do independent polls such as Gallup and Harris regularly sample public viewpoints on candidates, issues, and current problems, but prominent national politicians, especially in election years, develop their own polling organizations. Numerous accounts of Presidential campaigns testify to the importance politicians accord the findings of their pollsters.[57] Campaign style, issue selection, and the concentration of campaign resources are all influenced by opinions expressed by a randomly selected segment of the public. Even between elections, polls influence the course of Washington politics. Among other things they alter the strength of the President as he bargains with Congress and interest groups, affect the ease with which legislation is passed, and shape the political strategy of the opposition party.

In addition to scientific polling, less formal samples of public expression are gathered by many national officials. Most congressmen have newsletters that they send to many constituents, and in these newsletters constituents are encouraged to communicate their views. The enormous volume of casework that congressmen undertake also keeps them in regular contact with a significant portion of their constituency, and at least part of that casework touches on policy-relevant issues. The Congressional franking privilege, the huge administrative staff available to members of Congress, and the professional attention to constituent needs all facilitate this form of exchange between citizen and elected official.

Most of these elements are missing at the local level. Polling public opinion is almost as expensive among a relatively small population confined within one city as it is for the United States as a whole. But whereas the cost of a national poll can be borne by national polling organizations with a national audience or by national candidates with national constituencies, the cost of local polling is often prohibitive. Some newspapers do poll statewide constituences, and some local candidates do undertake their own scientific polls in preparation for electoral campaigns. But the practice is limited to candidates for important local offices, and even then it is not done with the completeness and sophistication characteristic of national electoral politics. Most locally elected officials have no scientific way of determining local public opinion at all. Nor do they have the less formal ways of sampling opinion available to congressmen. Without the franking privilege, without much of an administrative staff, and without the resources to undertake casework activities, most locally elected officials operate with only old-fashioned techniques for sensing the public's will. One does not know just how much the paraphernalia of modern scientific politics does in fact democratize national political life, but whatever its impact at that level may be, it is considerably less in local politics.

In summary, the structure within which citizen participation takes place at the local level is not especially conducive to group influence. The conduct of official business is more secretive, the coverage of local news media is less extensive and less issue-oriented, the local politician is less ambitious for reelection, and the local official has less wherewithal for estimating the state of public opinion. All of these factors serve to isolate public officials from their electorate. The chances that any particular act of citizen participation or group pressure will elicit a positive official response is thereby reduced. Therefore, individuals are less likely to participate, and groups are less likely to form.

Conclusions

Lower levels of citizen involvement in local politics can be understood as rational responses to the structural context in which the public finds itself. The cues facilitating political involvement in national politics are in many cases noticeably absent. Much of the time, political parties do not structure conflict, issues do not have as burning an importance, and candidates do not ambitiously compete for office. Information on local problems is hard to obtain from newspapers, and the decisions taken by local officials are made in obscure settings. Interest groups do not identify causes that mobilize mass involvement.

There are two consequences of low-pressure politics at the local level, both of which facilitate the pursuit of city interests. In the first place, formal channels of participation and communication are the mechanism upon which workers, minorities, the unemployed, and the poor are particularly dependent. As many have observed, it is primarily through elections, parties, trade unions, and group activity that the large numbers of ordinary citizens can counteract the prerogatives of smaller numbers of notables.[58] In their absence, access to decision makers is more likely to be reserved to the economically prosperous, the socially prominent, and the bureaucratically influential.

To the extent that local politics weakens the capacity for mass pressures, it allows for due consideration of city economic interests. At times the interest of one or another notable may run contrary to the economic interests of the city as a whole, but it is the interests of the disadvantaged which consistently come into conflict with economically productive policies. By keeping mass involvement at the local level to a minimum, serious pressures for policies contrary to the economic interests of cities are avoided.

Second, where politics are at a low pressure, informal channels of communication substitute for formal ones. In these channels the political resources that count are technical expertise, the power of persuasion, and the capacity to reason soundly. Threats of electoral retribution, on the other hand, are simply counterproductive. In such contexts those promoting a policy must show how the plan is consistent with the economic interests of the city as a whole. In this connection it is worth considering the role that reason and persuasion can play in local politics. When these factors are mentioned as contributing to the formation of a policy, it is usually implied that the reasons themselves were not as important as the persuaders' rhetorical skill, social prestige, or privileged access. Although the matter has never been subjected to systematic inquiry, it is quite probable that reasoned analysis itself affects policy outcomes when the economic interests of cities, taken as a whole, shape policy choice. If a particular policy can be shown to be of long-range economic benefit to the city, its chances for adoption are increased. And the way to persuade decision makers is through convincing argumentation, through presenting relevant facts, and, in general, through the development of a reasoned case that proposed legislation will produce desired consequences.

Finally, these broad comparisons between national and local political patterns must not be taken as a complete account of local politics. In subsequent chapters we shall identify significant differences among political practices in the three different arenas of local public policy. In chapter 7 we shall see that "power-elite" theories of local politics are most persuasive when applied to the politics of development, though even in this arena important qualifications to power structure theory must be made. In chapter 8 the politics of allocation will be shown to consist of a pluralist politics of group conflict and bargaining, with the contest between political machines and urban reformers forming the primary division in some communities. In chapter 9 the politics of redistribution is shown to be the politics of the nonissue. To appreciate fully the variety and complexity of local politics, the differences between these three arenas must be borne in mind. Yet this differentiation itself must be understood within the overall context we have just provided. Because party and group life have less of a role to play at the local level, one finds significantly different patterns of policy formation in the three policy arenas.

Seven

The Politics of Development

Public policy structures political relationships. What governments do affects the patterns of group formation, the way in which coalitions are formed, the channels of access to decision makers, and the range of demands communicated to policymakers. These points were first made by Eckstein in his influential study of the British Medical Association.[1] He showed that just as doctors influenced health policy, so government intervention in health services altered interest group activity. Other analysts, most notably Theodore Lowi, have expanded on Eckstein's insight by attempting to show that the type of public policy that is at stake affects the way in which the political process becomes organized.[2] In the next three chapters I shall follow Lowi by identifying varying political processes in each of three policy arenas. However, my principles of classification differ from Lowi's and apply with particular force to the local political arena.

The Three Policy Types

As was shown in part 2, policies may be usefully classified according to their effects on the city's economic interests. I argued there that each type of policy is both shaped by a different set of social and economic factors and characteristically performed by a different level of government. In the next three chapters I shall argue that each type of policy has associated with it the following distinctive patterns of group formation and citizen participation.

Developmental policies are those that contribute to the economic well-being of the city. Implementation of a developmental proposal can be expected to yield economic benefits that will protect the community's fiscal resources. The policy may even lead to growth and expansion. Plans to attract industry to a community, to extend its transportation system, or to renew depressed areas within the city are characteristic types of developmental policies. Such policies are often promulgated through highly centralized decision-making processes involving prestigious businessmen and professionals.[3] Conflict within the city tends to be minimal, decision-making processes tend to be closed until the project is about to be consummated, local support is broad and continuous, and, if any group objects, that group is unlikely to gain much support; only through lawsuits can it delay or forestall action. If there is more important opposition, it is usually generated by agencies or organizations external to the local political system—perhaps by a competing city or by a federal agency or by a private firm trying to achieve better terms in its negotiations with the city.

Allocational policies have only marginal and unpredictable effects on the interests of cities. They merely distribute local resources among residents by one or another set of criteria, either of which seems consistent with the economic prosperity of the area.[4] Although the issues are small when viewed from a vantage point external to the city, the residents of the city may feel that much is at stake. A good deal of bargaining and competition may ensue, and outcomes are compromises among the claims of various contestants. Each group can be expected to claim that its proposal is in the interest of the city as a whole, but a range of alternative proposals will be more or less equally persuasive in this regard.

Redistributive policies are those policies which, though they have a negative impact on the community's economic growth, still can gain some political support because the programs service needy members of society.[5] On humanitarian grounds alone a strong case can be made for some degree of redistribution. Also, given the large number of low-income residents in central cities, many redistributive programs are politically popular in these localities. As a result, redistributive policies are a type of local public policy likely to be proposed with some regularity, even when the economic consequences of these policies may be adverse. But because redistributive policies are usually at odds with the economic interests of the city, proponents will find difficulty in gathering support for them.[6]

Two factors qualify these relationships between public policy and political processes. First, citizen participation and group formation are affected only insofar as the economic consequences of a policy—over, say, the intermediate run—are recognized by policymakers. The distinctions that will be drawn cannot be applied to those policies whose consequences for the city—either positive or negative—are quite unexpected. Yet it is not unreasonable to assume that policymakers can perceive, at least in rough terms, what are the likely consequences of their policies at least in the short and intermediate run. Most political leaders are reasonably able men and women with fairly well developed systems of information. Although expectations are well worth deviant-case analysis, generalizations about policymaking are more likely to be correct if they assume a degree of intelligence, reasonableness, and rationality on the part of those entrusted with local authority.

Second, these are analytical distinctions among types of policies. Any particular proposal on a civic agenda may have elements within it that are developmental, others that are redistributive, and others that are purely allocational. For example, developmental policies designed to contribute to civic improvement and economic growth have allocational aspects to them. A proposal to establish an industrial park may provoke allocational politics concerning its exact location. To interpret the connections between policy and political process, one needs in such an instance to distinguish analytically the politics surrounding the decision to establish the park from the politics surrounding a decision to locate it in a particular area.

Bearing in mind these reservations, the differences in patterns of citizen participation among the three policy arenas are striking. The politics of allocation and redistribution are discussed in chapters 8 and 9. The remainder of this chapter is limited to specifying the politics of development, as identified by three research traditions: studies of independent authorities; community power studies; and analyses of the politics of urban renewal. By bringing together their findings, key features of developmental politics can be discerned.

Independent Development Authorities

The consensual politics of development is illustrated by the frequency with which responsibility for developmental policy is granted to groups and entities outside the mainstream of local politics. In smaller communities the Chamber of Commerce is as likely to direct developmental programs as is an agency of local government. In two of the four cities studied by Williams and Adrian, for example, "industrial development was handled by a nongovernmental body," with the Chamber of Commerce providing more leadership than the city council.[7] In larger cities and metropolitan areas, important developmental policies come under the direction of independent authorities. The best known examples are the Port of New York Authority and the Triborough Bridge and Tunnel Authority, the two entities that have the greatest impact on transportation and other growth strategies in the New York City area.[8] Other cities have similar institutions. Boston has had its Massachusetts Turnpike Authority, Massachusetts Port Authority, and Boston Redevelopment Authority; Oakland and Seattle their port authorities, and San Francisco its development authority. In addition, state highway departments, which "have tended to be a power unto themselves," make important decisions that impinge on the development of metropolitan areas.[9]

The secret to the autonomy of these independent authorities lies in their self-financing capacities. From the perspective of policymakers within these authorities, the goal is to provide "transportation facilities, paid for by the user, . . . to meet existing or predictable requirements."[10] By means of tolls, gasoline taxes, and license taxes earmarked for the work of their agency, those responsible for major developmental policies have a dependable source of income free of the usual political constraints. Consequently, they invest their monies in projects that are likely to generate the greatest possible return. The director of the Port of New York Authority once stated the objectives of these autonomous agencies with remarkable frankness and clarity:

> An authority is designed to put revenue producing public facilities on their own feet and on their own responsibility; to free them from political interference, bureaucracy and red tape . . . . This test of management, the administrative standards of a well-managed private corporation, is the test that should be applied to the [Authority's] responsibilities and duties.[11]

Operating like private firms, these independent authorities see little point in public discussion. Because it is in the city's interest to develop self-financing projects that enhance the productivity of the community, there is no place for the contentious group conflict that may characterize another policy arena. Thus, "for years, the Massachusetts Port Authority has conducted its business in closed session before opening up its regular monthly meeting in the afternoon. If there is any harsh debate or if there are any controversial issues the board members want kept quiet, the matter can be disposed of in closed session."[12]

No one was better able to wield the power potential inherent in the independent authority structure than Robert Moses. Even if one discounts the more one-sided passages in Robert Caro's unbalanced but fascinating account of this "power broker," the story he tells reveals the way in which power can be centralized when developmental policies are at stake.[13] The source of Moses's constantly renewed power and prestige was the tolls paid by those using the tunnels and bridges he controlled. As long as his resources were constantly expanding, so could his political reach. And because the economic demand for highways was continuously growing, Moses could act with secrecy and dispatch, gain the favor of one New York mayor after another, and build a political network of awesome proportions. Caro attributes Moses's power to his abuse of authority, his relentless attacks on opponents, and his use of Tammany Hall tactics in the name of reform. Moses seems to be guilty on all counts, but these techniques were not the source of his power. The secret to Moses's influence was his control over the largest source of autonomously generated public revenues in the nation's largest city. Had Moses not been the key figure in the formation of New York's transportation system, he never would have commanded the great influence he enjoyed.

In the mid-1960s, toward the end of his career, Moses encountered increasing opposition from neighborhood and environmental groups challenging his economic growth strategy. In Boston, Chicago, San Francisco, and many other cities, similar challenges to highway expansion also had noticeable success.[14] Developmental policy, which had traditionally been characterized by a consensual decision-making process, began to provoke debate of a more political nature. The factors accounting for these changes were both episodic and long-term. Of only temporary significance, perhaps, were the many groups and organizations spawned by the civil rights movement which in this period were challenging many aspects of local government. A decade later most of these organizations had lost their vitality. In the long run, the changing place of transport in the American economy is more significant. The economic benefits of an increasingly complex and sophisticated highway system have become ever more marginal. As the economic case for highway expansion weakens, those with environmental or other concerns that conflict with the goals of the highway planners gain in political strength. Highway issues are probably moving from the developmental to the allocational arena, and the politics of highways may in future take on a different character.

But even though highway politics may become more complex as energy resources become more constrained, for several decades they provided such a clear instance of developmental policy that responsibility for their promulgation could be delegated to highly autonomous independent authorities. Such delegation works best when the policy objective is clear and the means for accomplishing it are quite specific. In other cases developmental policies have such diverse effects and cut across so many jurisdictional boundaries that informal networks of power and influence must be built to accomplish the objective. To understand these processes, one must turn to the literature on community power.

Community Power Structures

Hunter, Miller, and the many others who employed the reputational method in the study of community power generated a significant number of little-appreciated findings about the politics of development.[15] Their work is of special interest because the method they employed readily identified those who were most active in developmental politics and because their case studies were characteristically drawn from the developmental policy arena. Within this arena they typically found that businessmen were most active, that decision-making processes were closed and consensual, and that individuals active in developmental politics were accorded considerable prestige by other members of the community. Because those employing this method attempted to generalize their findings to all of local politics, they opened themselves to serious criticism, which has never been effectively answered. As a result, their small but genuine contribution has not been fully recognized.

Indeed, hardly any respectable faction in academia now accords much significance to the work of Floyd Hunter and his followers.[16] To most urbanists, the studies are only of some historical interest, significant because they redirected inquiry away from a focus on formal governmental institutions to broader questions of power and democracy. It has been widely accepted that the methodology Hunter employed was woefully inadequate for identifying power distributions. Hunter identified only the reputation for power that some of the most prominent community residents enjoyed; he did not study the actual exercise of their influence. The critical work by Polsby, Wolfinger, and others not only convinced pluralists that they should employ a decision-making methodology instead, but also persuaded both neo-elite and Marxist urbanists that the reputational method was seriously defective. They rejected both decision-making and reputational methodologies in their search for the "other face of power."[17] As Polsby said recently about his earlier critique of the reputationalists, "I conclude that the argument...about the deficiencies of the [reputational approach and] stratification theory of community power is fairly well accepted."[18]

Many of Polsby's criticisms of Hunter's work are most certainly justified. Hunter's research was conducted in a casual manner; his writing fluctuated from sociological obscurantism to journalistic sensationalism; and the inferences he drew were not warranted by the findings produced. But enough time has now passed that it is possible to discern what substantive contributions Hunter and other reputationalist writers have made. If one sets aside Hunter's own inferences and concentrates on his findings, and those of others writing in this tradition, one notices a degree of regularity that requires more than a mere methodological explanation.

Their most durable finding is the high frequency with which prominent members of the business community are nominated as desirable members of a community-wide committee by well-informed observers of local politics. Other types of individuals are also given such recognition: the mayor, leading trade unionists, maybe a socially prominent benefactress, and perhaps a local politician with excellent state or national connections. But while the list has some diversity, the names that appear most frequently consist of industrialists, financiers, and the directors of large commercial enterprises.

Why does such a pattern emerge almost every time such a list is constructed? Neither the answer to this question given by reputationalists nor the explanation offered by their critics is very convincing. Hunter's own interpretation is that the list of names identifies the men of power who make the big decisions for the community. After they get together and call the "shots," they allow "front men" and "legmen"' to work out policy details. Hunter then tells a number of anecdotes that illustrate but hardly demonstrate the accuracy of his inferences. And as others have pointed out, it is hardly likely that his inferences are correct. Big businessmen are not likely to be united on all questions, they do not have time to examine the entire range of policy questions facing local governments, and other participants are likely to influence policies of particular interest to them.[19] If reputationalists infer too much from their findings, their critics incorrectly claim that they provide no useful information about local politics at all. Although Hunter and others may have gathered some information about the reputations of various potential participants in local politics, they provide no clue to actual power relationships. The individuals on the list may have some influence if they do become involved in political issues, but, it is said, this information is of little value because most people do not participate in most political debates.[20]

This argument seems to me to be as extremely stated as Hunter's own. If the list does not tell everything about power, it does not follow that the list provides no information at all. Reputation in a social system cannot be constructed out of nothing; there must be something in an individual's past that leads informed observers to concede him a political status of high rank. In baseball the reputation for being a great pitcher is usually deserved. Although the pitcher may be driven from the game on any given day, his reputation is not altogether unrelated to his ability to perform. So it is with the political game. Although politics is not baseball, where winners and losers can be so precisely ascertained, it "ain't beanbag" either. A person with a reputation for influence may not attain his objective in each specific political conflict, but it is unlikely that he will keep his reputation for long unless he has some policy impact.

If the reputational method provided no information about influence relations and if we accepted the pluralist argument that the decision-making method provides exact information about the distribution of power in a community, there would be virtually no overlap in the list of individuals identified by the reputational method and the list of decision makers. In even a small community, such as Oberlin, Ohio, with only 3,603 residents over the age of twenty-five, the chance that any individual would randomly appear on a list of the top forty-three influentials would only be 43 in 3,603, or .012. But in a study where both methodologies are used, the chance that a person with a reputation for power will appear on the decision-making list is approximately 1 in 2, or .5.[21] That is to say, if one is considered by reputationalists to be "influential," the chance that one will have actually participated in a decision is increased fortyfold (or, more precisely, by a factor of 41.6).

The intimate relationship between the "reality" and the reputation for power can be specified reasonably well, if we know the number of individuals who fall into each of the four cells in table 7.1. To be sure, power and reputation are continuous dimensions, not dichotomies, and this fourfold table, like most fourfold tables in the social sciences, can be only a rough guide to actual social relationships. But condensing information in this way does highlight all four of the elements in the power-reputation equation. Those in the upper left-hand cell are simply "powerful," for they deserve the reputation they hold. The "unappreciated" are those who participate in decision making but are not recognized as influential. "Bigwigs" are those overweight no-goods who hold a reputation they do not deserve.

Table 7.1: Relationships between Reputation and "Reality"

Reputation for Power	Power "Really" Exercised	
	High	Low
High	Powerful (22)	Bigwig (21)
Low	Unappreciated (86)	Nonentity (3,474)

And the "nonentities" are those who have neither influence nor the reputation for the same.

Although few studies of reputation and reality provide enough information to allow us to fill in the numbers of these four cells, Wildavsky's study of Oberlin is sufficiently detailed to make this possible. Since Wildavsky is critical of the reputational methodology, we can be quite sure that he did not massage his data in order to produce results that would enhance the reputation of reputationalists.[22] After studying all the issues that provoked political discussion in Oberlin, Wildavsky found that 22 individuals nominated as influential by activist members of the community had in fact participated successfully in decision making.[23] Another 21 individuals were just "bigwigs," who had a reputation for power but who had not in fact participated in decision making.[24] Wildavsky was so thorough in his study that he identified another 86 individuals who were either major or minor decision makers but were "unappreciated" by those nominating reputational leaders.[25] Wildavsky does not tell us the number of "nonentities" who had neither the reputation for power nor the reality of participating in decision making, but according to the United States census there were 3,608 adults twenty-five years or older living within the community in 1960. If we subtract the 129 individuals listed in the other three categories, we are left with 3,474 adults who were no more than marginally active and who quite correctly had no significant reputation for power and influence.

If we assume that Wildavsky's decision-making methodology gives an accurate picture of the reality of power in Oberlin, then it becomes a simple calculation to ascertain the relationship between reputation and reality. In this case the Q coefficient is .95. When two phenomena are found to be so closely correlated, in most areas of social inquiry they are treated as pretty much the same thing. That is what scholars within the reputationalist tradition have done. Undoubtedly, this is an exaggeration which critics are correct to point out, though the vehemence with which reputationalists have been criticized seems somewhat out of proportion to the size of their error.

Wildavsky's own conclusion from the information he has provided is that "reputation for influence is a curious compound: part reality, part myth; part guess, part knowledge; part what one does, part the position one holds; part observation, part assumption."[26] Although Wildavsky does not specify the size of the fraction to be attributed to each of these parts, the passage strongly implies that reputation is built roughly equally on myth and reality. His evidence for this claim is that there are approximately the same numbers of "bigwigs" as truly "powerful" individuals identified by the reputational methodology. But in calculating the accuracy of the reputational methodology, one must take into account the numbers in all four cells in table 7.1, not just the numbers in the two top cells. When an appropriate correlation coefficient is calculated, the relationship between reputation and reality approaches unity. Through a methodological error of their own, critics of the reputational method have seriously underestimated the information that can be obtained from this methodological device. At the very least, the reputational method provides an economical means of identifying a segment of those influencing government policy.

But can anything more precise be said? Probably the most sensible inferences about the meaning of such a list are those that remain close to the specific information that has been collected, which requires attention to the exact phrasing of the questions posed. In Hunter's own study and numerous studies since, a key question taking the following form, was asked: "Suppose a major project were before the community that required decision by a group of leaders that nearly everyone would accept. Which people would you choose, regardless of whether or not you know them personally?"[27] Notice that this question directs the informants to think about programs and policies that are beneficial to the city as a whole. It also refers to persons who are highly regarded by the community as a whole. Although the researchers have probably phrased the question in these terms to disguise their real analytical purpose (uncovering the community "power elite"), the question in fact asks the respondent to identify those who are best able to develop policies in the interests of the city as a whole. When the question is phrased this way, the respondent is invited to think about the politics of development.

The political issues most often discussed in studies of community power structures provide further evidence that this literature is concerned largely with developmental politics. In Hunter's study, the two local issues treated at greatest length are attracting an international trade association to Atlanta and getting a new industry to locate there.[28] Schulze's study of "Cibola" discusses the effort by city leaders to annex a neighboring township whose taxable wealth was deemed vital to the city's continued prosperity.[29] In Agger, Goldrich, and Swanson's four-city study, the issues which attracted the greatest amount of elite attention were matters of economic reorganization and civic improvement.[30] In still another study members of the economic elite of "Wheelsburg" were involved in such issues as downtown development, establishment of a metropolitan planning agency, improvement of airport terminal facilities, proposed sale of bonds by the city to finance construction of parking facilities, and proposed annexation of a suburban shopping center.[31]

Given the specific wording of questions used by reputationalists and given the kinds of issues in which their "power elite" tend to be involved, it seems reasonable to infer that these studies are largely analyses of the politics of development. Within this framework the preponderance of businessmen is no longer surprising. These are the people who are aware of the factors that could help promote the community's economic capacity, and they possess sufficient financial and other resources to influence it. Of course, not all businessmen are active in community-wide projects;[32] the value of the reputationalist methodology is that it tends to isolate those who are civic-minded. Hardly coincidentally, such civic-mindedness occurs most frequently when the businessman's own interests most closely match those of the city. Thus, many studies find that heads of banks, downtown retailing firms, newspapers, and home-owned industries are the most active participants in the politics of development.

Businessmen are not the only community residents that can contribute to the city's development. Wealthy socialites; prominent professional people; politicians, especially those with links to state and national governments; and even some public-spirited trade unionists have in some cases also demonstrated particular capacities to discern the public welfare or to secure resources for the city. The more a city's future depends upon actions by higher levels of government, the more politicians come to dominate the politics of development. For example, in Great Britain the prosperity of a community, insofar as it can be influenced by governmental actions, seems to depend as heavily on access to central departments as on its relations with the private sector. As a result, political leaders play a more prominent role in developmental policy in a British community than in comparable American cities.[33]

The reputationalist methodology does not reveal the processes by which developmental policies are determined. But much of the surrounding discussion emphasizes their consensual, covert quality. "There may be isolated dissatisfactions with policy decisions" in Atlanta, says Hunter, "but mainly there is unanimity."[34] "In Wheelsburg," Clelland and Form explain, "there was little evidence of basic differences in values among the economic dominants, the public leaders, and the elected officials."[35] The authors felt that this was related to the "tendency for community decision-making to be channeled to the private rather than public sphere."[36] In "Cibola," policy was formulated in "informal friendship groups," with officials of the Chamber of Commerce taking on the responsibility to "'feel out' the key economic units and the potentially concerned voluntary associations."[37]

Within the developmental arena, such consensual patterns of policy formation seem especially likely. If a policy can be readily defended as being in the interest of the city, there is less need to build public support for the proposal. On the contrary, public support will swell so rapidly that it is better to determine the feasibility of the policy in secret so that false hopes and expectations are not aroused. Indeed, when the project involves participants external to the city, local publicity can be downright counterproductive. By raising local enthusiasm, leaders only weaken their bargaining position vis à vis industries they are seeking to entice or federal agencies whose grants they want to secure. As public expectations rise, the terms external actors impose may become more stringent.

The research on community power structures provides better information on the kinds of individuals active in developmental policies than on the exact amount of power they wield. Even if all those nominated as members of the elite act together, they may still be unable to secure their objectives. Although the list of influential citizens gives some idea as to the rank ordering of individual political resources, the methodology provides little information about the quantum of power the nominated individuals have as compared with all other participants within the community. Even more, the composition of this list tells us nothing about their individual or collective capacity to influence decisions made by governments or private firms external to the city. Yet these are the entities that often determine a city's development. The very programs that can bring together a unified power structure tend to be those with only a marginal chance of success. The community may be competing with other communities for the location of an important scientific facility, access to the interstate highway system, or the siting of a manufacturing plant. Internal cooperation is needed to maximize the attractiveness of the community to outsiders. But as active as community leaders may become on such issues, they may still lose their objective to an equally unified leadership in another state or region.

Should they succeed, however, their reputations as civic leaders will be enormously enhanced. The politics of development is particularly enticing to otherwise apolitical businessmen, because successful effort on behalf of a project that benefits the community as a whole has a halo effect. The businessman becomes widely respected for his civic-mindedness, his firm becomes known as a pillar of the community, and little, if any, community controversy besmirches his name. No wonder that those active in the politics of development become widely appreciated as reputable civic leaders, men and women "everyone would accept" as members of a group to handle "a major project before the community."

In sum, community power studies that have employed the reputational methodology tell us many valuable things about the politics of development. Participants are well-regarded residents with control over economic resources or access to external governmental agencies. In most cases, the policymakers' special interests will not be in sharp conflict with the interests of the community as a whole. The processes of policy formation will be consensual and closed to the broader public, until technical and political feasibility is fairly well determined. Success at achieving policy objectives will redound to the reputation of the decision makers. The exact participants will vary with the type of developmental policy at stake. Where developmental efforts concentrate on the private sector, businessmen will be deeply involved. Where the resources to be secured are in the hands of higher level governmental agencies, the role of political leaders will be most central.

But suggestive as these community power studies have been, they still do not provide detailed information about the processes of policy formation in the developmental arena. Because they are more interested in structural arrangements than in political processes, their case studies are often cursory and elliptical. To obtain a sense of the texture of policymaking in this arena, one must turn to the politics of urban renewal, the one most systematic effort to plan the economic development of large, decaying central cities.

The Politics of Urban Renewal

James Reichley once wrote that the new mayor of Philadelphia, Richardson Dilworth, was the businessman's "able servant instead of their grafting, inefficient slave."[38] In these words he captured the two contrasting styles that characterize relations between the business community and local politicians on matters of developmental policy. On some occasions politicians quickly grasp that what is good for business is good for the community. In other contexts business leaders must organize quite independently of city government and campaign to show that their program is needed to sustain the local economy. Not surprisingly, both business and the city enjoy greater health with an "able servant" than with an "inefficient slave" in office. It is thus only an apparent paradox that business prospers most when its influence is least apparent. These points are most easily illustrated by reviewing two contrasting studies of the politics of urban renewal.

The Able Servant

Simply because a policy is in the interest of a city does not mean that only small efforts need to be made to achieve the policy objective. For one thing, each city competes with other cities; if the leaders of any particular city are slow to discern city interests or miscalculate the best techniques for achieving them, the city will lose to other contestants. Second, what is in the interest of the city is a collective good that benefits all residents, once it benefits any. But collective goods are difficult to supply, because most individuals do not have sufficient incentives to contribute to them. If they wait for others to provide the good, they can get the benefit at no cost to themselves. Wolfinger's engaging study of the "politics of progress" in New Haven demonstrates that securing public support for development taxes the ingenuity of even the most "able servant."[39]

There is little doubt that urban renewal enhanced the economic productivity of New Haven. The policy opened up traffic arteries into the central city, encouraging the utilization of downtown shopping facilities. It provided parking for automobiles that had previously clogged inner-city streets, made shopping more convenient for central-city and suburban residents alike, and permitted the construction of new high rise apartments, thereby providing appropriate accommodations for middle- and upper-middle-class residents who wished to live near the center of the community. Moreover, it protected Yale University, one of the city's most valuable resources, from the encroaching urban blight. All of these benefits were reaped with minimal expenditure by the local taxpayer. With great entrepreneurial skill, Mayor Richard Lee managed to find matching local funds for federal grants in ways that did not increase burdens on local taxpayers. Sometimes he even got federal funds to pay for public services that otherwise would have been locally financed.

Who could object to a program that raised the economic productivity of the area without adding to its public expenses? Lee's policies were so clearly in the public interest that only those whose own special interests were most directly threatened—for example, the small businessmen whose small-scale commercial enterprises did not justify their location on prime urban land—organized any sustained protest against it. Yet the mayor's task was by no means an easy one. Especially in the first year or two of local planning, when rewards were distant and uncertain, it was difficult to get much support. Prominent local businessmen did not want to waste their time on grandiose schemes that might go awry. Local politicians felt that such wholesale restructuring of the local space-economy might upset the political quiescence that had traditionally allowed them to secure modest side benefits from public service. Hidebound local bureaucrats were lovingly engaged in routine management of their specific enterprises; they did not want to bother with programs that cut across prevailing jurisdictions.

With almost herculean efforts, Mayor Lee succeeded in getting the necessary local support. He hired new administrators whose careers would be tied to program success, enlisted the aid of a developer who hoped to secure a windfall through urban renewal, and convinced Washington bureaucrats that New Haven could become a model "renewed" city. Mayor Lee even managed to bring together a group of community leaders who might have scored high on any list of influentials. His citizens' action committee for urban renewal consisted of downtown businessmen, financiers, industrialists, leading professionals, and one or two trade unionists. Yet bringing this committee together was a complicated, time-consuming process requiring skillful political leadership. It took months just to recruit the committee chairman.

Developmental politics are usually electorally popular. Mayor Lee was elected time and again at two-year intervals for more than two decades after he began his urban renewal drive. As Chicago's Mayor Richard J. Daley, second only to Richard Lee in his developmental successes, often observed, "Good government is good politics." By good government he did not refer to the patronage-free government that reformers have in mind when they use the term. Daley meant government that was in the interest of the community as a whole, a government that gave precedence to policies that strengthened economic productivity. If this objective were successfully pursued, political popularity would follow. Reputation, respectability, popularity, and power flow to those who take the city's interests as their own, or who are fortunate enough to have special interests that converge with those of the city.

The Inefficient Slave

Not every city is blessed with able political leadership that avidly pursues the city's economic interests. Wolfinger is in fact dubious about the prospects in most cities for the kind of leadership that Lee and Daley displayed.[40] Where this kind of political leadership is not provided by local politicians, then groups within the private sector, usually led by public-spirited businessmen, press for developmental policies. In Philadelphia a businessmen's reform group induced political changes that permitted the "able servant" Dilworth to become mayor.[41] In New York, city planner Robert Moses provided the impetus for developmental policies that seemed beyond the capacity of many of the city's mayors.[42] But it is that much-studied western city Oakland, California, which yields the best evidence on the politics of development when city government is only an "inefficient slave."[43]

In Oakland, urban renewal was implemented only hesitantly and belatedly after prolonged, disjointed community discussions. While Mayor Lee was busily putting New Haven's renaissance together as early as 1954 and had his initial projects underway in 1957, it was not until the latter date that Oakland created a redevelopment agency and developed an initial renewal plan.[44] By 1966 New Haven had spent $790.25 in federal funds per capita (compared with a mean of $53.51 for all cities);[45] but even as late as 1971 Oakland's program of "urban redevelopment" was reported to be "slow" in attracting "many middle class families" to central Oakland.[46]

Oakland's ineffectiveness at urban renewal was largely due to its fragmented, politically undernourished governmental system.[47] The city's mayor had a part-time, largely ceremonial set of responsibilities, the city council was elected on a nonpartisan, at-large basis, and few councillors had political incentives to promote ambitious new programs. Instead, the council only reacted to programmatic efforts initiated elsewhere; significantly, reaction was as likely to be negative as supportive.[48]

Because City Hall was unable to mount redevelopment on its own, a group of business leaders induced the mayor to appoint a special committee called the Oakland Citizens Committee for Urban Renewal (OCCUR).[49] This committee, which "included on it an impressive array of the economic elite, including, among others, three representatives from Kaiser Industries, one each from Sears Roebuck, Equitable Life Assurance Company and Wells Fargo Bank," was so effective that it "rapidly became the contact point for business and governmental groups involved in the process of urban renewal."[50] After several frustrations, including the outright rejection of their initial plan by the city council, OCCUR finally "overcame the politicians' objections"[51] and established a redevelopment agency in 1957. For all its efforts, OCCUR never equaled the success Mayor Lee enjoyed in New Haven. Since local government legitimacy and resources were not placed fully behind the plans, Oakland's urban renewal was undertaken much later than New Haven's, received far fewer federal funds, and was never implemented with the same resourcefulness. "The downtown merchants," Hayes reports, "who were intended to be the major beneficiaries of the program, have not come close to realizing their original goals."[52]

Power and the Politics of Development

Those who undertook the case studies of Oakland and New Haven reached contrasting conclusions concerning the power of business in local urban renewal efforts. Hayes's analysis of Oakland shows that OCCUR was comprised of high-ranking business leaders. Because the policy enacted was the result of OCCUR's efforts and because local government played at best a secondary role, Hayes concludes that "the active, direct involvement of the whole business community has been a prominent feature . . . in the city's recent history."[53] Wolfinger, on the other hand, found business interests in New Haven to be divided and in many instances uninfluential. Although Mayor Lee's "alliance with businessmen and Yale" is seen as one factor affecting the outcome, equal weight is given to three other "important advantages possessed by the Lee Administration: technical skill, public relations talent, [and] Lee's control of his government and party."[54] Business influence was more apparent in Oakland, yet it would seem that downtown business interests were better served in New Haven. Lee was such an effective leader that businessmen had to make fewer contributions to an urban renewal program that substantially aided the city's economic climate. In the western city, the mayor and city council were weak and ineffectual; to launch even an inferior urban renewal program, businessmen had to organize for political action. If it is correct to say that New Haven businessmen had less power, then the state of powerlessness would seem to be a blessed condition.

When developmental policies are considered, attempts to ascertain the power of one or another individual or group are probably pointless, if not misleading. In this policy arena the city as a whole has an interest that needs to be protected and enhanced. Policies of benefit to the city contribute to the prosperity of all residents. Downtown business benefits, but so do laborers desiring higher wages, homeowners hoping house values will rise, the unemployed seeking new jobs, and politicians aiming for reelection. Those who seem to have "power" over developmental policies are those who do the most to secure these benefits for all members of the city. In the developmental arena, capacities for social control are not as necessary as is the power of persuasion. Leadership that can entice others to contribute to a collective good is quite different from the capacity to squelch political dissent.

Very often, those who contribute to the collective well-being of the city have special interests that will also be served by the policy. Businessmen in Oakland were especially aggressive supporters of urban renewal, because improved downtown prosperity would yield especially significant economic benefits to them. Mayor Lee promoted the cause of urban renewal, because he hoped that his success as mayor would facilitate his election to higher public office. Yet business "influence" was not exercised in Oakland at the expense of the mayor or the city council, and political "influence" was not exercised in New Haven at the expense of the city's downtown business community. In the developmental arena, power is not best understood as a "zero-sum" game, where one person or group wins at the expense of another. Instead, power is better understood in systemic terms; it is the capacity of the community as a whole to realize its objectives. What is needed is not so much the capacity to enforce one's will over others as the leadership ability that can persuade others to contribute to a common cause.

In the politics of urban renewal the prizes to be won are partly in the private but mostly in the public sector. Although private interests need to be persuaded to participate in urban renewal efforts, the great prize is the federal grant, hopefully given on terms desired by the local community. To achieve this goal, political leadership by government officials is usually crucial. Since federal agencies characteristically contract and negotiate with their governmental counterparts at lower levels, private efforts are at best an inferior substitute for local political leadership.

Conclusions

The politics of development are conditioned by the fact that these policies redound to the advantage of the city as a whole. For this reason, developmental policies are often left to be developed and implemented by autonomous agencies that operate on income generated by their own projects, free of usual political constraints. When this is not feasible, policies are developed in a consensual fashion by respected community leaders, who are often businessmen well acquainted with the problems of fostering economic growth. These leaders can be enticed to participate in the promotion of developmental policy, because the benefits of the policy are widely enough distributed that policymakers are not likely to suffer much criticism for their efforts. It is good public relations to be known as a "public-spirited" community resident.

But even though the most "powerful" members of the community are often engaged in developmental policymaking, this does not mean their efforts are likely to succeed. Developmental policies come at the expense of other communities, and the local leadership can secure the benefit only if it wins a competition for resources. As a consequence, it is often of great benefit to a community, especially when negotiating with the federal government, if the formal governmental leadership also provides legitimacy for the policy. Its authority allows for a long-term commitment of local resources, and it usually has more administrative capacities available for projects and programs than does any private interest group. Without the enthusiastic backing of political leaders, a community may find it difficult to realize advantageous developmental policies.

The consensual quality of development policies does not hold in each and every case. Apart from factions and groups which may put their separate interests ahead of that of the community, under some circumstances community leaders may fundamentally disagree about the overarching interest of the community. Especially in smaller communities and in suburban areas, where economic and status interests may bifurcate, community leaders may split into "growth" and "no-growth" factions. While some express concern for the economic base of the community, others argue that the community should hold out against urbanization or attempt to survive as a residential enclave apart from the centers of commercial and industrial activity. If there is no agreement on the city's overarching interests, consensus yields to bitter, antagonistic ideological conflict. But these exceptions to the patterns are unlikely to characterize the politics of large and medium-sized cities. Residential exclusiveness is an objective that can be safely pursued only when immediately adjacent areas provide the economic bases that sustain residential prosperity. For cities of any size this option is not available, and developmental policies remain largely consensual.

Eight

The Politics of Allocation

Most of what is discussed as urban politics is the politics of allocation. It consists of conflicts over those policies whose impact on the economic interests of the city is so problematic that reasonable individuals can easily disagree about their effects. In this arena political bargaining affects policies, and the pattern of bargaining takes a characteristically pluralist form. On allocational issues, one finds acrimonious disputes among those who are at one and the same time united behind developmental policies and uniformly opposed to substantial redistribution. Patterns of coalition formation constantly change as participants find new allies with changing issues. Policy choice is characteristically a compromise among competing interests, the terms of which are influenced by the political leaders' electoral concerns.

Many political controversies fall within the allocational arena. Locational politics, which consumes much of the energy of urban politicians, usually involves the allocation of government resources to one or another part of the city.[1] Where should a school building be sited? What should be the route of a badly needed roadway? Should a new hospital be built on parkland? The housekeeping services of government compose another set of allocational issues. What streets should be cleared first? Which sidewalks need repairing? How often is the garbage to be collected? Where should fire stations be located? What should be city policy on the enforcement of parking and traffic ordinances? Even minor tax questions are largely allocational issues with little effect on the city's long-term interests. Should needed revenue be collected through increasing water and sewer fees, by charging admission to city museums, by increasing library fines, or by slightly raising the property tax?

The allocational policies that have provoked the most enduring local conflict have related to the terms and conditions of public employment. Their centrality in local politics has often been attributed to their material and divisible qualities. Jobs can quite literally be divided into ever smaller packages and distributed to ever more specific segments of the community. Policies controlling their distribution can be almost infinitely varied from one sector of public service to another and from one rank to another within the service. Different groups can each be given their own parcel of positions, whose recruitment and promotion policies can be geared to that group's interests. The benefit, moreover, is perfectly concrete and material, a tangible good whose value can be fairly accurately calculated.

Divisibility and materiality are well-known characteristics of public patronage. It is less appreciated that the allocation of public employment opportunities by one or another set of criteria has—with few exceptions—no known effect on the overall economic interests of the city. Of course, cities in principle need to recruit the most talented individuals with the most appropriate skills that can be obtained at competitive wage levels. In that way the city can operate public services at optimum efficiency, thereby maximizing its benefit/tax ratio. An efficient set of employment policies would favorably affect the overall productivity of the community.

But although one can state theoretically what a developmental personnel policy looks like, within the constraints of existing technology it has been impossible to achieve much efficiency in personnel recruitment. Even with the sophisticated diagnostic tools that personnel and guidance counselors can now employ, society does not know of any ascribed or achieved personal characteristics that can be codified into local ordinances in such a way as to allow for the recruitment of those with the most appropriate skills for public-service positions. There is the school of thought which claims that certain educational experiences are essential for the performance of certain public services, such as teaching or delivering social services or fighting fires or apprehending criminals. It has also been argued that performance on certain pencil-and-paper tests predicts competence in a variety of public-service activities. And, to be sure, laws that require some schooling and some minimum level of performance on aptitude tests help eliminate the altogether unqualified. But requirements are sometimes set well above these minimums, thereby eliminating individuals who may have quite appropriate expertise. Moreover, many who pass such tests and meet educational qualifications are still not able to apply their abilities in a work situation. The correlation between educational performance and job performance has always been modest, and it is even more difficult to show any relationship between performance on aptitude tests and skill in performing public-service tasks.[2] Indeed, Summers and Wolfe's careful analysis of teacher performance showed negative relationships between test performance and actual classroom effectiveness.[3] In short, it has proved to be very difficult to elaborate a "one best" set of recruitment and promotion policies in local government. A wide range of policies have roughly equal validity, leaving an unusually wide latitude for discretion.

It is that discretion that gives rise to the multifaceted politics of public employment, or of patronage, as the issue is often labeled in political debates. Patronage has been a central point of contention between political machine and good-government reformers, the coin of ethnic politics, a focus of minority group agitation, and, most recently, the cutting edge of local trade union politics.

Machine-Reform Conflict

Urbanists have emphasized the class conflict inherent in the battles between machine politicians and urban reformers.[4] The strength of the machine lay in the low-income ethnic communities just adjacent to the commercial and industrial heart of the city. Reformers appealed to native-born, middle-class residents living in more pleasant, outlying areas. Machine politicians themselves were often second-generation immigrants of working-class origin who used their political influence to enhance their economic well-being. Reformers consisted largely of professionals and progressive businessmen who had been educated at respectable universities and who had little in common socially with the "rowdies" controlling the ward organizations.

As far as they go, these are fairly accurate social portraits of machine politicians and their reform-minded opponents. All the talk about cleaning up government and improving the efficiency of public services veiled but thinly the social distance between Yankees and their Protestant allies, on one side, and the mostly Catholic immigrants, on the other. Yet one should not confuse the conflict between political machine and reform movement with open class warfare. On the contrary, class conflict took a particularly muted form. Neither side challenged businessmen's control of their private property, and neither questioned the central importance of economic growth to the welfare of the city. No one offered programs of sweeping social reform. Machine politicians wanted only a piece of the rewards that came from economic growth. The closest they came to proposing a set of redistributive policies was the passing of boodle to more and more claimants. At the same time, reformers were always more successful at structural than social reform. Although some reformers campaigned against tenement housing and child starvation, the most durable municipal reform triumphs involved only narrow political and governmental innovations.[5]

Machines and reformers of course differed over which mechanisms were best suited to the city's economic development. Reformers argued that through nonpartisan, at-large elections, leaders would be chosen who would guard the overarching interests of the city. Although the machine politicians were less articulate, scholarly defenders of the machine have argued that back-room deals and corrupt politics eased legal impediments to local capital investment. But machine-reform differences involved conflicts in style and technique, not in the goal to be pursued. Instead of debating economic prosperity or social distribution, machines and reformers have historically divided over questions of patronage and corruption. Every defeat of the Democratic party organization in New York City since 1900 has been the product of a campaign against political corruption.[6] Corruption has been the central theme of Chicago politics for decades, and the mayoral election won by reformers in 1924 followed the especially scandalous misapplication of public funds by "Big Bill" Thompson.[7] Political life in San Francisco has been so dominated by issues of corruption and patronage that the most comprehensive analysis of that city's politics concluded that "three major values—honesty, competency and adaptability—have shaped the origin and performance of urban governance here."[8] In the words of one contemporary observer, nineteenth-century municipal politics were

> like the sick man who finds no rest upon his bed, but seeks to ease his pain by turning from side to side. Every now and then the patient finds some relief in a drastic remedy, such as the enactment of a new charter and the expulsion at an election of a gang of knaves. Presently, however, the weak points of the charter are discovered . . .; civic zeal grows cold and allows bad men to creep back into the chief posts.[9]

Decades after many urban reforms had been instituted, these issues remained the currency of local politics. Conflicts between a patronage-bent Democratic organization and the forces of reform provoked critical elections in Philadelphia, Newark, Gary, St. Louis, Chicago, New York, and many other cities.[10] Although structural innovations were designed to curb patronage and corruption, it seems that "the pursuit of honesty" in any city "is not demonstrably related to structural forms."[11]

Issues of patronage and corruption dominate local politics not because local officials are particularly venal or devious, but because employment issues are one of the limited set of matters readily resolved at the local level. They have provided such a durable issue around which local divisions could express themselves simply becaase employment has been the allocational issue par excellence. In those cases where qualifications and professional expertise were in fact critically important, machine politicians were most willing to apply them. When local public health services needed qualified medical doctors to administer the wonder vaccines that by the late nineteenth century were beginning to eliminate fatal childhood diseases, even Tammany Hall conceded that partisan politics should have nothing to do with the administration of the service.[12] But genuine qualifications for most public-service employments could not be laid down in advance with the precision that was possible in the field of medicine. Instead, the politics of employment was fair game for competing political forces.

Both sides to the conflict could make a reasonable claim that their policies were good for the city. When machines took party service to be a major criterion for recruiting individuals to public service, they could argue the policy benefited not only the party organization but city government as well. Able performance in the complex and competitive processes of ward and precinct politics was probably a fairly reasonable predictor of competence as a bailiff, policeman, garbage collector, or tree trimmer. Moreover, whenever party loyalty was a condition of employment, a certain commitment to the larger objectives of governmental administration was shared by employees. At the same time, civil service legalisms insulating employees from partisan pressures made "firing even the most inept civil servant the eleventh task of Hercules."[13]

Reform critics of machine-style practices nonetheless had legitimate complaints. Recruitment and promotion within the public service for work done within the party organization weakened the hierarchical structure of the public service itself. Nominal superiors had a reduced capacity to exercise supervision over their employees. Moreover, party organizational work, however ably performed, did not necessarily qualify one for those administrative tasks in local government where skill at written communications was at a premium.

Over the years the reform movement has been increasingly successful in imposing its recruitment criteria on city governments, and it might be thought that their success is evidence that tests and education, as recruitment criteria, produce higher levels of governmental efficiency than the partisan criteria perferred by the machine.

But other factors can explain reform success. The parties themselves supported civil service reform whenever they anticipated electoral defeat; by such reforms they could keep their own friends in office. Public employees also appreciated the security of tenure that came with the increased rationalization of recruitment practices. Moreover, party organizations began to lose their grip on the electorate, as a better educated population began to rely on newspapers, radios, and television for voting cues. In Chicago, the one major city where a political machine still controls much of the recruitment to public service, the efficiency of public services seems on a par with that in comparable cities. Indeed, when Chicago–New York comparisons are made, most commentators think Chicago enjoys the greater efficiency in governmental performance. The comparison does not prove that the machine is more efficient than reformed government; many other variables can account for any observed differences between two of the nation's largest cities. The example only shows how difficult it is to establish that one set of recruitment practices is superior to the other.

The growth of political machines is due to a multiplicity of factors, including continuous social and economic change in nineteenth-century America; the mass immigration of European peasants until 1920; the fact that the democratization of urban government preceded industrialization; the widespread belief in opportunities for social mobility; and the individualistic rather than collectivist ethos that pervades American culture.[14] Yet the institutional setting within which the machine-reform conflict emerged helped perpetuate a particularly intense focus on issues of corruption and patronage. The politics of employment became dominant because it provided a practical issue that could be settled locally.

This becomes most evident when local politics are compared with national political campaigns and controversies. While corruption has been at the very core of local politics, it is only a secondary theme in Presidential campaigns. Even during the nineteenth-century heyday of the machine, national conflicts focused on issues of foreign affairs, economic policy, and interregional relationships. Not only did Civil War divisions fundamentally shape the bases of partisan power, but when war memories began to recede, tariff and monetary issues became predominant. With the growth of populism and the conversion of the Democratic party to Bryanism, issues like free silver, corporate monopolies, imperialism, and the exploitation of the natural resources of the West became central issues in American politics.

Patronage and corruption were certainly part of national politics. The disappointments of a job hunter cost James Garfield his life.

Sensational scandals caused the Grant, Cleveland, Harding, and Truman administrations considerable political damage. But in contrast to the dozens of mayors who were defeated and even jailed on charges of corruption, it was not until Richard Nixon that a national administration fell from power—or was even defeated in a subsequent election—for allegedly corrupt behavior. Grant was relected; Cleveland's greatest political disaster was the depression of 1893; Calvin Coolidge easily surmounted the Harding scandals that he had inherited; and Truman's popularity dropped rapidly only after the war in Korea had turned sour. In general, the issues that proved decisive in national politics related to sectional divisions and to the enduring quest for peace and prosperity. With such vital issues dominating the national agenda, corruption and patronage, though solid campaign issues, have necessarily been a subordinate element in all but the most unusual circumstances.

Ethnic Politics

Just as patronage questions fueled the contest between machine and reform, these same allocational issues contributed to the pervasiveness of ethnic controversy in local politics. Of course, patronage did not by itself produce enduring patterns of local ethnic conflict. The continuous flow of immigrants from all the countries of Europe, from Latin America, from Asia, and from the rural areas of the American South was another essential ingredient. But many expected ethnic politics to give way to class politics with the increasing assimilation of these immigrants into a modern industrial society. If this view were correct, ethnic politics should have all but disappeared for those groups for whom immigration was largely terminated by the Naturalization Act of 1920.

To the extent that political practice simply reflects discontent felt within the larger society, a decline in ethnic politics is to be expected.[15] But inasmuch as policy affects politics, what government does—and what government is able to do—affects patterns of political involvement. In several ways, the structure of local government helps perpetuate ethnic politics even when ethnic groups are becoming increasingly differentiated internally. In the first place, local governments can do little to foster class politics. The options available to local leaders do not allow for campaigns built around broad appeals to class interests. Instead, candidates tend to agree on giving economic development priority over social redistribution. This way, they avoid committing themselves to economically regressive public policies. But if there are few rewards for class politics, ethnic politics is another matter.

The dominance of ethnic over class politics at the local level is due to the relative ease with which politicians can satisfy ethnic aspirations. In Weber's categories, ethnic groups are status groups with differential access to the honors that society bestows. Demands by less respected status groups are demands for greater recognition and deference by other groups in the society. Ethnic groups want the legitimacy of their language, race, culture, or nationality to be affirmed by authoritative governmental action. And there are many ways in which local political leaders can give groups such recognition without adversely affecting the city's economic standing. Public officials can allow ethnic parades on various national holidays, name streets and buildings after ethnic heroes, attend the community celebrations of ethnic groups, utter phrases in the ethnic tongue, publicly enjoy ethnic cuisine, appoint leaders from the ethnic community to city boards and commissions, give members of the ethnic group special opportunities to secure positions of public employment—especially in those geographical areas where the ethnic group is concentrated—and, above all, run ethnic candidates for high public office. In most American cities a campaign day does not pass without a self-conscious effort by political candidates to win the support of one or another nationality group. And partly as a result, ethnic identifications have remained politically significant in local politics even for those immigrant groups that have resided in metropolitan areas for two and three generations.[16]

Jobs have been a crucial component of local ethnic politics, because "ethnic solidarity lets politicians economize on the indulgences they bestowed."[17] Not every member of an ethnic group has to be given a governmental position in order for a party to win favor in the ethnic community. "Rewards given to the few were appreciated vicariously by the many."[18] Or, in Lowi's words, "each appointment made on ethnic or religious grounds...reaffirmed the identification of the members of the group with each other."[19] Thus, the representation an immigrant group achieved in municipal bureaucracies became the mark of its standing in the community's political life. The Irish proved so successful that they in fact made government job-holding their chief channel of upward mobility.[20]

Ethnic appeals are not peculiar to local politics. The national government and national politicians seek political support through similar devices. Every four years candidates for national office are found marching in ethnic parades, eating foreign foods, and uttering phrases in foreign languages. A certain number of federal positions must be allocated with ethnic criteria uppermost in mind. Ethnic appeals may even appear decisive in tightly contested races. President Ford's misstatement that Poland is a free country and its implication that East Europeans support their Communist governments, Presidential sensitivity to Jewish fears for the state of Israel, and the care with which Presidential candidates address the abortion issue have all been noteworthy features of national campaigns. And when a candidate such as John Kennedy is from a readily identifiable ethnic group, the impact on voter alignments nationally may be considerable.[21] However, ethnicity seems to play a less significant role in national than in local politics. Candidate views on foreign policy and the economy are what give shape to most Presidential campaigns. The ethnically balanced ticket is a strikingly local phenomenon. Robert Lane observed that "in a real sense, the seat of ethnic politics is the local community, not the national capitol. This is evidenced by the fact that although ethnic groups often vote no more frequently than native white Protestants in national elections (with the Jews excepted) and sometimes less frequently, they usually vote more frequently in local elections."[22]

These differences between national and local politics parallel differences in the responsibilities of national and local governments. Where critical foreign and domestic issues are within the reach of political aspirants, these questions shape political strategies, the course of political campaigns, and voting behavior. But where governmental limits are more severely constrained, political strategies and political campaigns adapt accordingly. Candidates concentrate on those issues about which something can be done. Ethnic recognition is one of the limited set of policies local politicians can do something about without damaging the economic productivity of the city. Ethnic lines of differentiation are thus reinforced by political concentration on ethnically related public policies. Even where workers comprise almost the entire population of a central city, politicians use ethnic rather than class appeals to sustain a political following.

Minority Group Politics

Color changes the character of ethnic politics. The visibility of the minority group is much greater, and therefore group members are assimilated into the larger society more slowly and more painfully. In the case of black Americans, the slave experience left particularly deep social wounds that subsequent patterns of discrimination have kept from healing.[23] As a result, minority group politics has taken a more virulent form than older forms of ethnic politics.

Two factors seem responsible. In the first place, minorities of color seem to have a greater sense of grievance and deprivation. Their demands for social innovation have been more encompassing and

all-embracing than past ethnic demands. Black Americans in particular have been the most militant minority ever to surface in urban
areas of the United States. This is not just a matter of tactics, though
the riots, boycotts, sit-ins, and demonstrations that marked the
emergence of blacks as an organized political force were by themselves politically unsettling. Second, and more important, the demands themselves were far-reaching, and at the local level utterly
unrealistic. They included full-scale school and residential integration, absolute equality, even preferential treatment for minority areas
in the distribution of public resources and the allocation of special
funds to minorities to compensate for past deprivations. Blacks also
overwhelmingly supported a whole host of measures which, taken
together, would have implemented a welfare state rivaling any in
Western Europe: socialized medicine, guaranteed employment,
guaranteed minimum income, massive programs of publicly
financed housing, and equality of opportunity at all educational
levels. These items in "freedom budgets" called for a massive re-
allocation of the nation's wealth. The scale of the demands was
outside the mainstream of American political experience. Only the
particularly severe economic and political deprivations of black
Americans could account for a radicalism more characteristic of
Europe than North America.

The strength of these demands was countered by a particularly
negative and fearful white response. If black Americans wanted full
integration, white Americans reacted defensively to even small steps
in that direction. Neighborhood integration provoked white flight.
Black entrance into public schools induced the expansion of private
schools. When blacks campaigned to secure a share of the political
patronage, they were charged with advocating reverse discrimination. Only the most moderate black politicians could retain white
votes. Nationally, these black demands nearly rent the New Deal
coalition that had made the Democratic party the governing party of
the country.

Locally, minority group politics has not been as pluralistic as
traditional ethnic politics. Blacks themselves make redistributive
demands as part of their claim for group recognition, and whites see
even modest black allocational demands as redistributive in nature.
What benefits blacks is perceived as damaging white interests—and
thus it does. Token integration of community institutions is perceived by whites as the first step in an inevitable process of total
racial change, and in what becomes a self-fulfilling prophecy whites
stop using that community resource.[24] The result is that minority
group demands are often redistributive and therefore beyond the
capacity of local officials to grant.

The greatest victories won by black Americans have thus been in national politics. First and foremost, the Civil Rights Acts of 1964 and 1965 broke down institutionalized segregation and the denial of political privileges endemic to the Southern way of life. But federal efforts on behalf of black Americans have not been confined to the restructuring of social relationships in the old Confederacy. The Great Society programs, including Medicare and Medicaid, comprehensive health centers, food stamp programs, aid to the educationally disadvantaged, community action programs, manpower retraining and employment policies, and expanded social security programs, were among the nationwide efforts to redistribute economic and social opportunities and resources. Their passage came with a reforming vigor in national politics that owed much to the civil rights movement. Although many of these programs encountered great obstacles in the course of their implementation at the local level, there can be little doubt that national policymaking institutions were sensitive to the black power accumulated in the 1960s.

Local officials also responded to black demands but in a much different manner. Although they were not willing to carry out broad-scale desegregation or other programs of redistribution, allocational demands by blacks could be more readily accommodated. Streets and schools have been renamed after famous black heroes. In many cities Martin Luther King's birthday is now a public holiday. Black and other minority representatives are now regularly appointed to public boards and commissions, almost in proportion to their numbers.

Local governments have been most responsive to minority group demands for public employment. Before the civil rights movement gave blacks newfound power, deep-seated patterns of racial discrimination precluded them from obtaining their fair proportion of public jobs. Even in New York and Chicago, where blacks historically were provided the greatest opportunities for political participation, the only patronage in the gift of Harlem and South Side machines was low-ranking service positions.[25] In the 1960s pressure for sustained recruitment at all levels of local government rapidly intensified. As federal funds allowed for a rapid increase in locally administered programs, special efforts to recruit minorities for the new positions were undertaken. Community action programs, Model Cities programs, manpower and training programs, and community health centers were staffed primarily with individuals from minority backgrounds. At the same time affirmative action programs were undertaken by old-line governmental agencies. Although bureaucratic resistance to minority appointments was often considerable, government leaders gradually introduced new procedures with less obvious racial biases.[26]

As a result of these innovations, the public sector has been opened to black employees. David Greenstone and I compared the employment of blacks in local government positions with black employment in the United States economy as a whole.[27] We calculated an index of representation which took a value of 1.0 if the percentage of blacks employed by local governments in a particular occupational stratum was identical to the percentage of blacks employed in that stratum more generally. Values above 1.0 indicated black over-representation; values below 1.0 indicated underrepresentation. We found that in 1970 blacks were generally overrepresented in the local public sector; the index for all occupations took a value of 1.2. We also discovered that the index of overrepresentation increased in value, the higher prestige the occupational category. In service positions blacks were underrepresented in local government, but in professional and technical positions black overrepresentation attained a value of 1.7 and in managerial and administrative positions a value of 2.5. In all probability, this overrepresentation of blacks in the public sector is at least in part due to direct political pressures. In a comparative study of ten California cities, Browning, Marshall, and Tabb show that with the incorporation of blacks into local political processes, the ratio of blacks employed in City Hall, as compared with their numbers in the adult population, increases markedly.[28] And an analysis of Gary, Indiana, politics claims that the successful black mayor, Richard Hatcher, "replaced a white machine with a black one."[29]

"Why is recruitment . . . particularly likely to attract the attention of minority groups?" asks Frank Thompson in his study of Oakland's politics of employment. He answers that "this is the arena where their efforts bear the most fruit." Minorities shy away from redistributive policy proposals, he continues, because they sense "that the city has less money and controls fewer social services than other governmental levels." Their demands for affirmative action are "by comparison much less likely to provoke intense opposition."[30] Whether the changes in minority employment are due to particularly intense pressures in this arena, as Thompson thinks, or to a greater responsiveness on the part of government officials, or to both, racial politics seems to have different consequences in the allocational and redistributive arenas.

The responsiveness of governmental institutions to black demands for employment has in fact done much to soften the edges of racial conflict in America. Aided by a shift among blacks away from integrationist civil rights rhetoric and toward black power demands for affirmative action and community involvement,[31] city political leaders have found that responsiveness on issues of employment is a valuable mechanism for incorporating blacks into local political processes without sacrificing the local economy to broad-scale redistribution.

Municipal Employees

In recent years, employment politics has become even more directly a central issue in local government. With the passing of machine power in many cities, with some decline in old ethnic antagonisms, and with the increased political incorporation of the color minorities into local politics, employment politics has taken an ever more visible form. Municipal employees have always been active participants in local politics. More than any other segment of the community, employees of local government are directly affected by decisions taken by local public officials. Their salaries, their working conditions, their responsibilities, and even the existence of their positions depend on the decisions of elected officials. For these reasons, public-sector employees are more likely to be politically involved than are those working in the private sector.[32]

The greater involvement of public servants in politics seems to have little consequence in the national arena. Apart from those residing in areas around Washington, D.C., and a bygone concern with the welfare of postal employees, neither congressmen nor Presidents seem to feel that greater political dividends are reaped by attending particularly to the needs of federal civil servants. In national politics, long-standing partisan divisions, broad issues, and the personal popularity of candidates dominate electoral outcomes. Significantly, patronage is so minor a factor in national politics that none of the major studies of national voting behavior have even found it worthwhile to mention the particular rates of participation or the partisan orientations of government employees.[33]

At the local level public employees seem to have considerably more political clout. For one thing, voter turnout is much lower, and therefore a small number of public employees can have a significant political effect. The limiting cases seem to be "low-visibility" school board and school bond elections.[34] In this labor-intensive public service, the number of public employees who can potentially vote in local elections is very large. In the absence of a divisive political campaign they and their families can dominate electoral outcomes. It is well known to school superintendents, for example, that any school bond referendum campaign should be conducted quietly, with concentration on those most interested in maintaining a fiscally healthy school system. The probability of referendum defeat escalates with an increase in voter turnout.[35] More recently, New York City has instituted a system of neighborhood school boards whose members are elected at a time and place different from regularly scheduled elections. The initial election saw a voter turnout of only 14 percent, and the teachers' union decisively influenced many of the electoral outcomes.[36]

Municipal elections typically fall about halfway between national elections (with their 60 percent turnout) and the lowest visibility elections, where turnout may be as low as 5 percent of the adult population. In this middle range of electoral participation public employees probably do not dominate outcomes, but if they mount an organized campaign, politicians seem well advised to take them seriously. Lowi has in fact argued that in New York City the employees of public agencies are the "new machines" which provide the financing, election-day troops, and, according to one estimate, 20 percent of the votes.[37] With this kind of power "most of the larger city bureaucracies" secured "political representation in the inner core of the [Wagner] Administration."[38] Although the electoral influence of municipal employees has not been documented with the precision the subject deserves, other writers indicate almost in passing the regularity with which this force makes itself felt in local elections. Williams and Adrian discovered that in one of the four cities they studied "the most powerful political force was the city employees' union."[39] Wolfinger reports that in New Haven the policemen's and firemen's unions had "highly-politicized members," whose "opportunities for bargaining" seemed closely associated with local elections.[40] In Los Angeles "the members of the All-City Employees' Association, who are well disciplined and fairly evenly spread among elections districts, and who respond energetically to the directions of their leadership, are a preponderant force."[41] A factor seriously complicating the passage of charter reform in San Francisco was the "power of those working at City Hall."[42]

The traditional electoral influence of municipal workers has in the past decade been augmented by a new capacity to engage local governments in collective bargaining.[43] When public-sector unionism was legitimated by President Kennedy in 1961, the AFL–CIO undertook to organize white collar employees in local government. State laws forbidding strikes and other union activities among municipal employees no longer effectively precluded public-service employees from using their ultimate weapon. Local governments throughout the country were hit by a series of municipal strikes. Levi reports that work stoppages increased from 14 in 1958 to 386 in 1970 and that the workers on strike increased from 1,690 to 168,900.[44]

For a time it seemed that the combined economic and political power of public employees in local politics was about to remove the issue from the allocational arena. Worker demands were becoming so extensive and worker power reached such an unprecedented peak that some of the largest cities were reaching settlements that could only be financed with regressively high local taxation. In an early article on the urban fiscal crisis, Piven argued that public employees had taken advantage of weak political leadership, thereby winning economic concessions beyond the means of local governments.[45] Influenced by her writing, a number of Marxist writers began to speak of the "Fiscal Crisis of the State," perceiving the pressure on local government finances to be the cutting edge of worker-capitalist conflict.[46] Also, when I discovered that the Chicago Teachers Union had successfully bargained for 15 to 20 percent more in salaries than teachers were receiving in comparable situations elsewhere, I began to wonder if leaders could guard against "a longer range crisis of bankruptcy" when confronted by the "immediate crisis induced by uncollected garbage, unpatrolled streets, or unopened schools."[47]

With just a somewhat more distant perspective it appears that my first impulse to dismiss these developments as a passing phenomenon was probably more accurate. The concessions to public employees now seem to be aberrations resulting from "mistakes made by governing institutions during a transition period when they were adjusting to collective bargaining techniques."[48] Studies of the consequences of collective bargaining indicate that "the presence of collective bargaining leads to higher wage rates than in communities where it is absent but that the differential is, in most cases, small."[49] In a recent study of sixty-one cities Clark and Ferguson found modest correlations between the percent of the municipal force organized and employee salaries, but they found no correlation between the percent organized and the cost of public services. Whatever positive association between salaries and organization exists was offset by the negative association between percent organized and the number of municipal employees per capita hired. "Cities where employees are organized . . . pay more but hire fewer workers . . . . Municipal employees may be powerful enough to increase their compensation, but not to dirve up total expenditures."[50] Even in New York City, the fiscal crisis seems to have been due much more to long-term factors than to the celebrated effectiveness of unions in the late sixties (see chapter 10).

Municipal employees still have influence in local politics. As compared with federal employees, workers at the local level wield an unusually strong combination of political and economic power. But the exercise of that power is likely to focus on questions within the allocational sector: the terms under which recruitment and promotion take place, specific factors affecting working conditions, and long-term job stability. On matters of this sort concessions can be made without seriously jeopardizing the city's economy. As long as salaries, wages, pensions, and fringe benefits are only marginally in excess of the market price, cities tolerate the special political power of their employees without endangering their long-term economic interests.

Conclusions

There is no end to the politics of allocation. It is a continuing, thriving, potentially explosive political arena that fuels electoral contests and often subjects decision makers to intense political heat. Since any number of local controversies fall within the allocational arena, I have been able to provide only a condensed, simplified overview here. My emphasis has been on employment issues, which have been central in machine-reform conflict, in ethnic politics, and in the politics of racial minorities. Also, in recent years municipal employees have become powerful direct participants in local policy formation. In all these respects employment issues have played a greater political role in local than in national politics, simply because local politics emphasizes, perhaps exaggerates, the importance of allocational questions.

The significance of employment and other allocational issues highlights the constrained character of local political action. With developmental issues handled by consensus and redistributive issues seldom a matter for local resolution, local politics attends to matters which in national politics appear small and insignificant. When little else is under discussion, who gets what job and the conditions of employment that prevail can provoke a goodly row. Since most citizens are even less involved in local than national affairs, relatively small groups of citizens from a particular ethnic group or working for a specific public bureaucracy can exercise undue political weight. Their leverage is generally restricted to allocational issues, but for small groups this may be a profitable enough arena for political action.

The widely held view that local politics is an arena of bargaining, compromise, cross-cutting cleavages, and changing political issues is not incorrect. On the contrary, such a view depicts and characterizes the most visible aspects of local political relationships. But unless it is also appreciated how a city's interests limit its discretion, a bargaining understanding of local politics is itself limited. Local conflicts occur within a relatively narrow band of the range of controversies occurring within the nation. And even within this narrow band that we have called the allocational arena, local politics takes a special form. Because the larger public pays so little attention to local politics, the power over these allocational issues exercised by small groups is particularly potent.

Nine

The Politics of Redistribution

Redistribution is seldom a significant aspect of local government operations, and therefore the issue is largely excluded from the local political agenda. Although in central cities some redistribution occurs in the process of distributing similar services in all parts of the city, and even though wealthier localities can afford a higher level of redistributive services than poorer localities (see chapter 3), even under the most favorable circumstances there are sharp limits on the degree of redistribution that can easily occur. Because redistributive policies are usually at odds with the economic interests of the city, proponents will find difficulty in gathering support for them. Since the policies are manifestly unrealistic economically, even those groups which themselves would in the short run benefit from redistribution lend little support to such proposals. To contribute to a cause so unlikely of success is not worthwhile, whatever the possible benefits.[1] The policies of redistribution thus become what Matthew Crenson has called "unpolitics."[2] It is a policy arena where issue formation occurs only sporadically. When issues do arise, those responsible for protecting the interests of the city devise political strategies that enable the city to avoid implementing substantial redistributions.

Redistributive Policies:
Does Business Keep Them off Local Agendas?

The absence of a local politics of redistribution has led some analysts to conclude that at the local level a power elite keeps certain issues off political agendas.[3] Threats of economic reprisal and social ostracism are thought to be powerful enough to keep deprived groups from exercising their rights of expression and organization even in liberal democracies. Although instances of such repression can certainly be identified,[4] it is unlikely that this is the major explanation for the paucity of redistributive issues in local politics. Instead, it is the negative economic consequences of locally sponsored redistribution that shape this policymaking arena.

Crenson's study of air pollution politics is the most impressive empirical analysis of local non-decision-making. Even though the issue he studied is not redistributive in the same sense that we have been using the term, the adverse economic effects of strict pollution control create problems for local policymakers similar to those raised by low-income housing programs and other obviously redistributive questions. It is therefore important to consider whether the air pollution issue, as carefully observed by Crenson, had difficulty in reaching center stage on civic agendas because of the indirect influence of industrial elites, as Crenson believes, or because the structural constraints on local decision makers precluded addressing this kind of political question, as I argue.

Crenson's study has two separate data bases: (1) comparative case studies of politics in East Chicago, Indiana, and Gary, Indiana, in the 1950s, and (2) an analysis of the determinants of air pollution as a political issue in a sample of fifty-one American cities ranging in population from fifty thousand to seventy-five thousand. Data were collected using standard survey research techniques. In both sets of data, Crenson finds evidence leading him to conclude that industrial elites helped keep air pollution off the civic agenda.

In his comparative case studies, Crenson shows that conflict over air pollution arose more readily in East Chicago than in Gary; as a result, East Chicago passed an air pollution ordinance in 1957 when such a law was unthinkable in Gary. These differences between the two cities, in Crenson's view, were a function of (1) the availability in East Chicago of public hearings at which citizens could vent their civic complaints; (2) East Chicago's more competitive party politics; and (3) the larger number of manufacturing firms in East Chicago as compared with Gary, a town dominated by the presence of United States Steel. In general, he argues that in cities with little political and economic diversity, powerful industrial interests can keep issues such as air pollution off the local political agenda. His analysis of data from the sample of fifty-one cities yields similar results. In cities with high levels of air pollution, the appearance of pollution as an issue is negatively associated with industry's political influence. In cities with less pollution, industrial influence does not retard the injection of the issue into local politics but it does preclude full civic discussion. In sum, "the political power of polluters operates to diminish the survival and growth prospects of the pollution issue."[5]

Although Crenson's case-study research and analysis of survey data are impressive in many ways, key findings that Crenson reports are difficult to square with his own conclusions. For one thing, Crenson's regression analysis of the survey data provides only the weakest evidence for his main contention. When the degree to which air pollution becomes an issue is correlated with the level of industrial influence in the community, no significant relationship appears. Whether or not newspapers, the Chamber of Commerce, the labor council, or the local political parties took stands on the issue of air pollution had virtually nothing to do with the power of industry, as perceived by respondents. Crenson himself says that "most of the relationships are very weak."[6] Only when Crenson divided his sample into high- and low-pollutant cities did he find modest relationships, which were interpreted as indicating the presence of some industrial influence. Yet even these relationships, presented in table 9.1, are so modest and erratic that the most sensible interpretation would seem to be that industrial influence had no stable effect on whether pollution became an issue.

Similarly, one is puzzled by Crenson's interpretation of his case-study research. Throughout this section of his analysis, the author stresses the relative weakness of industrial elites in East Chicago as compared with Gary. Yet in his epilogue, Crenson writes that the law in East Chicago was implemented in the following way: "An informal agreement between the Inspector and local businessmen exempted from the pollution standards . . . all pieces of equipment installed prior to the enactment of the dirty air ordinance."[7] Although the ordinance seemed for a while to have had a positive effect on pollution levels, this "downward trend . . . was reversed" in 1962. It was significant that "the turning point coincided with the

Table 9.1: Industrial Influence and the Issue-ness of Air Pollution, Controlling for Suspended Particulate Level

| Industrial Influence on Air Pollution | Issue-ness of Scale Item | | | |
	Newspaper	Chamber of Commerce	Labor Council	Political Parties
High-pollution cities	−.34	−.23	.07	.03
	(18)	(18)	(18)	(17)
Low-pollution cities	.05	.30	−.24	−.36
	(27)	(28)	(26)	(28)

Source. Crenson 1971, p. 117.

adoption of a new steel making technique [at one of the East Chicago mills which generated] relatively heavy particulate emissions."[8] In other words, the ordinance was not effectively applied either to existing or to new installations in East Chicago. Altogether, it does not appear that in the end the air pollution question was handled much more successfully in East Chicago than in Gary.

Policies such as air pollution control, which can have an adverse effect on local economies, do not readily appear as local issues. Even when pollution control does become local public policy, effective implementation proves difficult without endangering the economic well-being of the community. Local governments which closely reg-ulate pollutants from industrial plants necesarily impose costs on firms not borne by competitors operating in less-regulated localities. *Ceteris paribus*, the more closely regulated company will suffer in market competition. In time it will be forced either to relocate or to relinquish its previous share of the market. The company's economic decline or outright departure saddles the community with increas-ing unemployment, declining property values, and declining local government revenues. Any potential gains in air quality come at a substantial economic cost. Even those who abhor the polluted en-vironment seem to understand that the costs of effective regulation preclude action by local officials. Accordingly, they tend to focus their attention on the activities of higher levels of government, whose policies apply equally to all companies in the industry.

Since local governments have difficulty resolving such questions as air pollution control, Crenson was correct in emphasizing the difficulty this question had in becoming a major local issue. Given the fact that industry bears the cost, it is tempting to explain the lack of pollution control on industry's political power. And if that power is not overtly expressed in local political activities, one might be further tempted to emphasize the weight of indirect industrial in-fluence on local agenda setting. Yet the limits to local air pollution control seem better explained by the more general limits on local policy imposed by the structural constraints which bind local gov-ernment. Not surprisingly, air pollution control became an integral feature of American public policy only when state and federal of-ficials worked together to develop nationwide standards. Crenson himself observed that "the political center of gravity for pollution policymaking has moved steadily higher within the federal sys-tem .... The federal government has taken on new responsibilities in the field of pollution abatement ... because ... lower levels of government have often failed to take action themselves."[9]

It is not the exceptional political power of local industry that has kept pollution control from becoming a local issue. Few important actors in the local setting have been eager to make pollution a major concern. Because air pollution control imposes significant economic costs on local industry and thus on the local economy, taken as a whole, even the most likely proponents of pollution control often do not become actively engaged. As we shall see, the same political passivity applies to the larger set of redistributive issues that one expects would be raised by working-class organizations and politicians.

Trade Unions

Trade unions are potentially the most powerful set of organizations likely to propose redistributive policies in big-city politics. At least since World War II, trade unions have commanded positions of great power in large industrial cities with predominately working-class populations. Even in the United States, where unions are less politicized than in Europe, mayors regularly consult trade union leaders as a routine part of governing the city.[10] Unions have representation on most local boards and commissions; many council and other minor elected officials are dependent upon unions for financing their election campaigns; and municipal unions, with their recently discovered capacity to strike, can cripple a city through industrial actions that can be undertaken quite outside the normal political process. On many issues of importance to the trade union movement, big-city politicians move with speed and alacrity.

Unions also have a strong, demonstrated interest in securing redistributional policies for their working-class constituents. Although much is made of the so-called conservatism of trade union leaders, the welfare state is difficult to conceive apart from union power.[11] Even in the United States, where unionization occurred later and unions have been less militantly socialist than in Europe, trade unions have formed an alliance with the Democratic party and, within that coalition, have campaigned with considerable success on behalf of welfare, housing, health, and educational programs.[12]

Union pursuit of redistributive objectives has been most vigorous at the national level. In big-city politics, union demands have seemed to many observers to be strangely narrow and self-interested. Unions press for city ordinances requiring that union labor be used in the construction and repair of local buildings. They have successfully gained control over entry into skilled labor occupations, thereby allowing members to secure higher wages for specialized services. Unions have been able to win wages and benefits for unionized employees in the public sector that are roughly comparable to those in the private sector. But local unions have done little to legislate high minimum wages for nonunionized labor, nor have unions aggressively campaigned at the local level for larger benefits for welfare recipients, for low-income housing, for extended medical services to the needy, or for welfare programs aimed specifically at the poor.[13] As Banfield and Wilson have said, "Local leaders are generally less ideological than national ones."[14]

In a comprehensive analysis of union politics, both nationally and in three large cities, Greenstone dwells at some length on these national-local differences. Distinguishing between a pluralist interest in allocational politics and a welfare-state orientation toward redistributive issues, Greenstone notes that

> organized labor's electoral participation locally . . . reflected a pluralist concern for the organizational interests of particular unions. [In Los Angeles] unions supported a conservative incumbent mayor in 1961 and displayed little enthusiasm for a liberal candidate in 1965. Yet, the same unions pursued welfare state goals in partisan election campaigns for state and especially national office on behalf of relatively liberal Democratic party candidates. Similar . . . differences between union behavior in national and local elections were apparent in Detroit and Chicago . . . . More generally, most labor efforts in local politics have remained the preserve of . . . relatively pluralist nonfactory unions . . . . But as we have seen, a great number of ideological industrial unions have devoted most of their resources to national politics.[15]

One explanation for the peculiar conservatism of local trade unions is their small constituency. McConnell has observed more generally that, if a constituency is small and homogeneous, "the ends it most probably seeks will be narrow, specific, concrete, and usually material in character. If the constituency is large and heterogeneous, its ends will be large, general and sometimes vague."[16] From this perspective, the nonredistributive orientation of unions at the local level is attributable to the smaller, homogeneous constituency of the local labor movement. Greenstone's own interpretation of the national-local differences in union politics takes this form:

> Homogeneous constituencies are much more common in local as opposed to national politics. The federal government is far more diverse in terms of the number of citizens and variety of interests it comprises than are the states and localities . . . . In local politics, with fewer interests to be satisfied than in national politics, the possibilities of making particular arrangements with individual interests . . . are increased.[17]

A complementary explanation is that broad-scale redistributive policy proposals are inappropriately addressed to local governments. For example, if a city-wide minimum wage is passed, it will drive business outside the city's boundaries. If good-quality, subsidized housing is built with local funds, not only must it be paid for out of local tax dollars, but it might very well attract low-income families from other places. Other redistributive policies have similar consequences. As a result, unions instead concentrate on securing from local governments those particular benefits that can be limited to their own members. Their redistributive impact is sufficiently curtailed that they have few adverse economic consequences.

Unions press for narrow allocational benefits. But they also participate enthusiastically in the politics of development. Plans for the economic expansion of a community are often drawn up with the participation of at least some union leaders. Subsidies for business firms migrating into the community are supported because they will increase employment opportunities. For such statesmanlike contributions to a community's welfare, union leaders win a respected place in a local community's institutionalized bargaining process. In a consensual world of mutual deference and consideration, the particular interests of greatest concern to the movement are protected. Redistributive demands, which create class conflicts in national politics, have little place in local politics. Significantly, the limits on what the city can do often work to the advantage of local union leaders. In an atmosphere of local harmony and good will, unionists win a respected place in the community without sacrificing reasonable worker demands.

Working-Class Party Organizations

Political organizations heavily dependent upon working-class votes are also likely proponents of redistributive policies. Especially in central cities where the working class constitutes an overwhelming majority of the population, these parties may feel compelled to pursue a redistributive approach to urban problems simply to sustain their working-class support. Certainly, these political parties send representatives to the national legislature who align themselves on the redistributive side of most national political issues. Even in the United States the distinction between the Democratic and Republican parties on redistributive issues has been fairly clearly drawn since the New Deal. Moreover, the elements within the Democratic party most supportive of redistributive policies have been those representing urban areas.

At the local level this redistributive orientation is much less apparent. Democrats who in national politics favor a national health insurance program are unwilling to extend the public health services to low-income groups within the city. Democrats who vote for increases in national minimum wages oppose increased wages for local public employees. Democrats who support national financial aid for the education of economically deprived children tolerate the redirection of these funds to middle-class children within the local community. Significantly, systematic studies of state and local public policies in the United States seldom find that partisan political differences have policy consequences.[18] Once socioeconomic factors are taken into account, the balance of power between the political parties has only modest policy consequences. In an extensive review of the literature on the determinants of public policy, Fried finds a "lack of party impact that may be disturbing from the perspective of the 'responsible party governments' model of urban democracy."[19]

The lack of a distinctive partisan impact on local policy outcomes does not prevent local campaigns from being at times addressed to the needs of workers and the poor. Out of either ideological conviction or political necessity, candidates regularly seek to identify themselves with the needy and deprived of the community. But when they do, they usually select policies that do not have negative economic consequences. A variety of strategies are available. Candidates may call for policies that produce economic growth and therefore more employment opportunities for workers. If they call for redistributive policies, such as better housing or improved welfare benefits, they will recommend that the policies be funded with revenues from higher levels of government. Sometimes liberal candidates may propose locally funded programs for the needy, but, however popular, these will be relatively inexpensive programs, such as recreational programs for young adults or low-cost transportation fares for the elderly during off-peak hours.

Even modest plans for redistribution that have little more than symbolic value may not always be supported by local officials. Open-housing legislation in Wisconsin in the late 1960s is a case in point.[20] The proposed legislation prohibited racial discrimination in the housing market. But the legislation had little more than symbolic significance, both because the federal Constitution, as interpreted by the courts, already forbade such discrimination, and because establishing the fact of discrimination in any particular case was particularly difficult. Laws passed at the state and local levels have been both redundant and ineffectual. Yet Henry Maier of Milwaukee, a popular and effective mayor with liberal credentials, was unable to give open-housing policy his full support. He strongly endorsed this symbolically significant civil rights reform when proposed on a statewide basis for all of Wisconsin, but opposed any local ordinance applicable solely to the city of Milwaukee. A local ordinance passed without comparable laws covering surrounding suburban communities would only hasten white flight from the central city, he claimed.

Protest Groups

Although local redistributive policies are seldom proposed by either trade unions or big-city politicians and very few interest groups propose major schemes for redistribution, a new brand of protest group was spawned in the United States in the 1960s by the civil rights movement and the Vietnam War. These groups were new participants in the local political game, generated by a wave of citizen participation and often subsidized by federal agencies and national foundations which had little sense of economic limits on local policy. Analysis of their agitation is instructive in several ways: (1) the divergence of their demands from the traditional patterns of local politics clarifies just how nonredistributive local issues typically are; (2) the processes by which the local system responded to these demands demonstrate the capacities local systems have for handling vigorously stated redistributive demands; and (3) the decline of these groups in local politics shows the fragility of the politics of redistribution in the local arena.

Michael Lipsky's study of the rent strikes of Harlem in 1964 remains a seminal analysis of the politics of protest, and it is worth examining the ways in which the events he describes reveal the limits of city politics.[21] In the first place, the demands of the New York City rent strikers involved massive redistribution. They demanded nothing less than comprehensive rehousing or rehabilitation of existing housing for the poor minorities of New York. This could be accomplished (a) by insisting that private landlords maintain low-income housing at a standard that met the city's building code; (b) by public assumption of the properties in the hands of private landowners and the allocation of public funds to bring properties up to standard; or (c) by the construction of new, adequate housing for low-income residents. In pursuit of one or a combination of these policies, a collective withholding of rents to landlords was organized until code violations were repaired. To achieve an effective strike, the strike leaders launched a publicity campaign designed to reach the hundreds of thousands of poor living in housing that failed to measure up to the New York City code.

Second, the rent strike was quite successful, given the redistributive objectives that the strikers were pursuing. Jesse Grey, the leader of the protest movement, was able to enlist several hundred participants in his strike—a much larger number of activists than are usually mobilized in local political controversies. He secured the assistance of college students and other volunteers from outside the community, who lent their technical skills to a cause otherwise short on canvassers, typists, and pamphleteers. In addition, newspapers found the subject newsworthy and hence gave the rent strike much more free publicity than would be given activist groups in later years. Moreover, many in City Hall recognized the legitimacy of the rent strikers' complaints. New York was governed by a liberal mayor, Robert Wagner, many of whose advisers and departmental officers were sympathetic to the needs and objectives of the strikers. Grey also benefited from the highly politicized context in which policy was being formulated. The Wagner administration was nearing its conclusion, and many candidates were searching for issues, allies, and liberal credentials for the forthcoming election, in which John Lindsay would emerge as the winner. Since poor minorities numbered in the hundreds of thousands, their demands could hardly be ignored. In short, one can hardly imagine a local political context better suited to a group calling for redistribution.

But even all these politically favorable factors did not yield much substantive fruit. Adequate response to striker demands was simply not within the limits of the government of New York City. For one thing, it could not enforce the building code. At one level this was a function of the shortage of building inspectors and of the organizational routines of the building department, which did not concentrate inspectors in the areas of greatest need. At another level these organizational factors were themselves conditioned by the fact that proper enforcement of the city's building code would have driven most low-income housing in New York into receivership. Maintaining the buildings at code level would have escalated costs for many landlords far beyond any return they received in rent. And since buildings in low-income areas had little, if any, capital value, the landlord could be expected to relinquish control of the property to the city through failure to pay taxes. Many such properties had already become "nationalized" through just such a procedure.

City assumption of slum properties had its own difficulties. To avoid simply replacing one exploiting landlord with another, the city would have to repair and rehabilitate the housing. The costs of rehabilitation could not be covered by the rents low-income residents could afford. And if the city chose to subsidize the housing, the burden to local taxpayers might well become astronomical. An alternative was the destruction of tenement housing and erection of modern low-cost housing in its stead, but this, too, would be fiscally prohibitive, if financed out of local funds. Since federal funds were limited, there was little that could be done to meet the broad-scale demands of the rent strikers.

The task of local political leaders in such circumstances is to manage conflict. The demands of the strikers cannot be rejected out of hand, and their protest cannot be suppressed through punitive action unless the protestors seriously disturb public order. In the early 1960s poor minorities and even liberal-minded middle-class residents of the city were sympathetic to these redistributive demands. Outright suppression might only provoke a wider and more virulent political agitation. On the other hand, the strikers' demands could not be met in any substantively significant manner. To do so would have undermined the economic viability of the city. In these circumstances political symbols are of extraordinary value.

New York City's government employed a wide range of political symbols, all of which were designed to give the appearance of responding to the protest—but which at the same time did not require significant redistribution. Horror cases were given special treatment. These incidents, particularly frightening to the public at large, provided dramatic stories for the news media, and some government response was essential. For example, federal funds were used to establish an emergency heating program for tenants whose buildings were without heat on bitter-cold winter days. A federally funded rat extermination program was created in response to stories of rodents biting small children. On a longer range basis, a city commission was established to investigate the possibility of reorganizing the departments responsible for housing policy. Plans for new federal housing programs in low-income areas were announced with considerable fanfare.

Lipsky's detailed analysis shows that, substantively, little was changed in the housing markets of New York's low-income communities. Any visitor to the city can soon discover that the residential slums of the city remain; if anything, their boundaries only enlarged in the decade and a half following these events. However, the protest movement itself subsided. It proved impossible to maintain enthusiastic involvement in protest action for more than a few months. Almost inevitably, Jesse Grey made tactical errors. Newspaper reporters discovered he had exaggerated the size of the rent strike. Strikers realized that, to be effective, they had to pay rent into a court-designated fund while their dispute with the landlord was being resolved. Without a financial incentive for joining the strike, their continued cooperation proved hard to sustain. In the meantime public attention drifted to other issues. By manipulating political symbols, New York political leaders were able to minimize the impact of a vigorously asserted campaign for redistribution.

Managing Conflict

On the basis of the research by Lipsky and other students of protest politics, it is possible to specify a range of techniques available to local political leaders whenever demands for redistribution are forcefully articulated. They can be grouped under three general headings: (1) delay substantive response, thereby allowing the demanding group to become discouraged; (2) convert the redistributive issue into an allocational one; and (3) convert an economically redistributive issue into a political one.

The delay strategy is the most convenient and the easiest to implement. In the beginning, public leaders simply ignore demands they do not have the resources to grant. The fact that the demands seem so unreasonable makes the group illegitimate and the motives of leaders suspect. In the expectation that others will see the demands in this same light, public officials simply continue with business as usual. High-level officials refuse to see the group, to concede that the group has any public support, or to allow that any significant problem exists. However, if the group gathers support or is able to gather public attention or manages to disrupt a vital service of the community, the official employs more complex delay tactics. He may at long last grant an interview to the group, which sometimes is sufficient by itself to satisfy complaints. The mere fact that the authorities recognize the legitimacy of a complaint will be enough to dampen it. A certain satisfaction comes from having been able to ventilate a complaint or from having been able to tell an official off. Perhaps at the moment of recognition—in the sanctity of the mayor's office, say—the group itself begins to realize the unreality of its proposals.

If mere political recognition does not dampen protest, the government has other delay techniques available. Establishing a committee or commission to study the problem is probably the tactic most frequently employed. Since the group demands a major change from present policy, it is necessary to consider the matter at length before determining what can be done. Moreover, since the group's own proposals seem so unrealistic, it is evident that the matter must be handed to a group that has experience and expertise in the field.

The outstanding examples of this form of response were the numerous riot commissions established at both national and local levels in the late 1960s.[22] These commissions were set up only after several years of protest by black organizations. They were appointed in an atmosphere of potential violence that threatened the stability of the political regime. Simply ignoring the concerns of the black community was no longer a safe political strategy. Instead, broadly representative ad hoc commissions were established to investigate race-related problems and to come up with comprehensive solutions. The work of these commissions usually took several months to two years to complete, and once completed the commission itself had no power to implement them. But in the meantime, political leaders, without actually implementing economically redistributive policies, could declare that something positive was being done. By the time the commissions reported, pressures for change were no longer so intense and the most redistributive of the recommendations could be set to one side.

Authorities resort to a more sinister version of the delay strategy only in extremis. Protesting groups are sometimes able, through extralegal tactics, to capture physical resources that authorities consider vital. Inhabitants of houses that need to be torn down in order to make way for a major thoroughfare may sometimes refuse to leave their condemned property. Or environmental action groups may chain themselves to trees. In these circumstances the government needs to make an effort to negotiate—to give the appearance of reasonableness—without sacrificing its ultimate objective. In such cases, the glove of negotiations covers the mailed fist of coercive force. In the most extreme cases of terrorist skyjackings, authorities may make false promises to allow time for coercive action; the isolation of the terrorist group from public opinion allows for outright dissimulation on the part of the authorities. In the case of local protest, authorities try to persuade groups to cooperate without making false promises. On the other hand, the more isolated from public opinion the group becomes, the easier it is to utilize a combination of dissimulation and coercive force.[23]

A second strategy of political leaders is to convert redistributive issues into allocational ones. When groups demand redistributive reforms at the local level, government leaders explore ways of disaggregating the proposals so that from the resources available to them they can make some reponse. One of the most useful approaches is to meet very specific demands of the group calling for major change, while doing little or nothing about the overall problem. For example, in the rent strike the complaints of the group engaged in the strike were given first priority by city departments. To placate the unrest, efforts were made to satisfy the immediate problems of specific complaining groups, though the elimination of substandard housing throughout the city could hardly be considered.

This technique is valuable, but it can sometimes be counter-productive. If complaining is rewarded too quickly and easily, others will be induced to make similar demands. For example, when groups in two New York communities obtained community development funds from the juvenile delinquency program, their success encouraged the formation of many more like-minded groups in other parts of the city.[24] And when special benefits, such as winter clothing allowances, were given to active members of the Welfare Rights Organization, the concessions only encouraged other welfare recipients to join the organization and make similar demands.[25]

To avoid these kinds of difficulties, government agencies often sponsor experimental programs. Ostensibly, the policy is called an experiment because the government wishes to discover whether the plan will work in one specific context before being applied more generally. In fact, the agency simply does not have the resources to implement the policy throughout its jurisdiction, no matter how well the approach might resolve a given social problem. But by calling the project an experiment, the authority is able to respond to pressures from some particular group without conceding that a far more costly general policy of this sort is at hand. Consequently, the authority does little in the way of experimental design research to determine whether the policy is effective at treating the problem, and few, if any, redistributive experiments are generalized.[26]

An alternative form of this disaggregation strategy involves identification of group leaders and giving them special concessions. If used effectively, this approach need not consist of outright bribery. Instead, group leaders can be employed in relevant public-service positions, given an honored position in policy deliberations, or invited to participate in conferences at distant places. Although these techniques are usually called "cooptation," they can also be understood as providing training in public policy analysis. By being exposed to the problems of formulating adequate responses to redistributive demands, these leaders, without necessarily giving up their objectives, are encouraged to channel their energies into more realistic approaches.

Another useful method of disaggregation is to concentrate on the tip of the iceberg. Addressing the most visible aspect of a problem allows authorities to give the appearance of responsiveness to political pressure without sacrificing the larger interests of the city. The treatment of horror cases in the New York rent strikes is an obvious case in point. The availability of emergency rooms at hospitals is another. Although medical services may not be distributed evenly, in life-and-death situations medical treatment is available to anyone.[27] More generally, local plans for relief of the poor, though hardly adequate welfare assistance programs, have for decades taken the edge off demands for a more equitable distribution of wealth.[28]

Delay and disaggregation are familiar techniques available to authorities faced with demands to which they cannot respond. A third device, less frequently used, is the conversion of a demand for redistributive government services into a demand for the redistribution of local power. Changing the governance structure of a city in response to political protest is usually undertaken only after prolonged disputes. Because officeholders are reluctant to share their positions of power, they change the governing structure only when pressed. But political changes by themselves do not affect the economic productivity upon which the city's long-range welfare depends. Political innovation is thus a final measure that can be used to protect a city from economically redistributive policies.

The community action program of the War on Poverty provides one illustration of government responsiveness to demands from disadvantaged racial minorities for a sharing in political power. The requirement included in the poverty legislation, that community residents should have opportunities for "maximum feasible participation," became the vehicle for widespread involvement by racial minorities in the policymaking processes for a variety of local government programs.[29] Such participation changed allocational policies to some extent; racial minorities received a larger share of government services, and they were particularly favored in the recruitment of new employees to staff these innovative programs. But even though allocational decisions were affected by these changes in political power, local government undertook very few new redistributive commitments.[30]

School politics in large cities of the United States offers another instructive example of the way in which political forms can be altered to accommodate protest.[31] As a by-product of the civil rights movement, central-city schools in the late 1960s came under increasing scrutiny by black leaders and neighborhood groups. School boards were subjected to a variety of unrealistic redistributive demands, including demands for racial integration, massive increases in school funding, reallocating of teachers, complete equalization of educational resources, and even compensatory educational policies that would allocate extra resources to schools serving low-income areas. However, school boards in most central cities did not capitulate to the most redistributive of these demands, even where blacks made up a large proportion of the city's voting population. Every strategy for deflecting civil rights demands was brought into play. Protest groups were ignored. When that was no longer possible, study groups and investigatory commissions were asked to write reports, which, when concluded, were either drastically revised by the board or not implemented at all. To make some concessions to political pressures, boards established experimental programs and pilot projects. They gave positions of responsibility within the school system to community leaders. But in some cities none of these strategies proved sufficient, and public officials devised a more dramatic policy alternative, namely, decentralization of school governance to neighborhood boards throughout the city. In Detroit and New York, the two cities where this change in political organization was most fully executed, it proved successful in reorganizing the basis of political conflict. Instead of demands for massively redistributive policies by a central board, community groups concentrated on improving schools in their area by electing members to local boards. These local boards had limited resources, were dependent on other agencies for financing, and were constrained by policies determined at higher levels of government. Although allocational policies were changed, substantial redistributions in the delivery of educational services remained beyond the economic capacity of the local boards.

Conclusions

The politics of redistribution at the local level is thus an arena where certain kinds of citizen needs and preferences seldom become demands; an arena where demands, when voiced, do not gain much support; and an arena where redistributive questions, even when posed as major political issues, are treated by a variety of strategies designed to forestall, delay, and preclude their implementation. Some have concluded from these facts that a powerful elite keeps redistributive issues off the agenda of local politics.[32] It is said that this elite is so potent that groups favoring redistribution, fearful of economic sanctions or social ostracism, are dissuaded from making these topics local political issues. But in our view the absence of redistributive political issues is seldom due to the suppressive activities of an organized economic elite.[33]

It has also been claimed that the very structure of local governing institutions discourages local groups from raising redistributive issues, that these institutions are so structured that there is little hope there will ever be a response to redistributive demands. Put in these terms, the claim that the local political system is "biased" is more persuasive.[34] As chapter 7 shows, proposals for economic growth gain access to the local political agenda with greater ease than do proposals calling for social redistribution. Moreover, the consensus that often is formed behind developmental proposals seems to be due to the structural characteristics of local governments, which are called upon to raise revenues out of their own resources and finance capital expansion through transactions in private bond markets. Conversely, these same structural constraints limit the redistributive plans of local governments.

But even though local political systems in the United States are biased against redistributive issues, one cannot generalize from this fact to the character of politics in the United States as a whole. What may be difficult to achieve at the local level is open to bargaining in national politics. If redistribution is not an appropriate function of local government, that does not mean that the United States, taken as a whole, has no capacity to redistribute socially valued things. National political systems in a market economy are constrained by international flows of capital and credit, but the constraints are not as severe as they are at the local level. Nations control human migration, they erect tariff walls, and they prohibit the flow of capital outside their boundaries. These and other powers make redistribution a possible focus of national government action. The extent to which it occurs in any national political system is open to investigation. Demands which at the local level may be rejected out of hand or dealt with through symbolic manipulation and tactical maneuvering may in national politics be given due consideration.

4

Changing the Limits
on Urban Policy

Ten

Is New York a
Deviant Case?

On 16 November 1975 President Gerald Ford announced to the country that he would recommend to Congress new legislation that would allow the federal government to "provide a temporary line of credit to the State of New York to enable it to supply seasonal financing of essential services for the people of New York City." He said he was undertaking this unusual step, because "in the next few months New York will lack enough funds to cover its day-to-day operating expenses." Since the city had accumulated a large short-term debt, "the private credit market remained closed to them."[1] In other words, New York was financially bankrupt in all but name, and only the direct intervention of the federal government would save the investments of New York's creditors.

This dramatic conclusion to a year-long flirtation with outright default seems both to confirm and to question the argument advanced in the preceding chapters. On the one hand, the events in New York highlight the economic constraints that limit local public policy. If these limits are systematically ignored over a substantial period of time, the consequences for a local government can be nothing short of disastrous. On the other hand, these events raise doubts about the capacity of local government leaders to safeguard the economic interests of the city. New York's near-default seems to suggest that local governments are fundamentally responsive to short-term political forces within their cities regardless of the long-term economic consequences of their policies.

Opinion concerning the causes of the New York fiscal crisis has been divided. Many have said that the difficulties are the result of

Margaret Weir, University of Chicago, is coauthor of this chapter.

187

long-term socioeconomic trends that have had an adverse effect on the city's fiscal resources. Social and economic changes in the larger society are leaving New York with fewer resources to support the services its residents need. Others have said that the sources of the fiscal crisis are essentially political. New York City's financial situation deteriorated rapidly in a relatively short period of time; the causes of the deterioration were significant short-term changes in New York politics. In a sense, both perspectives are correct, for each view captures one dimension of the fiscal crisis. Yet both perspectives are limited, because neither distinguishes the factors affecting changes in the overall size of the New York City budget from the factors affecting the level of short-term loans necessary to finance the budget. In the analysis that follows we show that short-term political factors are best reserved for an explanation of increases in New York's debt in the sixties and seventies, while long-term factors account for the overall growth in local expenditures.

Long-term Economic Factors

For many, the New York fiscal crisis was externally determined, by long-range socioeconomic forces and by national policies that facilitated suburban growth. According to this view, new forms of communication and transportation have allowed individuals and firms to locate in less densely populated areas, where grass and space are more plentiful and noise and pollution less intense. Migration outward from New York City dates back to World War I, and since World War II the greatest areas of metropolitan growth have been outside the central city. At the same time, regional shifts have occurred, as businesses and individuals have been attracted to a warmer, drier climate. Finally, in the past fifteen years smaller cities and towns have grown at the expense of larger areas. With an improved transportation system and with the telephone reducing the need for face-to-face interactions, firms are finding that the disadvantages of locating at some distance from major population centers are offset by the lower wage levels, lower levels of unionization, and more dependable workers found in smaller communities.

As a result, middle-class residents and businesses have migrated from New York City, leaving the metropolis an attractive place for only low-income groups. Blacks, Puerto Ricans, and other Spanish-speaking people have come to New York searching for the same economic opportunities that attracted the struggling immigrants from Europe two and three generations ago. Increases in the percentages of blacks, Puerto Ricans, and other low-income residents have been a mixed blessing. While they still provide a work force that sustains New York's large service industry, the crime, unsanitary conditions, and fire hazards that accompany the presence of low-income groups, together with the greater need for social services, create substantial costs for the municipality.

These socioeconomic trends have been abetted by a variety of public policies. The continued racial discrimination in the South and the lack of adequate economic opportunities in Puerto Rico provide incentives for minorities to migrate to New York City. Federal support for the interstate highway system facilitated the decentralization of residence, commerce, and industry within metropolitan areas and improved the access of smaller communities to major population centers. The preference of the Federal Housing Authority and the Veterans Administration for recently constructed housing and the practice of "redlining" black and racially mixed communities further encouraged migration away from central cities. Also, the location of major military and space complexes in the "sunbelt" accentuated the rate of interregional change.

The effects of these changes on New York's fiscal policy were gradual but cumulative. Eventually, the external forces negatively affecting the city's economic capacities became so powerful that it was unable to support the municipal services its citizens needed. The fiscal crisis was the inevitable outcome.

In its purest form, this view is probably held most firmly in New York by recent municipal leaders.[2] But a view along these lines has also been cogently expressed in a background paper prepared by the staff of the Congressional Budget Office. Although they consider a broader range of factors that helped contribute to the fiscal crisis, they give great emphasis to the long-term factors that have forced many cities to "assimilate a new wave of rural migrants into the industrial economy just when the industries offering employment opportunities are shifting their bases of operation out of the cities." According to this study, the fact that the "city's tax base has failed to grow as rapidly as its revenue requirements" is due to factors that "are both complex and difficult for the city to change."[3]

Short-term Political Factors

While this "socioeconomic" view of the fiscal crisis has been popular among New York City officials, it has been given only limited credence nationwide. When the federal government exhibited great reluctance before coming to New York's assistance, it disseminated widely the belief that politicians were themselves largely to blame for the city's fiscal problems.[4] This political interpretation attributes the crisis to changes in the late 1960s that generated unprecedented increases in public spending to the point where the city was no longer able to pay its bills. Among these changes were the unionization of municipal employees, the increasing demands on local government by minorities, the economically imprudent policies of an ambitious politician, Mayor John Lindsay, and the pressure that numerous state and federal programs placed on local finances.

In its final report on the fiscal crisis, the city's own Temporary Commission on City Finances generally endorsed this interpretation. Although it noted economic trends unfavorable to the city, the commission rejected the view that New York was the captive of events beyond its control. Instead, the commission criticized the tendency of the city's politicians "to engage in policies and practices that were inconsistent with rather obvious long-term needs." The view of the commission is so widely held that it warrants quoting in some detail:

> Taxes were raised beyond the point of economic rationality and helped drive out mobile businesses and individuals; debt was issued beyond the capacity of the market to absorb it at competitive rates and, ultimately, to absorb it at all; salaries and benefits were negotiated beyond the capacity of the local government to finance the increases except by reducing the work force, cutting essential public services, and worsening the quality of life in New York City. In each instance, it clearly was in the short-run interest of City officials to pursue policies that were destructive to the future.[5]

Although the exact groups and personalities responsible for the precedence given to short-run interests over long-term needs were left unspecified in this public document, urban scholars have taken up the slack. In an early essay on the urban fiscal crisis, Piven identified the set of political factors that many studies since have accepted as critical: "Periods of political instability," she writes, "nurture new claims and claimants. This is what happened in the cities in the 1960s, and it happened at a time when the urban political system was uniquely ill-equipped to curb the spiral of rising demands."[6] In her view, it was the "urban blacks who made the trouble, and it was the organized producer groups . . . who made the largest gains."[7] In New York City, for example, "the municipal payroll expanded by over 145,000 jobs in the 1960s, and the rate of increase doubled after Mayor John V. Lindsay took office."[8]

Writing after the full effects of the fiscal crisis in New York had become evident, Shefter developed and extended Piven's analysis: "The current New York City fiscal crisis is above all a political crisis. Its origins lie in a set of political changes the city experienced in the

1960s, which led municipal expenditures and indebtedness to grow at an explosive pace."[9] Shefter argues that the "politicians who governed the city during the 1950s" were sensitive to fiscal and budgetary constraints, if only because they "paid special heed to the views of the city's tax-conscious lower-middle-class homeowners."[10] As a result, the city's "expense budget increased at an average annual rate of only 6.6 percent between 1953 and 1960."[11] However, "this political calm was shattered ... by the emergence of three new political groups ... the Democratic reform movement, the school-integration movement, and the movement to unionize city employees."[12] Because politicians allied themselves with these movements, the old regime was destroyed, initiating "the present era of budgetary inflation."[13]

David and Kantor's analysis is developed along similar lines. They report that the "growth in the city's budget and the sources of the city's revenues remained remarkably stable from the later 1940s to the early 1960s. From fiscal 1949 to fiscal 1962, the average annual expenditure increase was 6.5 percent."[14] Operating within this stable context, the New York City Board of Estimate "imposed various procedures which provided tight control over expenditures."[15] But in the "eleven years after 1963 a transformation of the city's political system induced major changes in the expectations of budgetary participants. The consensus underlying the postwar system was shattered by politicization among the city's minorities and public employees."[16] As a result, "the growth in the size of the budget was unparalleled."[17]

David and Kantor, Shefter, Piven, and the report of the Temporary Commission all stress the short-term political changes that occurred in New York during the mid- to late 1960s. Civil violence, strikes, and demonstrations, when combined with a Presidency-seeking liberal politician, eventually produced widespread fiscal chaos. Given that these political transformations occurred over a relatively short span of time, the role of long-term social and economic trends must necessarily be subordinate. "To account for the rapid growth of the municipal budget and debt," Shefter observes, "one must explain why public officials responded as they did to ... changes in the city's demographic and economic base."[18] The economic changes only provide a backdrop for a performance in which New York's politicians and political groups played leading roles.

The Long- and Short-term Factors

Although both the short-term political and the long-term economic analyses of the New York fiscal crisis seem convincing in many ways, there is a tendency in many discussions to treat the short and long term as roughly equivalent to the political and the economic. Instead, these are two quite separate dimensions, as table 10.1 illustrates. Two major kinds of economic factors can affect a city's fiscal well-being. The long-term factors are those that affect a city's competitive position vis-à-vis other localities and regions. They are the continuing changes in national and international economics that affect the city's capacity to export its products. As a city loses its competitive edge, it may be slowly but increasingly unable to sustain its previous level of public services. The short-term economic factors that affect fiscal policy are largely a function of fluctuations in the business cycle. If the national economy is experiencing a recession, local revenues may be less than anticipated. Or if the national economy is undergoing rampant inflation, local costs may increase much faster than inelastic local revenue sources, such as the real estate tax.

Just as economic factors can be either long or short term, so can political factors. In most discussions of the political dimensions of the New York fiscal crisis, short-term factors receive greater consideration. But two long-term political factors may be of greater importance in accounting for certain aspects of the crisis: the impact of public policies on the local economy, and the effect of structural arrangements on the system of party and group representation.

These distinctions allow for a more precise specification of the sources of New York's fiscal crisis. In brief, we shall show that the immediate cause of default, the city's heavy dependence on short-term loans, was a function of short-term influences that were mostly political in nature. Continual increases in the city's operating budget, the financial reason the city had to turn to short-term financing, occurred over a much longer span of time and therefore must be attributed to long-term factors. Although obvious socio-

Table 10.1: Factors Affecting Urban Fiscal Policy

Type of Factor	Duration of Time over Which Factor Influences Policy	
	Short-term	Long-term
Political	Rapid mobilization of new groups	Policy effects on migration of residents and firms
	Civil violence	System of representation
	Imprudent leadership	of party/group interests
Economic	Fluctuations in business cycle (depressions, inflation)	Secular changes in social composition of population
		Migration of commerce and industry

economic trends beyond the control of city officials were a major factor affecting the city's fiscal capacity, structural features of New York's political system also had their own effect.

Growth in the City's Debt:
The Role of Short-term Factors

The emphasis on short-term factors, whether economic or political, is particularly appropriate in accounting for the rapid escalation in short-term debt financing of the New York City municipal budget. Although by law the city was required to produce a balanced budget each year, in fact the city in the 1960s and 1970s was beginning to depend heavily on its previously strong position in the bond market to finance its operating budget. As can be seen in table 10.2, while long-term debt grew no faster in the 1960s than in the preceding decade, short-term debt, which had increased (in constant dollars) by only 4.3 percent annually during the 1950s, grew by 35.1 percent annually from 1963 to 1967 and by 27.2 percent from 1968 to 1972. Even in constant dollars New York City's total debt had more than quadrupled between 1963 and 1975. Stated in different terms, the total debt per capita increased (in constant dollars) from $710 in 1967 to $1,021 in 1975, and the total debt as a percentage of the personal income of the residents of the city increased from 17.6 percent in 1967 to 24.3 percent in 1975. Debt financing was in fact so important to the provision of public services that, for the period between 1967 to 1976, short-term debt on the average was used to pay for about 6.4 percent of the operating expenditures paid of out local resources. With local revenues steadily and consistently falling short of locally financed expenditures, this kind of budgetary mismanagement eventually culminated in virtual bankruptcy.

Table 10.2: Increases in Long-term and Short-term Debt of New York City in Constant Dollars

Period	Long-term Debt		Short-term Debt	
	Amount for Final Year of Period ($m)	Average Annual Percent Increase	Amount for Final Year of Period ($m)	Average Annual Percent Increase
1952–62	4747.2	1.2	141.3	4.3
1963–67	5070.0	1.3	635.0	35.1
1968–72	5091.8	.1	2115.0	27.2
1973–75	4818.2	−1.9	2816.4	10.0

Source. Citizens' Budget Commission 1979.

Such dramatic changes in local fiscal policy call for short-term explanations. Both economic and political interpretations have been advanced. The Congressional Budget Office study emphasized as critical the downturn in the national economy.[19] David and Kantor also noted that "between 1969–1972 the city lost 250,000 jobs, reflecting an employment decline not only in manufacturing but also an unprecedented loss of jobs in non-manufacturing sectors."[20] But while these economic changes were fully apparent only in the 1970s, debt was rapidly escalating well before 1967. Moreover, the economic recession was affecting all local governments, not just New York City's. Yet when New York was compared with a sample of fifty-one American cities, it was found that the "Big Apple's" short-term debt per capita was ten times that of the average city, or more than six standard deviations above the mean. Whatever difficulties inflation, recession, and falling employment levels were creating, by themselves they could not account for New York's peculiar fiscal problems.

As an explanation for the city's increasing reliance on debt financing, a political analysis along the lines developed by Piven, Shefter, and David and Kantor would seem to be quite convincing. Faced with escalating demands from minorities and challenged for the first time by well-organized, strike-prone municipal unions, public officials responded to their money-demanding constituencies at a level which their local tax revenues could not support. The response in New York to these constituencies was even greater than in other cities, because low-income groups were particularly well organized in New York, unionization had proceeded more quickly there than in other cities, and public officials, including Robert Wagner and John Lindsay, were eager to maintain a liberal image in their search for higher public office.

Neither should one exclude the special importance of the city's powerful banking community. Although the power of a banking elite in municipal affairs is usually thought to entail fiscal restraint, New York bankers exhibited unusual tolerance for politically popular but financially unsound governmental policies. The building boom of the 1960s, which seemed to promise large tax revenues in the future, the relative liquidity of the banks in this period, and the handsome profits to be made by financing New York's debt all seem to have contributed to the banks' fiscal myopia. When the First National City Bank decided in 1970 to review in detail the city's long-term financial position, it found that "because of the current bout of inflation, there might be a tendency to underestimate costs [and] revenue easily could be overestimated."[21] Yet the bank concluded that "in sum, the outlook for the future may not be completely negative. There are some signs that point to a moderate easing in the growth rate of expenditure pressures [and] municipal income can continue to grow, both through increases in intergovernmental aid and through increases in the city's collections of taxes and charges."[22] The document reveals the extent to which the banks buried their fiscal heads in the sand and entrusted large amounts of their investors' money in New York tax anticipation warrants. With national and international resources at their disposal, the banks were able to assist public officials to an extent that would simply have been prohibitive in any other American city.

Growth in Operating Expenditures:
Long-term Forces

Although a political explanation convincingly accounts for the increased dependency of New York on short-term debt financing, it proves to be a less satisfactory explanation for changes in the overall size of the city's budget. The growth in the budget has been relatively constant throughout the postwar period; percentage increases in the 1960s and 1970s were on the average no greater than in the preceding decade. The forces affecting the locally financed operating costs seem to have been constant, long-term factors rather than any vagaries of the politics of the 1960s.

Changes within New York over Time

Examination of the raw data on New York's operating expenditures at first glance seems to confirm the impact of dramatic short-term transformation. As can be seen in table 10.3, the operating expenses increased from $2,275 million in 1961 to $11,654.4 million in 1975, an average annual increase of some 12.4 percent. When these rapid increases in the budget in the 1960s and 1970s are compared with the 6.5 percent annual increases in the 1950s, one is tempted to look for a short-term explanation for changing fiscal policy.

Other aspects of table 10.3 also seem to call for a political explanation. Not only was the budget increasing by 12.4 percent per annum during this fifteen-year period, but the increases were concentrated on redistributional expenditures. Whereas the annual increment in expenditures on development and such allocational programs as police, fire, sanitation, and transit averaged only 9.5 percent, expenditures for redistributive programs increased by 15.7 percent and for educational programs by 11.9 percent. The cost of servicing the city's debt also increased by 14.9 percent per annum. Not only was the New York City budget increasing rapidly, but its focus was shifting away from traditional services most clearly within the economic interests of the city to programs more directly targeted to the needs of low-income groups.

But as suggestive as these data are, the figures are controlled neither for inflation nor for the amount received from state and federal sources. The first factor, inflation, is beyond the control of local officials, and the second, increases in the local budget due to increases in intergovernmental revenues, can hardly be said to reflect adversely on the prudence of local authorities. If anything,

Table 10.3: Annual Percentage Increase in the Operating Expenditures of New York City

	Expenditures			
	Millions of Dollars		Annual Percent Increase	
Functions	Current $ 1961	Current $ 1975	Current $	Constant $ᵃ
Redistributive				
Housing	14.7	178.3	19.5	14.5
Addiction services	. . .	83.9	. . .	. . .
Youth services	4.7	43.1	17.1	12.1
Welfare	345.8	3115.2	17.0	12.0
Health services	50.4	277.4	13.0	8.2
Hospitals	179.5	726.1	10.5	5.8
Human resources	. . .	144.5	. . .	. . .
Subtotal	595.1	4568.5	15.7	10.8
Educational				
Elementary & secondary	587.5	2572.1	11.1	6.4
Higher	53.2	537.3	18.0	13.0
Subtotal	640.7	3109.4	11.9	7.2
Developmental & allocational				
Environmental protection	131.5	435.9	8.9	2.8
Corrections	19.6	109.6	13.1	8.1
Pensions (unallocated)	66.9	327.5	12.0	7.3
Police	236.1	928.8	10.3	5.6
Transit	108.1	345.0	8.6	4.0
Fire	122.0	389.3	8.6	4.0
Judicial	43.5	135.2	8.4	3.8
Libraries	20.6	59.4	7.9	2.7
Parks	45.0	124.7	7.6	3.0
General government, legislative, & other	208.2	516.3	6.7	2.2
Water supply	45.4	59.4	1.9	2.5
Cultural				
Subtotal	964.2	3450.9	9.5	4.0
Debt servicing	75.2	525.6	14.9	10.0
Total	2,275.2	11,654.4	12.4	7.2

Source. Temporary Commission on City Finances 1978, p. 56.
ᵃPrice fluctuations estimated from United States Department of Commerce 1977, p. 43.

local officials should be congratulated on securing new resources from higher levels of government.

When these two factors are both taken into account, changes in the city's finances appear in a much different light. In the last column of table 10.3 the inflationary factor is held constant by reporting the percentage by which constant-dollar expenditures increased. Stated in these terms, the average annual increase in the New York City budget between 1961 and 1975 was not 12.4 percent but only 7.2 percent. In table 10.4 the second factor is also controlled. Only increases in that part of the budget that were paid for out of local taxes are included in the last two columns. For these locally financed expenditures, the average annual percentage increase was only 5.4 percent. In other words, much of the 12.4 percent annual increase in the size of the New York City budget during these years was a consequence of two factors for which local officials could hardly be blamed: (1) inflation, and (2) increased assistance from state and federal governments.

In table 10.4 one can also see that locally financed expenditures continued to be allocated in a more or less stable fashion across the major types of city services. We were able to obtain information on tax-levy expenditures for only the seven major local government functions, but at least for these services there did not appear to be

Table 10.4: Comparison of Total Budget and Tax-Levy Expenditure Growth for Seven Major Services

Functions	Budget Expenditure ($m)			Tax-Levy Expenditure ($m)		
	1961	1975	Annual Percent Increase	1961	1975	Annual Percent Increase
Total of all expenditures	2,695.4	7,227.5	7.3	2,077.7	4,338.3	5.4
Redistributive						
Welfare	394.1	1,931.9	12.0	152.4	476.8	8.5
Hospital	204.6	450.3	5.8	145.5	244.3	3.8
Total	598.7	2,382.2	10.4	297.9	721.1	6.5
Educational						
Elementary & secondary	669.5	1,595.1	6.4	435.2	847.7	4.9
Higher	60.6	333.2	12.9	24.7	119.2	11.9
Total	729.5	1,928.3	7.2	459.9	966.9	5.5
Developmental and allocational						
Police	269.1	576.0	5.6	248.4	530.4	5.6
Fire	139.0	241.4	4.0	122.7	232.2	4.7
Environmental protection	149.9	220.3	2.8	105.7	199.6	4.6
Total	558.0	1,037.7	4.5	476.8	962.2	5.1

Source. Temporary Commission on City Finances 1978, p. 57.

dramatic changes in patterns of allocation. Although expenditures for redistributive services—health and welfare—increased at the somewhat higher rate of 6.5 percent per annum, the increase for police, fire, and sanitation was only a short distance behind—5.1 percent per annum. If there was a marginal shift in local priorities in response to minority demands, liberal reforms, and Presidential aspirations, the changes were far less wholesale than a glance at the raw figures initially suggests.

A more detailed analysis of the data sheds even greater doubt on the proposition that dramatic changes occurred in expenditure patterns in the late 1960s. In table 10.5 it can be seen that during the administrations of O'Dwyer and Impellitteri locally generated revenues increased by an average annual rate of 4.9 percent. During the first two Wagner administrations, when city politicians were supposedly responding primarily to tax-conscious lower-middle-class homeowners, the rate of increase was 4.7 percent. During the third Wagner administration, when liberal forces were apparently gaining

Table 10.5: Increase in New York City Expenditures from Local Sources under Five Administrations

Administration	Expenditures during Final Year of Administration ($m)[a]		Average Annual Percent Increase (for constant $)
	Current $	Constant $	
O'Dwyer/Impellitteri (1949–54)	$1221.1	$1516.9	4.9[b]
Wagner I & II (1955–62)	1930.2	2191.2	4.7[c]
Wagner III (1963–66)	2533.6	2686.6	5.2[d]
Lindsay I (1967–70)	3644.3	3289.0	5.2[d]
Lindsay II (1971–74)	5404.0	3868.3	4.1[d]
Beame (1975–76)	7043.1	4227.5	4.5[d]

[a]Although the fiscal year ended six months after the administration concluded its term of office, it is assumed that expenditures for that year are influenced primarily by the policies of the outgoing administration.

[b]Data calculated from the New York Chamber of Commerce 1960.

[c]Increase in revenues from local sources. Data on tax-levy expenditures not available to us for this time period. It is assumed that inasmuch as short-term debt for this period increased from a very low base at a comparatively low rate, increases in local revenue flow correspond closely to increases in expenditures paid for out of local sources. Data calculated from Citizens' Budget Commission 1979.

[d]Data calculated from Temporary Commission on City Finances 1976, tables I and II.

strength, the increment in the local operating budget averaged 5.2 percent, somewhat higher than in earlier administrations. But during the first Lindsay administration, when economic constraints were purportedly thrown to the wind, New York's local budget increased once again by just 5.2 percent. The increase was only 4.1 percent during the second Lindsay administration, while the first two years of the Beame regime showed an increment of 4.5 percent.

Not much should be made of the variation in the percent of budget increase from one administration to the next. The rate of increase is not so much lower in Lindsay's second administration that he should be congratulated for his fiscal prudence. But the data clearly do show that any changes in New York politics during the 1960s had only minor effects on expenditure patterns. Instead of New York's lavishing its resources either on the poor or on city bureaucrats at an ever-increasing rate, it seems as if the pattern of civic expenditure remained at a relatively constant rate of increase. Whatever forces induced a 5 percent rate of increase in New York's budget were in place at least as early as 1949.

There is, however, a factor not taken into account in table 10.5 that may lend some credence to the argument that short-term political factors swelled the local budget in the 1960s. This is the matter of the promises made during the Lindsay years concerning city employee pension funds. These promises committed the city to increases in payments which would not be felt immediately but which would, in time, constitute a significant expenditure. Pensions comprised 9.4 percent of the total budget in 1975, and the city had incurred unfunded liabilities which in 1976 totalled $8.5 billion. But even though Lindsay's pension policies were open to question, by themselves they did not induce the fiscal crisis. The actual expenditures for pensions up until 1975 did not mark a drastic departure from those of the previous decade and were, at least partially, the result of forces outside the city. Retirement costs jumped from $290 million (in constant dollars) in 1961 to $707 million in 1975, a 6.6 percent annual increase. From 1970 to 1975, however, these costs mounted from $559 to $707 million, an annual increase of only 4.8 percent.[23]

Even these figures overstate the extent to which the promised increases in pensions were the result of choices made by city leaders. In the first place, the total cost of retirement benefits includes Social Security benefits, an area over which the city has no control. The increases in Social Security in this period were not minor: in 1975 the cost of Social Security to the city was $250 million, or 22 percent of the total costs of retirement benefits.[24] Second, some of the retirement benefits were granted by state legislators, not by city officials; this was particularly true during the first Lindsay administration.[25]

Comparing New York with Other Cities

There is no question that New York's expenditures have been higher than those of localities in other parts of the country. New York City's per capita tax burden in 1974 was $699, while that for the next fourteen largest cities in the United States was only $257. Total city and state taxes per capita for New York were $1,186, as compared with an average total of $632 in the other cities.[26] No doubt New York's figures are high relative to the average simply because it provides some services that in other parts of the country are handled by counties and special districts. But when New York is compared with cities whose populations are five hundred thousand or more (see table 10.6), its per capita outlays for just the common services provided by most local governments still are relatively high. In 1973 they were $273, as compared with $194 in cities losing population and only $122 in cities gaining population. Table 10.7 shows that the number of city employees performing common functions per one thousand residents living in the city was considerably higher in New York than in the cities gaining population, and the wages these employees received were well above wages paid in the other big cities. In short, the cost of public services is considerably higher for the residents and firms of New York. And if these differences are strong and consistent even when New York is compared with other large cities, they are most certainly even greater between New York and the smaller cities and suburbs which are the growing areas in American society.

But while the comparatively high cost of public services in New York is indisputable, the differentials between New York and other cities do not seem to be of recent vintage. Although on some indicators the rate of increase in service costs is somewhat greater in the "Big Apple" than in other large cities, the trends are not uniform and differences are generally modest in nature. It is true that per capita revenues from city sources increased between 1970 and 1976 at a slightly higher rate in New York than in other cities (see table 10.6); on the other hand, per capita outlays for common services did not increase as rapidly in New York as elsewhere. And even though in table 10.7 one notices that the wages of municipal employees increased more rapidly in New York than in other cities during the five years 1967–72, the number of employees per one thousand residents remained constant in New York while growth occurred elsewhere.

Table 10.8 provides additional information about the total cost of services paid for out of local revenues over a somewhat longer span of time. In this table note once again the comparatively high level of per capita expenditures in New York. But while New York starts

Table 10.6: Expenditure and Tax Policies of Central Cities with a Population of More than 500,000

	Per Capita Outlays for Common Services[a] (constant $)			Outlays as Percent of Resident Income (common services)		Per Capita Revenues from City Sources[b] (constant $)		
	1969–70	1972–73	Aver. Annual % Increase	1969–70	1972–73	1969–70	1972–73	Aver. Annual % Increase
New York City	$220	$273	7.5%	6.9%	8.4%	$391	$503	8.8%
Declining cities[c]	147	194	9.7	5.4	6.9	184	216	5.5
Growing cities[d]	88	122	11.5	3.1	4.0	107	133	7.5

Source. Muller 1975, pp. 82–83.

[a]Services provided by most local governments and usually paid from local revenue sources.
[b]Includes all city services, not just common sources.
[c]Those cities experiencing declining population between 1960 and 1973. They were Baltimore, Buffalo, Cincinnati, Cleveland, Boston, Chicago, Detroit, Milwaukee, New Orleans, Philadelphia, Pittsburgh, St. Louis, San Francisco, and Seattle.
[d]Those cities experiencing increasing population between 1960 and 1973. They were Dallas, Columbus, Denver, Houston, Indianapolis, Los Angeles, Memphis, Kansas City, Honolulu, Jacksonville, Phoenix, San Antonio, and San Diego.

with a very high base (in part because it offers services provided elsewhere by other governmental jurisdictions), the average annual percentage increase is only a half percentage higher than the median percent increase for the other nine cities.[27] In sum, when New York is compared with other cities, the trend data for the 1960s do not show a pronouncedly higher rate of increase in locally financed expenditures.

Table 10.7: Employment Policies of Central Cities with a Population of More than 500,000

	City Employees per 1,000 Residents (common functions)[a]		Monthly Average Wages of City Employees (common functions)		
					Aver. Annual
	1967	1972	1967	1972	% Increase
New York City	12.2	12.2	$709	$950	6.0
Declining cities[b]	11.3	12.5	598	717	3.7
Growing cities[c]	7.9	8.9	556	635	2.7

Source. Muller 1975, pp. 39, 49.
[a]Services provided by most local governments and usually paid from local revenue sources.
[b]Those cities experiencing declining population between 1960 and 1973. They were Baltimore, Buffalo, Cincinnati, Cleveland, Boston, Chicago, Detroit, Milwaukee, New Orleans, Philadelphia, Pittsburgh, St. Louis, San Francisco, and Seattle.
[c]Those cities experiencing increasing population between 1960 and 1973. They were Dallas, Columbus, Denver, Houston, Indianapolis, Los Angeles, Memphis, Kansas City, Honolulu, Jacksonville, Phoenix, San Antonio, and San Diego.

Table 10.8: Per Capita Expenditures from Local Sources in the Ten Largest United States Cities

City	1964 (constant $)	1974 (constant $)	Aver. Annual % Change
New York City	$407	$578	3.6
Median of other nine cities	156	208	3.1
Washington	392	719	6.3
Los Angeles	203	240	1.7
Baltimore	192	259	3.0
Philadelphia	171	252	4.0
Detroit	156	139	−1.2
Cleveland	151	208	3.3
Dallas	139	189	3.1
Chicago	119	162	3.1
Houston	114	61	−6.5

Source. Temporary Commission on City Finances 1976, pp. 10–11.

Long-term Political and Economic Characteristics

Inasmuch as the increase in locally financed operating expenditures (in constant dollars) has been consistent and steady throughout the postwar period, it is important to examine other long-term characteristics and trends in order to ascertain the underlying causes of the city's eventual incapacity to balance its local revenues and its local expenditures. In this regard, it is important to consider first the long-term secular decline in the competitive capacity of the New York economy.

Economics: Competitive Capacity

At first glance, New York's economy appears stable through most of the period since World War II. For example, the report of the Temporary Commission treats the postwar years as an equilibrium period, the 1960s as a decade of moderate growth, and the years following 1969 as a recessionary period. Although the commission recognized longer-term secular declines in manufacturing, it felt that until 1969 these were largely counterbalanced by growth in the corporate office sector. It was because past trends had been uneven that the commission believed that "there is a reasonable basis to assume that in the [1980s] the decline of the local economy can be slowed significantly and perhaps even halted."[28] If the proper political decisions are reached, desirable demographic and economic changes can be anticipated, it suggested.

The commission's analysis looks at changes within New York City largely in its own terms. But when the city is compared with the United States as a whole, the trends no longer appear uneven but point uniformly in the direction of secular decline. In order to isolate the particular place of New York in the nation's society and economy, New York characteristics are considered in Table 10.9 in relation to characteristics of the United States as a whole. For example, as the first row reveals, the population of New York as a proportion of the national population declined from 5.66 percent in 1940 to 3.51 percent in 1975, a reflection of the fact that the city's population has decreased somewhat while the population of the United States has nearly doubled in size. All other figures in the table are similar ratios of New York characteristics to national characteristics.

New York's decline on all indicators in the table provides impressive evidence of the city's long-term secular decline. Whereas in 1950 median family income was well above the national average, by 1975 it was significantly less than the norm. The number of new housing starts in New York as a percentage of new housing nationwide fell almost to the vanishing point in 1975. If that figure can be discounted by suggesting that New York already has a viable housing stock in place, the dramatic drop in total employment, a decline which is considerably more steep than the population decline, can hardly be considered as complacently. The reduction in employment opportunities is especially severe in the manufacturing sector, as industrial plants no longer find New York an inviting place to locate. Even in finance, real estate, and insurance, the areas in which the city is still thought to be dominant, growth within New York City has lagged behind growth elsewhere in the United States. As a result, the city's relative position has sharply deteriorated. The one sector of the economy in which the city has enjoyed considerable net

Table 10.9: Economic and Demographic Changes in New York City as Compared with the United States

New York/U.S. Ratio	1940	1950	1960	1970	1975
Population size[1]	5.66	5.23	4.34	3.80	3.51
Nonwhite population[1]	3.55	4.93	5.27	6.62	5.67
Median family income[2]	NA	1.17	.88	1.16	.94[a]
New housing starts[3]	NA	2.91	2.68	1.43	.30
Employment (total)[4]	6.32	5.85	4.25	3.56	3.14
Employment (sector)					
Manufacturing[5]	7.05	6.29	5.11	4.01	2.74
Finance, real estate, and insurance[6]	20.99	17.54	14.04	12.56	11.00
Government[7]	NA	10.78	11.53	15.03	17.46
Employment (occupation)[1]					
Professional, technical	9.35	6.77	4.67	5.38	NA
Managers, proprietors	7.68	7.47	8.01	3.87	NA
Clerical	NA	8.91	9.66	6.08	NA
Craftsmen, foremen	6.53	4.89	5.91	2.08	NA

Sources. (1) United States Bureau of the Census, Characteristics of the Population. (2) United States Bureau of the Census, Characteristics of the Population; Bahl, Campbell, and Greytak 1974. (3) United States Bureau of the Census, Census of Housing, Nonfarm Housing Characteristics, 1950; United States Bureau of the Census, Census of Housing, Housing Characteristics for States, Cities, and Counties, 1970; United States Department of Housing and Urban Development, Statistical Yearbook, 1974; United States Department of Commerce, Bureau of the Census, Construction Reports, series C-20. (4) United States Bureau of the Census, Characteristics of the Population; New York State Statistical Yearbook, 1977. (5) United States Bureau of the Census, Characteristics of the Population; New York State Statistical Yearbook, 1977; United States Department of Labor, Bureau of Labor Statistics. (6) United States Bureau of the Census, Characteristics of the Population; New York State Department of Labor Employment Review; United States Department of Labor, Bureau of Labor Statistics. (7) United States Department of Labor, Bureau of Labor Statistics: New York State Department of Labor Employment Review.

Note. NA = information not available.

[a]Computation relied in part upon projection of New York City data for 1972. The Consumer Price Index was employed to bring the data to projected 1975 levels.

growth has been the area of governmental employment. Some say that is one of New York's problems.

When changes in employment are considered by occupation, the impact of the marked decine in the manufacturing sector is evident. Both managers and craftsmen are leaving New York in especially large numbers. The number of professionals and clerical workers living in New York relative to elsewhere has dropped somewhat less steeply. The one area in which New York is gaining relative to other parts of the country is the number of nonwhite and Spanish-speaking residents. Given the relatively weak financial situation of these groups together with their greater dependence on redistributive services, this can scarcely be considered to be in the city's economic interest.

On the basis of these long-term trends in New York's competitive position, it is quite possible to conclude that its fiscal crisis was in many ways externally determined. It can be argued that, except for an unusual dependence on short-term debt financing in the early 1970s, New York has maintained a fairly consistent set of public policies. Only the long-term decline in the city's economic position, not peculiar responsiveness to either minorities or public employees, accounts for the city's present fiscal difficulties. It might be said that public officials in New York, as elsewhere, have been framing their public policies within the economic constraints that limit all local governments, but inasmuch as socioeconomic trends have all been to the disadvantage of the central city, even prudent public policies have not spared New York from an externally determined, but nonetheless painful, virtual bankruptcy.

Politics: Fiscal Policies

The increasing pressure on the fiscal capacity of many central cities suggests that externally determined factors may in large part account for fiscal crisis, even as they account for much of urban politics and policy formation. But certain aspects of New York's fiscal policies are not easily squared with this interpretation. Although socio-economic factors have affected New York's competitive position, the city's own fiscal policies seem to have aggravated its economic position.

On many indicators, it seems as if New York officials did not pursue their city's economic interests as efficiently as officials elsewhere have done. As is shown in tables 10.6, 10.7, and 10.8, New York's taxes are higher, its expenditures for common services are higher, its wages are higher, and the number of municipal employees per one thousand residents is higher than in growing cities. Not only are New York expenditures per capita much higher than in other cities, but the taxes levied to pay for them seem to be unusually progressive for local government. For example, it is estimated that in 1973, the average United States resident with an income of $7,500 paid 1.1 percent in state and local income taxes; on an income of $50,000, the tax was only 3.7 percent. For New Yorkers, the scale ran from 2.0 to 11.1 percent. The only city in which state and local income taxes were anywhere near as progressive was Minneapolis, where the percentage paid in taxes increased from 3.9 to 6.9 percent.[29] New York seems to have a particular penchant for dissuading its more prosperous and productive residents from remaining in the community.

Two long-standing characteristics of New York City probably account for its liberal commitment to high expenditures and redistributive tax policies. First of all, New York was at one time the city which more than any other locality could afford to provide high-quality redistributive public services. It was the richest city in the world. It was the world's greatest center of trade and commerce. It was—and in some ways remains—the financial center of the world. It was the central point of exchange between the great industrial complex located in the northeastern and midwestern heartland, on one side, and the capitals of Europe, on the other. Although New York had competitors, it had no peer. Just as the wealthiest states have the highest levels of redistribution (see chapter 3), so the richest city in the United States could afford more lavish levels of public expenditure. Consequently, New York assumed responsibility for the operation of seventeen hospitals and financed a comprehensive system of higher education when more modestly endowed cities and towns found these activities utterly beyond their means.

Once a city assumes responsibility for a public function, it cannot easily discard it. New York has tried for many years to shift at least some of the financial responsibility for its colleges and universities, its welfare system, and its complex of hospitals to state and federal authorities. In 1966, for example, the Temporary Commission on City Finances proposed that "the State of New York should assume financial responsibility for the City University of New York."[30] But state leaders were unwilling to undertake this responsibility, and much of the financial burden remained at the local level. Unfortunately, at the very time when the demand for these services was steadily increasing, New York was losing the economic capacity to finance the necessary supply. The high level of taxes necessary to support these unusual local services became increasingly painful for the city's remaining businesses and residents.

But New York City's wealth did not by itself produce a liberal commitment to redistribution. In addition to its wealth, New York has had an unusual system of competitive politics and group activity not characteristic of local politics elsewhere. Even before the fiscal crisis, Greenstone and Peterson discussed the city's group politics in language that still seems appropriate enough to allow lengthy quotation:

> Nowhere have [group] interests been more frequently recognized, have potential groups been more likely to become 'real' organized groups, have possible conflicts the greater likelihood of breaking out than in New York City. [The] fragmentation of power at the very top levels of government as well as the division of electoral strength between the Democratic organization and the reform coalition frees city agencies from close central direction and opens them up to pressures from the host of civic groups in the city. Inasmuch as both political factions must seek support from interest groups, neither side can effectively eliminate them from their spheres of influence .... The vulnerability of city agencies to group pressures in turn encourages the formation of even more groups in the turmoil of New York politics.[31]

Because group life finds nourishment in New York, political forces within the city place particularly strong pressures on local public officials, even when these may be at the expense of the city's long-term economic interests. It is in this sense that New York has been exceptional in its disregard of the limits usually placed on city policies. Yet even in New York City these limits have had to be given their due respect.

Conclusions

However suddenly New York lurched toward bankruptcy in the mid-1970s, the forces pressing in this direction had been in place throughout the postwar period. While New York's competitive position vis-à-vis other parts of the United States was steadily declining, its operating expenditures were edging upward by 5 percent per year (in constant dollars) and its tax structure remained both comparatively burdensome and relatively progressive. The fiscal crisis was not generated by a massive deviation from a concern for the city's economic interests by any one particular mayor. Instead, the trends were so slow and gradual that even the First National City Bank could conclude as late as 1970 that "the outlook for the future may not be completely negative."[32] If public officials were not pursuing the city's economic interests as effectively as possible, the errors were not wholesale but on the margins. Incremental decisions were being taken which in the long run would have seriously negative consequences.

The interaction between long-term economic trends and firmly entrenched patterns of political relations brought New York to the point where its liberal fiscal policies could be financed only by massive borrowing. The degree to which the city had reached its limits by the mid-1960s remained obscured so long as the banks were willing to underwrite city debts. Debt financing permitted municipal politicians of the 1960s to close their eyes to the city's ever-decreasing competitive advantage and allowed them to pursue politics "as usual" precisely at a time when economic calculations would have counseled policies of belt tightening.

Alarms were sounded from various quarters in the early 1960s, however, warning public officials of the dangers inherent in the increases in local government costs. In 1961, Robert Wood noted that for the previous fifteen years experts had been predicting "gaps between revenues and expenditures ranging from $200 million to over $500 million annually."[33] The New York Chamber of Commerce, in a document entitled "The Coming Crisis in New York City Finance," analyzed the long-range outlook in much the same terms as Wood did. "One of the significant developments of recent years," they began, "has been the rapid and continuing increase in the expenditures of local governments."[34] The trends in New York City were particularly alarming: "If the New York City budget continues to grow in future years at the same rate it has grown since 1948," they predicted, "the $3 billion mark will be reached in 1965, and the budget will exceed $4 billion by 1970."[35] After projecting these trends, the report argued that "the City of New York cannot continue indefinitely to increase its expenditures at a rate substantially faster than the growth of the tax base. To continue this trend for any length of time will be to court financial disaster."[36]

Not only did the Chamber of Commerce accurately project the economic consequence of the city's policies, it also evaluated the political factors which had produced such policies and proposed a plan to correct the situation. The difficulty was that "there seems to be no overall consideration of the interest of the City, as a whole. Responsibility for policy-making is highly diffused .... It is virtually impossible to determine where the responsibility actually lies for the formulation of municipal policy in any given area." To correct these deficiencies, the Chamber of Commerce proposed "the appointment of an advisory committee of distinguished citizens to explore, with the Office of City Administrator, the activities of the hunded or more departments, agencies and activities of City Government, and to form judgments regarding the relative essentiality of each service."[37]

One and one-half decades later, the arrangements established to pursue a more economically rational set of public policies took a form that closely resembled the Chamber of Commerce proposal. The major difference was that the "distinguished citizens" had a good deal more than just advisory powers. The establishment of the Municipal Assistance Corporation and the Emergency Financial Control Board in the wake of default cut deeply into the policy-making prerogatives of the mayor, the Board of Estimate, and other elected officials. In the words of David and Kantor, "the real locus of power in the budgetary process has shifted to financial and business elites who virtually set up and then came to dominate the emergency boards." As a result of their management of the city's fiscal affairs, "the whole purpose of the budgetary process has changed to one of political coordination and economic planning."[38] Significantly, these stringent economic measures were politically popular; New York's next mayor would prove to be as fiscally conservative as he was socially liberal.

New York pursued a set of economically problematic fiscal policies for a much longer period of time than less well endowed cities could have afforded. But even in the city that was once the nation's wealthiest and most powerful, the importance of economic interests became so painfully apparent that the political changes needed to bring about their effective pursuit were finally introduced. If New York once deviated from the pattern followed by most cities, the city's business elites, politicians, and voters have all ensured that such deviation no longer continues.

Eleven

Redistribution in the Federal System

Nothing highlights the differences between national and local government more than the federal government's rescue of New York from virtual bankruptcy. By pursuing policies beyond its economic limits, New York incurred fiscal deficits that reached a peak of $1,645 per capita in 1975. Yet at the time the federal government intervened, its own debt was no less than $1,863 per capita and it was running an additional annual $66.5 billion deficit.[1] Actions not possible by local governments, separately or in combination, become Washington's responsibility. After summarizing what the foregoing analysis has revealed are key features of the federal system, I shall sketch briefly the direction reform must take.

Local Political Economies

Fiscal crises in New York, Cleveland, Chicago, and elsewhere demonstrate with special clarity one of my central contentions: redistribution is not and cannot ordinarily be a constituent part of local government policy. If a city expands its services to needy citizens, it only increases its attractiveness as a residence for the poor. Other things being equal, consistent, concentrated pursuit of such a policy leads to bankruptcy. Most localities therefore resist the temptation to redistribute, and as a result, only about 12 percent of local fiscal resources in the United States as a whole are so allocated. By contrast, over one-half of the domestic federal budget is spent on programs of redistribution.

Economic limits shape not only urban public policy but also the pattern of local politics. Local issues are less pressing, local conflicts are less intense, and local political parties either are appendages of national parties or are dispensed with altogether. Group life is underdeveloped, and rates of voter participation are depressed. Liberal demands for egalitarian reform are notable for their absence, and in those special circumstances when minorities champion the needs of the poor, their proposals often fail to acquire the legitimacy necessary for reasoned local discussion. Although economic development is assiduously promoted by civic elites, the contentious aspects of local politics consist, in the main, of petty disputes over patronage, ethnic appointments, and service delivery. As important as these questions can be for particular individuals and groups, one must understand that the politics of patronage and ethnicity lacks the stature of issues of war and peace, unemployment and inflation, inequality and redistribution, which give intensity to national political debates.

Notwithstanding these central tendencies in local politics, the patterns I have identified are hardly invariable. Under some circumstances egalitarian political pressures yield policy consequences. In general, their effect is greatest when economic resources are least constraining.

National politics provides the best illustration of this tendency. Because the national government has fewer constraints on its policy options, group pressures in the context of competitive party politics have produced a range of welfare-state policies, including minimum wage laws, compensatory education, welfare assistance, low-income housing, food stamps, and unemployment compensation. Of course, even at the national level redistributive policies are not continuously pressed upon government officials. Cycles of innovation and reform alternate with prolonged periods of consolidation, even dismantlement. Yet welfare-state reforms, once introduced, are not easily withdrawn. Once a governmental program has been established, an administrative staff recruited, a set of clientele groups with a direct stake in program maintenance actively formed, and a particular policy direction legitimized by a Congressional decision, the political inertia that often weighs against redistribution now acts to perpetuate it. Eisenhower chose not to revamp the New Deal, and even the Nixon administration discovered that the Great Society programs inaugurated by Lyndon Johnson had surprising durability.

While these political patterns are especially evident in national politics, one finds at least a shadow of them locally. For example, chapter 3 revealed that more services are offered to low-income groups in states and localities that have a larger fiscal base. In these more affluent areas local governments can levy taxes no higher than their neighbors' and still have more revenue to respond to the urgent needs of less fortunate citizens. Liberals, reformers, and low-income groups in these communities, it would seem, are able to make a case that at least some of the "surplus" revenue be used for redistributive purposes. Once such policies are enacted, they tend to become an institutionalized part of the local policy system.

New York provides perhaps the most dramatic instance of this pattern. A city which once boasted exceptional economic resources gradually accumulated a wide array of government programs not typically financed at the local level. As its economic capacities became more circumscribed, it taxed its residents and firms at increasingly high levels in order to maintain its sophisticated array of public services. Public policy began to contribute toward economic decline; outward migration of firms and residents was aggravated by high-tax, high-expenditure policies. Adverse effects notwithstanding, these policies were so entrenched that the city lurched toward bankruptcy before corrective policies were introduced. This pattern, so obviously manifest in New York City, has repeated itself elsewhere in many central cities of the Northeast and Middle West. Migrational shifts that have coincided with national prosperity have had a centrifugal effect on many once-august major cities, exacerbating their problems and accelerating their comparative decline.

Federal Influences on Local Political Economies

Significantly, even as central cities were coming under increasing economic constraints, the national government selected a set of new public policies specifically designed to increase local pressures for redistribution. As a centerpiece for these policies, the federal government sponsored a community action program which called for "maximum feasible participation" of low-income and minority groups in policy formation. Local leaders, already experiencing resource limitations, suddenly were faced with federally sponsored groups which insisted upon added redistributive service-delivery programs. When city officials resisted, even while professing their own liberal social-reform commitments, low-income groups queried their veracity. Civic disputes became so cantankerous that in Douglas Yates's words "conflicts engendered by street-fighting pluralism" produced "an increasingly ungovernable city."[2]

In one crucial respect, the community action program of the war on poverty was a resounding success. At a time when black Americans and other minorities were confronting publicly their systematic exclusion from political life, new government programs provided a means for accommodating the narrowly political aspects of their demands. Through its juvenile delinquency, community action, manpower training, Model Cities, and compensatory education programs, with their emphasis on citizen participation and affirmative action, the federal government legitimated minority demands and opened up employment opportunities. By so doing, they contributed substantially to the easing of racial tensions in America. In this respect, these programs, like the machine-style politics of earlier decades, demonstrated the unusual capacity of the American regime to respond to the political needs of ethnic minorities.[3]

Yet political recognition of racial minorities cannot be treated as identical to economic redistribution. As William Wilson has noted, poverty remains a problem in black America, despite civil rights legislation and affirmative action programs, which opened up new opportunities to college-educated, middle-class blacks.[4] To the extent that Great Society programs were concerned with reducing economic poverty as distinct from racial exclusion, the mechanisms they chose for addressing the problem were hopelessly inept. At a time when many central cities were undergoing tightening economic and fiscal constraints, they could only "hunker down" and resist the bludgeoning that they were receiving in the "poverty wars." After the political tumult was over, local governments, taken as a whole, had not significantly modified their commitment to redistribution. The increase in local resources allocated to redistributive programs increased by less than 1 percent (see chapter 4). Even in New York City, where minority political protest was supposed to have had dramatic policy effects, the locally financed portion of the budget, in constant dollars, did not increase at a rate any greater than in the previous two decades.

The underlying theory of many of these Great Society programs understood bureaucratic imperatives and group processes to be the primary obstacles to local redistribution. It was thought that local government agencies administered a potpourri of uncoordinated services in haphazard fashion to a predominantly middle-class clientele. The foci of many of these local services, it was said, had simply not been altered in years, even though the racial composition of urban centers had greatly changed. To redirect local services to the poor, the federal government needed to galvanize the political resources of low-income and minority communities. At the same time it was believed the federal government could entice existing agencies into innovative programs by distributing grants to reform-minded applicants. In this way, a limited amount of federal resources would leverage much larger local resources in a redistributive direction.

This theory assumed that cities operated under economic constraints that were no different from those under which the federal government operated. It assumed that the obstacles to redistribution

were local elites, bureaucratic ineptitude, insufficient group formation in low-income areas, and noncompetitive local politics. Instead
of seeing that these were the symptoms of an underlying structural
problem, Great Society leaders attempted to "muscle" local officials
into a set of policies they could not afford. In the end the federal
government only strained the New Deal coalition that had made
possible the national commitment to Great Society reforms.

Conceivably, these federal policies also contributed to the fiscal
crises of older central cities. At a time when central cities were
losing their competitive edge, the federal government was pressing
them to increase their programs for low-income residents. While
they seem to have resisted pressures for expansion of these programs, it was more difficult for cities to pare programs already in
place. Only in the seventies, when federally sponsored community
action groups had all but disappeared from local politics, did older
central cities begin their retrenchment drive.[5]

The limits on cities, therefore, constrain but do not eliminate local
politics. Where cities have more resources, redistributive politics
becomes more likely. Even when economic constraints increase,
both bureaucratic and group politics can retard needed policy ad-
justments. Yet as the New York City case makes clear, once the
economic and fiscal limits have been reached, the political system
accommodates itself to them.

What Is to Be Done?

There are three views on what is to be done about redistribution: (1)
nothing, (2) everything, (3) something. Each view is embedded in a
view of industrial society that encompasses a large set of public
policies. Although it is inappropriate at this late point in the analysis
to discuss in detail the larger political perspectives surrounding
each view, certain connections warrant consideration, if only to
elaborate a point made in my preface: how decisively the liberal,
progressive view has been pushed to the periphery in policy-
relevant debates.

Do Nothing

For many analysts, especially those with training in economics, the
incapacity of cities to redistribute goods and services is not a cause
for alarm. The present drift toward retrenchment is accepted not just
as inevitable but as simply desirable. For these scholars industrial
societies are plagued by the negative impact on societal productivity
of an inefficient public sector. If local governments have become
increasingly responsive to the market forces pressing upon them and

if central cities no longer have quasi monopolies, then local public policies are beginning to match more closely the public's economic demand for them. As migration occurs and as local governments adapt their policies to attract productive immigrants, the efficiency of the public sector begins to match that of the private sector. The long-term productivity and prosperity of the society as a whole are being enhanced. The issues I have raised simply require "benign neglect."

For these neoconservative analysts, there is a substantial trade-off between efficiency and productivity, on one side, and equity and redistribution, on the other. The trade-off occurs because individuals place a value on their time. People are willing to engage in productive activity only until the marginal value of their earnings no longer exceeds the marginal value of the foregone nonproductive activities in which the individual would otherwise participate. As the marginal value of productive time declines, the individual substitutes marginal leisure activities for the now decreased value of time engaged in production. Taxes paid for inefficiently provided public services or for services provided by non-taxpayers decrease the marginal value of productive activity. At the same time public services specifically directed toward non-taxpayers subsidize their leisure time. The difference between the average value of highly taxed productive activity and the average value of subsidized leisure may for many people be so small as to induce very little productive activity at all. If individuals place a high value on their marginal leisure time, then redistributive taxation and expenditure policies incur high costs in societal productivity.

From this neoconservative standpoint, my analysis has exaggerated the differences between national and local governments. Although these analysts would agree that local redistribution is dysfunctional, they probably feel that I have underemphasized the economic constraints that also limit the capacity of national governments to promulgate programs for the poor. National governments, like local governments, must make painful choices between what is politically popular and what is economically essential.

Although the declining rate of increase in productivity in the United States makes this argument especially persuasive in the 1980s, the size of the trade-off between productivity and equality remains difficult to specify. And until research is able to specify more exactly the loss of productivity entailed by increased redistribution, Western democracies are unlikely to forego their simultaneous commitment to both liberty and equality. Although the United States and other industrialized nations will continue to allow citizens to engage freely and autonomously in private, productive activity, they also will continue to utilize some of society's resources to care for the needs of the deprived and dispossessed. To do otherwise runs counter to the egalitarian ideals that legitimate their political regimes. If inequality is unlikely to be abolished, neither will political leaders abandon attempts to alleviate its most visible effects. Yet redistributive, egalitarian policies implemented through inappropriate governmental structures only aggravate inefficiencies in the public sector. Recommending that nothing be done in the hopes that redistribution will disappear from the public agenda is as unrealistic as it is insensitive.

Do Everything

Another school of thought, generally neo-Marxist in orientation, sees few alternatives other than the total redesign of Western societies. Although the picture of the utopian world they envision is sketched with little more precision than Marx's own suggestion that distribution be "from each according to his ability to each according to his need," these scholars are quite convinced that nothing short of revolutionary reconstruction can resolve the contradictions in the existing political economy. Many in this tradition will accept the argument that local redistribution is next to impossible to achieve. But instead of treating the problem as one of local political structures and arrangements, they argue that the economic imperatives of advanced capitalism perpetuate and accentuate existing inequalities.

In their view, too, I have exaggerated the differences between national and local governments. The fiscal crisis of the city is the fiscal crisis of the Western nation-state.[6] What has been observed in New York City and elsewhere in the central cities of industrial areas is only the most visible aspect of a fundamental contradiction between the economy's need for capital accumulation and the state's need for social legitimacy.[7] Because the rate of return from capital investment falls continuously, public incentives to increase capital formation continuously expand. At the same time, the increasing supply of surplus labor (which takes the form of unemployment, underemployment, and departure from the labor market altogether) increases the state's need to extend social services and maintain social control (through its police and military forces). Caught between these competing imperatives, the state finds it increasingly difficult to resolve its fiscal difficulties. New York's virtual bankruptcy is only a harbinger of developments at all levels of government.

Because politics at the local level provides so many useful examples for this thesis, neo-Marxists have taken the urban setting as one of their most important research laboratories.[8] In their studies they have uncovered community "power structures," revealed the naked fist behind the "other face of power," discovered the "trenches" into which leaders of protest have fallen, and discerned a dual economy which leaves central-city fate in the hands of corporate capitalism. Every rejection of the demands of low-income groups, each program for economic development, and all imbalances in the provision of city services are interpreted as critical evidence concerning the limits of advanced corporate capitalism.

The neo-Marxist, like the neo-conservative, builds a sweeping argument that is just as powerful as it is impossible either to document or to falsify. Even as the neoconservative is unable to specify the trade-off between productivity and equality, so the neo-Marxist is unable to specify the way in which capital accumulation and social legitimacy become mutually incompatible goals. In neither view are the virtues of moderation appreciated; both views escalate tendencies and difficulties into inexorable laws over which those in political authority have little, if any, control. The distinction between national and local government is collapsed, because all nuance, modification, and variation become trivia in a grand schematic that incorporates within it the entire direction of Western civilization.

Neo-Marxist analysis, though apparently bold and revolutionary, is in fact as reactionary as neoconservative analysis. Because no meaningful change is possible unless everything is altered, any reformist impulse is stultified except during those rare historical moments when ordinary citizens are on the verge of civil violence. In their recent work Piven and Cloward argue against any form of organization for political reform other than mass agitation to induce societal disruption.[9] In other, more systematic statements of the neo-Marxist position, scholars have become so obsessed with the system-maintaining functions of the Western state that they have all but defined away the capacity of the capitalist system for radical change.[10] But if revolution remains a utopian dream and reform an immediate impossibility, then the neo-Marxist and neoconservative analyses converge.

Do Something

If I have taken economic tools of analysis seriously and if I have accepted the limits that economic contexts place on local decision making, my argument still allows room for political action. The structural arrangements that limit the possibility of local redistribution and impede the effectiveness of intergovernmental programs are not an irrevocable concomitant of the national political economy. Once the governmental arrangements which structure our political life are adequately understood, the possibility for effective political reform emerges. Not only are alternative governing structures possible, but they in fact exist in societies not fundamentally dissimilar from our own. The federal system which limits the policies and politics of local governments in the United States is not an inevitable part of a capitalist system, nor is it essential for achieving a modicum of efficiency in the public sector. On the contrary, it is an aberration in the Western industrial world. The introduction of structural changes would basically alter the peculiarly American arrangements which impede the effectiveness of redistributive programs. If by themselves they would not ensure equality, they would at least provide one structural precondition that would make greater equity more possible.

1. *The full faith and credit of the federal government should stand behind all state and local government indebtedness.* This policy innovation would remove the threat of bankruptcy, which is the last and final constraint on local government fiscal policies. Although many factors direct local attention to a city's economic limits, the one constraint which cities simply cannot ignore is their standing in the credit market. As cities see their bond rating slip first from AA to BBB and then slide to a point where no viable credit options exist at all, a crisis in local politics generally develops. Whatever the city's past political orientation, public attention is now focused on restoring economic order to the city's household. Redistributive programs in such an atmosphere become especially vulnerable to the budgetary ax, because these programs contribute little, if anything, to the economic well-being of the community. Were the issue of a city's credit removed from city politics, the most important constraint on local redistribution would be removed.

To institute this policy, the federal government would, of course, also have to place its own controls on local government debt management. In the United States, capital investments by local government are regulated by the private bond market; if the investment is desired by local officials (and by local voters), credit can be obtained as long as both the purpose of the investment and the stability of the local government meet the standards of the financial community. Under the arrangements suggested here, any such proposal would have to be considered by an agency of the federal government. The agency would have the responsibility of determining whether the proposed policy was technically sound, likely to be of benefit to the community, and consistent with overall national policies. In making its decisions this agency would wish to consider both the nation's overall strategy for economic growth and questions of balance among different areas of the country. For example, it could provide a coherent framework to address complex issues such as "reindustrialization" and dilemmas inherent in "investment and dis-investment" decisions.

Although many might balk at the creation of such an awesome power in the nation's capital, in Britain "local authorities must obtain the consent of the [appropriate central department] before exercising their borrowing powers."[11] For example, whenever a local educational authority (LEA) in England or Wales wishes to build a new school, it must include the proposed capital investment in its building program, which is submitted annually to the Department of Education and Science. The department exercises control over LEA decisions in three ways: (1) by giving or withholding approval of specific building proposals; (2) by imposing minimum standards of accommodation; and (3) by limiting the costs that can be incurred in the construction of the school. Only after permission has been granted in these areas can the LEA obtain capital financing for its building program. While some may object that such regulations in application will inevitably be cumbersome and rigid, Griffith's careful analysis of the way in which the regulations work in practice concludes on the optimistic note that,

> as they are operated, the regulations are not unduly restrictive, ... experimentation is perfectly possible ... and ... generally, therefore, the regulations provide a proper and necessary level of performance which it would be undesirable to lower while not, in administrative practice, being so strictly applied as to stifle the development of new ideas.[12]

2. *The federal government should institute a revenue-sharing plan that would attempt to equalize per capita fiscal resources available to each state and local government.* As the economy of a local community declined, its claim on the United States Treasury would increase. As the economy of the community improved, increasing its local fiscal resources, its portion of revenue-sharing resources would decline. Such a policy would greatly reduce the local government's fiscal incentive to promote economic growth through either tax concessions to business firms or cutbacks in services to low-income residents. Improvements in the local economy might still be pursued, but the local government itself would receive fewer fiscal benefits.[13] Every increase in local revenue sources would be offset by a declining portion of federal revenue.

The technical difficulties of this policy innovation are so great that it would probably be impossible to achieve in its entirety. For one thing, the amount given to each lower-tier government would have to take into account the range of functional responsibilities it performed. At present the distribution of functions varies widely from state to state and among areas within states. In some parts of the country the state assumes a large responsibility for financing public services; in other parts of the country over two-thirds of the services are paid for out of local government accounts. In some places, notably New York City, one single government is responsible for the full array of services provided by the local government. In other places, notably Chicago, service delivery is shared among municipal government, county government, a sanitary district, a board of education, a park district, a regional transportation authority, and a host of other specialized districts. A revenue-sharing plan would have to either standardize the structural arrangements through which local governments exercise their responsibilities or find a formula for resource distribution that took into account the great variability presently experienced.

The costs of local government also vary from one part of the country to another. Heating costs are greater in the Northeast; labor costs are greater in central cities than in rural areas; transportation costs are greater in the Mountain states; capital costs, including the purchase of land, are higher in more densely populated areas; and concentrations of poor people in certain areas greatly increase the welfare and social service costs of these communities. A formula that equalized the per capita resources of local governments but did not find some way of accommodating the variable costs faced by local governments would leave their fiscal well-being still dependent upon their local economy.

In addition, it would be difficult to determine an acceptable standard for determining what local resource capacity might be. The amount of revenue that could be raised by a specific property tax rate is one possibility. But localities would then have an incentive to underestimate the value of their property and to remove significant portions of their property from tax rolls (through, say, tax concessions to businesses or institutions which seemed to have an eleemosynary purpose). Also, a community may have economic resources which are not readily apparent in land values but which nonetheless yield considerable income or sales tax revenues. The capacity of resort areas to tax receipts paid largely by tourists is one example.

Difficulties such as these require careful research attention. Yet these technical problems, which probably preclude an ideal solution, should not obscure the fact that at the present time federal policies in the United States do very little to equalize the resources available to local governments. By contrast, many European governments have for decades struggled with these technical problems and seem to have worked out programs of intergovernmental assistance which in large measure have freed localities from the economic and fiscal constraints that so dominate local policymaking in the United States. In Britain the primary mechanisms for equalizing local fiscal resources are the general grant and rate deficiency grant. All authorities share in the general grant, which allocates resources among authorities according to population size, population density, number of school-age children, and other indicators of local fiscal needs. The rate deficiency grant compensates those authorities whose local taxes at any given rate raise fewer revenues per capita than can be raised nationally at that rate. Since London and other southern coastal areas enjoy a large share of the nation's resources, four-fifths of the local authorities share in the rate deficiency grant, and 40 percent of the revenue for some local governments comes from this source.[14] When taken together, government grants have such an equalizing effect on local expenditures that the coefficient of variation in expenditures among local authorities is less than .1 in England and Wales, as compared with .32 among the fifty states of the United States.[15] Moreover, variation in British local government expenditures is only weakly and inconsistently explained by variations in the wealth of local communities.[16]

3. *Minimum standards of service provision should replace existing grants-in-aid programs.* Many of the existing federal programs which generate continuous intergovernmental disputes, endless administrative difficulties, and contradictory principles of resource distribution could be eliminated in favor of a comprehensive revenue-sharing plan. Local governments would then be able to allocate resources among service sectors in a way consistent with local needs and preferences. To guard against the misuse of federal funds, the national government might find it appropriate to set minimum standards of service provision in order for local governments to become eligible for revenue sharing. Also, programs of welfare assistance might be appropriately administered directly by the national government in much the way the Social Security program directly operates. Since only a small percentage of welfare assistance is at present provided locally, national direction in this policy area could be achieved without much sacrifice in local autonomy. Taken as a whole, the restructuring of federal arrangements would leave local governments with far greater flexibility to experiment widely and to respond differentially to local interests and concerns.

Many will object that these proposals are technically impractical, constitutionally questionable, and politically infeasible. National politics today is concerned primarily with economic development, energy conservation, and government deregulation. Yet inasmuch as the liberal impulse has not evaporated altogether, it could find renewed substance almost overnight for reasons that cannot now be anticipated. Even in today's conservative atmosphere, we find steady increases in federal responsibilities for health, welfare, and education policy. The first step toward political feasibility is identification of the objectives worth pursuing. Liberal reform is in retreat today, not least because it has lost intellectual vitality and creative ingenuity. Before discarding a proposal for its political unattractiveness, the substantive merits first must be addressed.

But even if fully promulgated, these policy innovations will not introduce an egalitarian utopia, where the needs of low-income groups are carefully met by liberally minded public officials.[17] The choice between productivity and redistribution, or, in an older terminology, between liberty and equality, will continue to require a search for an appropriate balance among competing values where no final resolution is possible. With the amelioration of one problem, new difficulties will emerge, compelling both scholarly and practical attention. The proposed structural changes will nonetheless permit the trade-off between equality and productivity to be debated within a local framework that at least resembles the one that shapes our national debates. Whatever possibilities there are for a more equal distribution of the nation's resources will be explored almost as assiduously at local as at national levels. Once the structural impediments to local redistribution are set aside, a new range of local policies will become possible. Even more, local political life itself may acquire a new meaning.

Appendix

Determinants of Local Expenditures, a Review of the Literature

Although at the local level methodological problems muddy the waters considerably, the evidence for distinctions among redistributive, developmental, and allocational policies persists. The results of the pioneering study by Brazer are particularly striking, especially since his treatment of methodological problems is usually sound.[1] In table A.1 fiscal capacity and expenditures for educational purposes are strongly correlated. On the other hand, the correlation between fiscal capacity and developmental expenditures is small and usually statistically insignificant. Instead, developmental policy expenditures seem more a function of demand. For allocational policies, the correlation with economic demand is greater than the correlation with fiscal capacity in the sample of large cities, but when all cities are taken into account, the two are both moderately influential, much as was hypothesized.[2]

Bahl and Weicher, in separate studies, have also examined expenditures for functions commonly performed by city governments. Bahl gathered expenditure data for various allocational and productive policies in 198 central cities of metropolitan areas for the years 1950 and 1960.[3] As shown in table A.2, 1960 expenditures for allocational policies were associated with indicators of both fiscal capacity and demand/supply. Similar but weaker relationships were obtained for allocational expenditures in 1950. Developmental policies, on the other hand, had, as hypothesized, no significant relationship with the indicator of fiscal capacity but a fairly strong negative association with density.[4] Weicher's study of 1960 expenditures for 206 central cities provides only unstandardized regression coefficients, and therefore comparisons in table A.3 can be made only down the columns, not across the rows.[5] Although the

Appendix

Table A.1: Determinants of City Expenditure—the Brazer Study

	Determinants of Expenditure	
Type of Policy	Fiscal Capacity: Income	Demand-Supply: Density
Educational		
Large cities	.36	...
All cities	nc	nc
Allocational		
Police		
Large cities	...	.51
All cities	.16	.33
Fire		
Large cities	...	.24
All cities	.13	.16
Sanitation		
Large cities	...	.26
All cities	.14	.15
Developmental		
Highways		
Large cities	...	−.46
All cities	.18	−.30

Source. Brazer 1959, table C-1.
Note. Table gives beta coefficients generated by a thirteen-variable regression analysis; statistically insignificant correlations not reported; nc = not calculated.

Table A.2: Determinants of City Expenditure—the Bahl Study

	Determinants of Expenditure	
Type of Policy	Fiscal Capacity: Home Value	Demand-Supply: Density
Allocational		
Police		
1960 data	.19	.45
1950 data	.07	.19
Fire		
1960 data	.19	.26
1950 data	.04	.09
Sanitation		
1960 data	.16	.23
1950 data	.25	.11
Developmental		
Highway		
1960 data	−.02	−.19
1950 data	.04	−.17

Source. Bahl 1969, table 38.
Note. Table gives beta coefficients generated by a ten-variable regression analysis.

Table A.3: Determinants of City Expenditure—the Weicher Study

Type of Policy	Fiscal Capacity: Income	Demand-Supply Density	Demand-Supply Jan. Temp.[a]
Allocational			
Police	.24	3.56	3.96
Fire	.21	.38	2.33
Sanitation	.03	1.85	−1.45
Developmental			
Highways	.02	−2.14	−6.0

Source. Weicher 1970, p. 384.
Note. Table gives unstandardized regression coefficients generated by a twenty-one variable analysis.
[a]The colder the weather, the greater the cost of street maintenance.

twenty-one variables introduced into the regression greatly increase problems of multicollinearity, Weicher's findings are quite consistent with Bahl's 1960 results. Allocational policies are responsive to fiscal capacity, while developmental policies are not. Both policies are responsive in expected ways to appropriate measures of demand and supply. Weicher himself notes the varying patterns of association for different types of public policy, but he is unable to account for the contrasts:

> If we compare the regressions ... it is immediately apparent that ... the results for police and fire protection are very similar, and the results for sanitation and highways are also similar, but there is little similarity between the two pairs ....
>
> It would seem plausible that income is insignificant [in the sanitation and highways regressions] because of correlation with some omitted variable or variables .... As a measure of fiscal capacity, income should have generally similar effects on all services.[6]

Weicher's puzzle is resolvable, once one considers the possibility that fiscal capacity has quite differing effects on public policies, depending on whether they are allocational or developmental. Governments may expend resources on developmental policies even if they have limited fiscal resources. The level of allocational and especially redistributive policies, on the other hand, depends on differential fiscal resources, which generate variable levels of revenue at uniform tax rates.

The Brazer, Bahl, and Weicher studies analyzed expenditures of municipal governments. When data on local government expenditures are aggregated at the county level, similar results obtain. In a national study of counties, Schmandt and Stephens reported only simple correlation coefficients, and their findings were heavily influenced by variations in the amount of state aid local governments received for redistributive and developmental policies.[7] But, as can be seen in table A.4, once these factors are taken into account, the findings are consistent with those of the other studies. Correlations between expenditures for redistributive purposes and local environmental variables are reduced by the especially large amount of state assistance provided for this type of policy. Yet the correlations between expenditures and fiscal capacity are uniformly greater than those between expenditures and demand/supply variables. State aid also reduces the size of the correlations between expenditures and local environmental variables in the developmental policy arena. However, the pattern is exactly the reverse of the one obtained for redistributive policies. In this case, demand variables were more closely associated with expenditures than was the indicator of fiscal capacity. For allocational policies, all correlations were much stronger, because the role of the state was much reduced in this policy arena. But, significantly, fiscal capacity and demand/supply factors seem to have roughly similar effects. A more complex analysis of data aggregated at the county level has been performed by Adams.[8] To achieve comparability among his units of analysis and

Table A.4: Determinants of County Expenditures—the Schmandt and Stephens Study

		Determinants of Expenditure		
Type of Policy	State Aid	Local Fiscal Capacity: Income	Demand-Supply	
			Size	Density
Redistributive				
Health and hospitals	.17	.32	.16	.21
Welfare	.53	.18	−.02	.02
Educational	.46[2]	.33	−.19	−.18
Allocational				
Police	.26	.55	.46	.51
Fire	.05	.53	.65	.62
Sewerage	.10	.39	.24	.26
Sanitation	nc	.40	.51	.52
Developmental				
Highways	.50	.17	−.27	−.26

Source. Schmandt and Stephens 1963, table IV.
Note. Table gives simple coefficients of correlation.

to eliminate the problems associated with variations in state assistance for redistributive and developmental policies, he performed his regression analysis only on allocational variables. But his analysis confirms Schmandt and Stephens's finding that both demand/supply and fiscal capacity variables were significant determinants of expenditures.

Because of the important role of the state and federal governments in financing redistributive policies, most studies do not provide reliable information on the local determinants of expenditures for this purpose. For this reason, we have reported only the problematic data from the Schmandt and Stephens study and educational expenditures from the Brazer study. But there is one study by Sharkansky of county expenditures for general welfare assistance to the poor that carefully isolates the variation in expenditures for redistributive purposes by local governments. This study is particularly interesting, because Sharkansky explicitly focused on the extent to which fiscal capacity or the need for redistribution seemed to determine the level of expenditures for this program. In almost every state Sharkansky found that, for the locally determined program of general assistance, expenditures were significantly influenced by fiscal capacity—and only rarely influenced by need levels. As Sharkansky concluded, "Among the public assistance programs General Assistance is the least subject to federal and state supervision; it shows the greatest inequalities among the counties of most states and the clearest tendency to vary with county economic resources."[9]

Notes

Chapter One

1. Cf. Fried 1975, p. 308, who warns against "the automatic transferability of concepts and empirical relationships between levels of government" but nonetheless asserts that "the urban level provides a much larger universe of politics to be studied than the national level, though one of similar complexity."

2. Dahl 1976, p. 47, writes, "In the American system (insofar as New Haven is a fair prototype)...the growth of oligarchy is inhibited by the *patterns* according to which political resources are allocated and by the ways in which resources are actually *used*."

3. Hawley and Wirt 1968 provide a useful collection of readings and a lengthy bibliography. Other bibliographies are mentioned in a review of the literature by Polsby 1980.

4. The classic statement is by Hunter 1953. See also Miller 1970 and Vidich and Bensman 1958.

5. Dahl 1961; Banfield 1961; Sayre and Kaufman 1960.

6. Bachrach and Baratz 1962, 1970.

7. Also, see criticisms of this approach by Wolfinger 1971 and Polsby 1980.

8. I have discussed the machine-reform conflict more fully in Peterson 1976 and, with J. David Greenstone, in Greenstone and Peterson 1976, chapter 1.

9. Banfield and Wilson 1963; Hofstadter 1955; Hays 1964; Elazar 1970; Tyack 1974; Cronin 1973; Wiebe 1962.

10. Bryce 1910; Ostrogorski 1910.

11. Wolfinger and Field 1966.

12. The findings of Lineberry and Fowler 1967 have often been cited as evidence showing class-relevant policy consequences of machine and reform insitutions. But Liebert 1974 has shown that most of their findings are spurious. J. David Greenstone and I discovered that the impact of machine

and reform institutions on the implementation of the poverty program in the five largest American cities was far more complex than that predicted by the class model. See Greenstone and Peterson 1976.

13. Compare Ira Katznelson's discussion of the separation of trade union conflicts and partisan conflicts in nineteenth-century urban politics in *City Trenches* (forthcoming).

14. Scott 1972; see also Merton's 1957, pp. 71–82 and 192–94, discussion of the machine.

15. Peterson 1976, chapter 1.

16. Hofstadter 1955.

17. Holli 1969 makes this distinction but then tries to show (with limited success) a strong commitment to social reform in Detroit.

18. Fried 1975 gives this literature an authoritative, detailed review.

19. Lineberry and Fowler 1967.

20. Clark 1968.

21. Weicher 1970.

22. Fabricant 1952; Brazer 1959.

23. Dye 1966.

24. Clark 1968; Lineberry and Fowler 1967.

25. Liebert 1974.

26. Brazer 1959; Schmandt and Stephens 1963; Adams 1967.

27. Sharkansky 1970, chapter 7.

28. For example, some states reserve the financial responsibility for welfare policy almost entirely to themselves, while others delegate much of this responsibility to local governments. As a result, the degree to which the state itself accounts for the total of all state and local expenditures within a state varies considerably. And it is not very helpful to include this variation in the assignment of financial responsibility as one of the independent variables in the analysis. When so included, it accounts for much of the variance in expenditures by statewide institutions, leaving only residual amounts to be explained by other variables. The analytical problem this creates can be posed in two ways. Technically, the analyst has committed the cardinal sin of including the same variable on both sides of the equation, thus producing a spurious correlation. The equation takes the following form:

$$SE = a + b \left(\frac{SE}{SE + LE} \right) + b_1 x_1 \ldots b_n x_n ,$$

where SE = expenditures by the state, LE = expenditures by local governments within the state, a = a constant value, and $x_1 \ldots x_n$ = all other independent variables.

Less technically, one may ask in what way the assignment of functional responsibilities can be treated as an independent variable influencing state expenditures. The decision to assign responsibilities to local authorities and the concomitant reduced expenditure level by statewide institutions are part and parcel of one single policy with respect to the division of labor between state and local governments. It makes little sense to "explain" through some correlation analysis the one aspect of this policy in terms of the other. For an extended treatment of this problem and some useful suggestions for handling it, see Clark and Ferguson (forthcoming).

29. Sharkansky 1968, p. 10.

30. Dye 1966.

31. Another problem with which the expenditure literature has grappled is the manner in which intergovernmental transfers are treated. A favored solution is to include all expenditures by a unit of government, including those expenditures which are the product of intergovernmental transfers of funds. But when this total is related to variables endogenous to the state or locality, it explains policy outcomes in terms of characteristics of the state when they are in part the product of decisions taken at a hgher level of government. Some analysts "correct" for this misattribution by also including intergovernmental transfers as independent variables. But this enters the same variable on both sides of the equation, creating spuriously high levels of correlation (Morss 1966). Substantively, it creates special problems of interpretation. To the extent that the higher level of government takes local "needs" into account in dispersing its funds (as it does in its allocations for highways and natural resources) and to the extent that the lower level government also allocates its resources in response to the economic demands that these needs generate, then the "need" variable and the "federal assistance" variable will be highly correlated. When both are included in the regression analysis, some of the impact of the need variable is obscured by the inappropriate inclusion of the federal assistance variable. The best— though not perfect—solution is to deduct the intergovernmental transfers from both sides of the equation. I am unaware of any previous study that has used such a procedure on data aggregated at the state level.

32. Grodzins 1966.

33. Wright 1975, p. 109; United States Senate, Committee on Government Operations 1969.

34. Elazar 1966, p. 2.

35. Kaufman 1960.

36. Elazar et al 1969.

37. Elazar 1966, p. 2.

38. Diamond 1969.

39. Grodzins 1966; Elazar 1966.

40. There are exceptions. Brown 1978 has an excellent analysis which, while developed independently, parallels the one presented here. Also, Wirt 1974 devotes considerable space to "external influences" on local policy; and Williams 1971 appreciates the importance of location and social access.

Chapter Two

1. Flathman 1966.

2. Banfield 1961, chapter 12.

3. Tiebout 1956.

4. Ibid., p. 419.

5. Ibid., p. 420.

6. Bruce Hamilton, "Property Taxes and the Tiebout Hypothesis: Some Empirical Evidence," and Michelle J. White, "Fiscal Zoning in Fragmented Metropolitan Areas," in Mills and Oates 1975, chapters 2 and 3.

7. See Weber, "Class, Status, and Power," in Gerth and Mills 1946.

8. For a more complete discussion of roles, structures, and interests, see Greenstone and Peterson 1976, chapter 2.

9. Cf. Thompson 1965.

10. I treat entrepreneurial skill as simply another form of labor, even though it is a form in short supply.

11. Elazar 1970.

12. Weber 1921.

13. United States Department of Commerce, Bureau of the Census 1977.

14. Williams and Adrian 1963.

15. Eulau and Prewitt 1973, p. 542.

16. Ibid., p. 543.

17. Ibid., chapters 26 and 27.

18. Williams and Adrian 1963, p. 192.

19. Oates 1969; Pollakowski 1973.

20. Oates 1973; Pollakowski 1973; McDougall 1976; King 1977; Rosen and Fullerton 1977.

21. Cebula 1974.

22. Babcock 1966; Mills and Oates 1975.

23. Tiebout 1956.

24. Just how inefficient this can be is demonstrated by a comparison of the relative costs of public and private garbage collection in New York City. Even though the conditions for collection are more or less the same, the costs of public collection are double those in the private sector. Savas 1976.

Chapter Three

1. Cf. Lowi 1964a.

2. Levy, Meltsner, and Wildavsky 1974, chapter 4.

3. Ostrom et al. 1973.

4. This is possible because I have a "unitary" model of state-local policy-making processes. This is made explicit in Peterson 1978, 1979a.

5. Peterson 1978, 1979a.

6. One of several difficulties with which the expenditure literature has wrestled is the problem of multicollinearity. When independent variables are correlated with one another, it is difficult to distinguish their separate influences. In the research reported in the text, I have given as much attention to simple correlation analysis as to multiple correlation analysis, I have preferred findings from regression analyses where fewer rather than more independent variables have been introduced, and I have given special weight to research where analysts have taken special pains to reduce problems of multicollinearity. Such selectivity is especially important in an area

of research where so little attention has been given to developing a theoretically defensible rationale for the selection of independent variables and where scholars, taking advantage of high-speed computers, run "barefoot" through the data.

7. Fisher 1964.

8. Dye 1966.

9. Ibid., p. 169.

10. Cnudde and McCrone 1969.

11. Ibid., p. 864.

12. Tompkins 1975.

13. Sharkansky and Hofferbert 1969.

14. We are using the simple, not the partial, correlations that Sharkansky and Hofferbert provide on p. 877 because the partial correlations control for political variables. Sharkansky himself has elsewhere pointed out that these are theoretically inappropriate variables to use in an analysis of the combined expenditures of state and local governments.

15. Dye 1966.

Chapter Four

1. Elazar et al. 1969.

2. Diamond 1969.

3. Grodzins 1966.

4. Greater autonomy allows for greater redistribution from the better off to the less well off. It may be, however, that even in an entirely self-contained economy, there remain tradeoffs between efficiency and equality. Too high and too progressive a rate of taxation to finance too elaborate a welfare state may weaken incentives for capital formation. Yet, some minimum standard of welfare provision seems necessary to ensure a steady, healthy, capable working population. These are highly debatable issues, beyond the scope of our analysis (see O'Connor 1973). But there is one set of constraints on local redistribution that does not restrict decision making at the national level: taxpayers cannot easily flee to other jurisdictions while incoming recipients flood the social-delivery system. In this regard, national governments have a much greater capacity to redistribute goods and services than do local governments.

5. Greenstone and Peterson 1976, chapter 7.

6. Musgrave 1959.

7. Meltsner 1971.

8. United States Advisory Commission on Intergovernmental Relations 1974.

9. I am excluding local revenues received from user charges and intergovernmental grants.

10. United States Advisory Commission on Intergovernmental Relations 1964, pp. 83–84.

11. This is not the place to discuss all the relevant arguments. First, one must distinguish between the portion of the property tax that is common to

all parts of the economic system and the portion which varies from one local jurisdiction to another. The portion of the tax levied differentially is borne entirely by the property owner, because the capitalized value of the tax differential will be reflected in the market price of the property. The portion of the tax common to all parts of the economic system must itself be subdivided into the tax on land and the tax on buildings and improvements. The tax on land is borne by the landowners. Whether the portion which is a tax on improvements is an excise tax borne by the consumer or a tax on capital depends on assumptions concerning the finite limits on the supply of capital in an economy. These issues are discussed in Netzer 1966.

12. United States Advisory Commission on Intergovernmental Relations 1974, p. 55.

13. Piven 1976.

14. We have included general control expenditures among the housekeeping services of government, and it is this that accounts for the 3.8 percent of federal expenditures on allocational activities.

15. State and local government deficit spending does not have the countercyclical effects that federal deficits are expected to have (Hansen and Perloff 1944; Sharp 1965; Rafuse Jr. 1965). Consequently, it is not appropriate to classify local interest payments as expenditures for developmental policies unless the project that the debt financed "paid for itself."

16. See chapter 5.

17. Marsh and Gortner 1963, p. 53.

18. Ibid., p. 40.

19. Ibid., p. 41.

20. Ibid., p. 42.

21. Ibid., p. 87.

22. Wirt and Kirst 1972; Murphy 1971; Orfield 1969; Hughes and Hughes 1972; Goettel 1978.

23. United States House of Representatives 1977.

24. Ways 1969, p. 620.

25. Macmahon 1972, p. 84.

26. Peterson 1978.

27. "We have not in recent years had much of an extension of domestic programs run *directly* by the national government, but we have had a great extension of programs operated by states and localities with federal funds and with varying . . . degrees of federal policy control." Reagan 1972, p. 12.

28. Hunter 1953. For a collection of readings from this literature and a general bibliography, see Hawley and Wirt 1968.

29. Bachrach and Baratz 1962.

30. Bachrach and Baratz 1970.

31. Ibid., pp. 79–80.

32. Ibid., p. 97.

33. Ibid., p. 89.

34. Ibid., p. 71.

35. Greenstone and Peterson 1976; Peterson and Greenstone 1977.

36. Chicago Urban League 1977.

37. Truman 1951; Riesman 1950; Dahl 1961.

38. Pressman and Wildavsky 1973.
39. Ibid., p. 94.
40. McFarland 1969.
41. McConnell 1966.
42. Derthick 1972.
43. Ibid., p. 101.
44. Murphy 1971; Pressman 1975.

Chapter Five

1. Heidenheimer, Heclo, and Adams 1976.
2. This definition of an efficient school system assumes no societal returns to education other than those for which those who incur the costs are compensated. It assumes that there are no ripple or neighborhood effects, which otherwise would justify public subsidy of education. Although some educational economists have argued that such ripple effects exist, their evidence is dubious. More and better education provides individuals with credentials that allow them to jump ahead of others in the queue for the higher paying and more prestigious occupations, but it is much less clear that societal productivity, taken as a whole, increases more by investments in human than in physical capital. And only societal benefits above and beyond those received by individuals in return for their own educational investments provide a warrant—by the efficiency criterion—for publicly subsidized education.
Efforts to reduce poverty through manpower retraining illustrate the point. Although one can show that individuals trained in such programs jump the unemployment queue and receive increased earnings at least over the short run, their employment only displaces other workers, unless the training program has somehow increased the overall employability of the work force. When this does not occur, it is just a game of "musical chairs." Even if the new effect is to increase productivity—to add more chairs to the game—this does not make a public subsidy efficient unless the societal benefits are greater than the sum total of benefits received by the individuals who paid for their training. On these issues, cf. Psacharopoulos 1973; Becker 1964; Jencks et al. 1972; Levin 1977; and Thurow 1972.
3. Tiebout 1956.
4. Miner 1963.
5. Miner 1963; James, Thomas, and Dyck 1963; Sacks, Harris, and Carroll 1963; James, Kelly, and Garms 1966; Hickrod 1971.
6. Grubb and Michelson 1974.
7. Ibid., p. 56.
8. Morgan et al. 1962.
9. Hirsch 1960.
10. Sacks and Hellmuth 1961.
11. Fischer 1967; O'Shea 1970; Harvey 1969.
12. Rosen and Fullerton 1977; McDougall 1976.
13. Oates 1969; Peterson and Karpluss 1978; Rosen and Fullerton 1977; Meadows 1976; Edel and Sclar 1974. In a study of the San Francisco Bay area

by Pollakowski 1973, the results were inconclusive, but this study was hampered by an inadequate sample size (nineteen cities).

14. Callahan 1962; Tyack 1974; Peterson 1976.

15. Burkhead et al. 1967.

16. Katzman 1971, pp. 135–36.

17. Levy, Meltsner, and Wildavsky 1974.

18. Katzman 1971, p. 144.

19. Grubb and Michelson 1974, pp. 64ff.; Owen 1972; Burkhead et al. 1971.

20. Hanushek 1972; Murnane 1975; and Summers and Wolfe 1977 find that experience positively affects high achievers, negatively affects low achievers.

21. Owen 1972, p. 33.

22. Ibid., p. 33 fn.

23. Coleman et al. 1966.

24. Smith 1972; Jencks 1972.

25. Heyns 1974; Alexander and McDill 1976; Summers and Wolfe 1977.

26. Morgan et al. 1962.

27. The National Center for Education Statistics, charged with the responsibility of maintaining this historically important archival resource, informed me that they have the right to distribute the information to the Educational Testing Service (ETS) in Princeton, New Jersey. Unofficial but apparently well informed sources allege that the National Center has simply "lost" its copies of the tapes and has made no effort to obtain new copies. ETS explains that its tapes, to which the National Center now generously refers interested scholars, are no longer "readable" by a computer. It has been so many years since anyone has used their tapes, which in fact contain information only in the original "raw" preanalyzed state, that the quality of the tape has deteriorated to the point where data can no longer be retrieved. I have contacted numerous scholars who have published findings from the Coleman study. Although none had any obligation to assist me, all were more helpful than the National Center. But even though I have been given many "leads" and explored each to its end, I have yet to obtain a usable copy of this study.

28. However, the data in this form do not permit any comparisons of the relative importance of the four family background characteristics.

29. Smith 1972.

Chapter Six

1. Pressman 1972, p. 513.

2. Downs 1957.

3. Key 1949, 1964.

4. Hibbs 1977.

5. McConnell 1966.

6. Piven and Cloward 1971.

7. Burnham 1970; Ladd 1970.

8. Politics in Lindsay's New York are given a sophisticated, thorough review in Bellush and David 1971.

9. Peterson and Kantor 1977.

10. Fried 1975.

11. Dahl 1961, pp. 44–51.

12. Banfield and Wilson 1963, p. 46.

13. This and the following three paragraphs follow closely the argument developed in Peterson and Kantor 1977. I thank Paul Kantor for his permission to use this material here.

14. Fletcher 1967.

15. Bryce 1891, pp. 543–44, 550.

16. Gilbert 1964.

17. Stokes 1967, pp. 192–98.

18. Lee 1963, p. 80, table 7.

19. Alford and Lee 1968.

20. Hansen 1975.

21. Hawley 1973.

22. Lee 1960.

23. Prewitt 1970.

24. Downs 1957, chapter 12; Truman 1951.

25. Truman 1951; Latham 1952; Lowi 1969; McConnell 1966. But see the dissent from this view in Bauer, Pool, and Dexter 1972.

26. Caputo 1976, p. 196.

27. Banfield and Wilson 1963, p. 254.

28. Ibid., p. 255. They draw upon Clark 1959.

29. Crecine 1969, p. 189.

30. Caputo 1976, p. 195.

31. Wood 1958, p. 186; see also pp. 161–66. In Oakland there is such a "lack of organized politically interested groups" that when a group of students tried to form a coalition, they found "there was no one to coalesce with." Pressman 1972, pp. 513–14.

32. Gardiner 1968, p. 167.

33. Derthick 1968, p. 256.

34. Dahl 1961.

35. Wolfinger 1974, p. 12.

36. Alford and Lee 1968, p. 803. Eulau and Prewitt 1973, p. 380, say that "only about a third of the eligible voters in the 82 Bay Area cities cast ballots in council elections."

37. Caraley 1977, p. 338; data computed from table 15-1. During the period 1948–52, the percentage of the adult population voting in Presidential elections in eighteen cities averaged 59 percent, while the percentage voting for mayor averaged 41 percent. Calculated from data in Banfield and Wilson 1963, p. 225.

38. Verba and Nie 1972, p. 31.

39. Wildavsky 1964, p. 289.

40. The surveys are cited in Caraley 1977, p. 339.

41. Olson 1968; Wilson 1973.

42. A quotation of a local public official in Derthick 1968, p. 255.

43. Olson 1968. The particular formulation we find most convincing is in Frohlich, Oppenheimer, and Young 1971.

44. Hirschman 1970.

45. See Agger, Goldrich, and Swanson 1964, pp. 504–5.

46. Olson 1968 points out that small groups can form even when large groups cannot, because in small groups it is possible for each individual to notice how his contributions to group action influence the actions of others, and therefore it is easier to combine forces. But this kind of interpersonal noticeability among participants is possible only in the very small group—and, as it applies here, in the very small community. In most localities the thousands, hundreds of thousands, or even millions of residents living within the jurisdictions of a local government form much too large a group for appropriate application of Olson's small-group thesis.

47. The classic description of local decision-making processes is in Vidich and Bensman 1958, pp. 109–14. Also, see my description of the decision-making processes of the Chicago School Board in Peterson 1976, chapter 5. Even in New York City, Gittell 1973, p. 213, found that "public participation in school policy formulation is circumscribed by the lack of visible decision-making, the shortage of information available to the public on most issues, and a deficiency in the means for participation." About Oakland, Pressman 1972, p. 516, writes, "Most decisions [of the city council] are made at special 'work sessions' before the council meetings [even though] citizens' groups and the press have raised pointed questions about the secrecy of such meetings."

48. Banfield and Wilson 1963, p. 321.

49. Cox and Morgan 1973, p. 136.

50. Banfield and Wilson 1963, p. 321.

51. A local paper "trains most of the incomers to the profession, only to lose many of the best of them." Cox and Morgan 1973, p. 8.

52. Fiorina 1977.

53. Prewitt 1970. The diverse motives involved in recruitment to public office are characterized in Barber 1965.

54. Wolfinger 1974.

55. Ibid., p. 398.

56. Prewitt 1970, p. 14.

56. For some examples, see White 1969, pp. 61, 145, 279.

58. Key 1964, chapter 1.'

Chapter Seven

1. Eckstein 1960.

2. Lowi 1964a, pp. 677–715. See also Froman 1967, pp. 94–103.

3. When the "power-elite" literature turns from sociometric analysis to a study of local issues and policy formation, it tends to concentrate on developmental policies.

4. The locational decisions to which Banfield 1961 gives much attention are a well-known instance of allocational politics.

5. There are a few instances where redistributive policies are not regres-

sive but instead have a positive impact on the local economy. For example, where there is a shortage of unskilled labor, a local government might provide subsidized housing for unskilled workers to attract them to the local market. Instances of redistribution that have positive economic benefits occur seldom enough that they are excluded from this analysis.

6. Crenson 1971.

7. Williams and Adrian 1963, p. 304. See also pp. 192–93, 305.

8. Doig 1966; Danielson 1965.

9. Lupo, Colcord, and Fowler 1971, p. 181.

10. Ibid., p. 211.

11. Doig 1966, p. 34.

12. Lupo, Colcord, and Fowler 1971, p. 243.

13. Caro 1974.

14. Lupo, Colcord, and Fowler 1971; Hartman et al. 1974, p. 66.

15. Hunter 1953; Miller 1958; Clelland and Form 1968.

16. For an interesting survey of the literature as well as an extensive bibliography, see Hawley and Wirt 1968.

17. Bachrach and Baratz 1962.

18. Polsby 1980, p. 145.

19. Ibid.; Banfield 1961; Wolfinger 1974.

20. "Answers to [the reputationalists'] question may mean many things, and their meanings are in any case irrelevant until concrete instances of policy formation are examined." Polsby 1963, p. 64.

21. Wildavsky 1964, p. 312; also see Presthus 1964, pp. 112, 147.

22. Wildavsky 1964, chapter 20.

23. The figure is the total number of decision-making individuals mentioned by activists as members of the general elite, housing elite, water elite, and education elite. Numbers calculated from data in column I of table 83, Wildavsky 1964, p. 313.

24. This is the total of individuals who did not participate in decisions but who were nominated by activists as members of one of the four types of elites identified in column II of table 83, Wildavsky 1964, p. 313.

25. These numbers are calculated from columns III-A and III-B of table 83, Wildavsky 1964, p. 313.

26. Wildavsky 1964, p. 319.

27. Agger, Goldrich, and Swanson 1964, p. 710; for Hunter's wording of the question, see Hunter 1953, p. 62.

28. Hunter 1953, pp. 160, 164ff., 175ff.

29. Schulze 1961.

30. Agger, Goldrich, and Swanson 1964, chapter 6.

31. Clelland and Form 1968, p. 85.

32. Ibid.; Jennings 1964; Schulze and Blumberg 1957.

33. Miller 1958.

34. Hunter 1953, p. 111.

35. Clelland and Form 1968, p. 86.

36. Ibid.

37. Schulze 1961, p. 67.

38. Reichley 1959, p. 61, as quoted in Banfield and Wilson 1963, p. 272.

39. Wolfinger 1974.
40. Ibid., chapter 12.
41. Reichley 1959, p. 61.
42. Caro 1974.
43. Hayes 1972.
44. Ibid., pp. 108–9.
45. Wolfinger 1974, p. 195.
46. Hayes 1972, p. 120.
47. Pressman 1972.
48. Hayes 1972, chapter 5.
49. Ibid., p. 112.
50. Ibid., pp. 112–13.
51. Ibid., p. 115.
52. Ibid., p. 120.
53. Ibid., p. 194.
54. Wolfinger 1974, p. 346.

Chapter Eight

1. Banfield's 1961 study of political influence in Chicago focuses almost exclusively on locational issues. His study demonstrates the diversity and complexity of political controversy in the allocational sector.
2. "Supervisors' ratings have an average correlation of about .30 with workers' IQ scores in most occupations. There is enormous variation from one employer to another, and in many settings the correlation is actually negative." Jencks 1972, p. 186. See also Berg 1970.
3. Summers and Wolfe 1977.
4. See citations in chapter 1.
5. Holli 1969.
6. Lowi 1964b.
7. Counts 1928. See also Salisbury 1970.
8. Wirt 1974, p. 131.
9. Bryce 1910, pp. 654–55.
10. Reichley 1959; Meyerson and Banfield 1955; Lipsky and Olson 1976.
11. Wirt 1974, p. 130. The observation is about San Francisco, but it seems to be generalizable.
12. Shefter 1976.
13. Wirt 1974, p. 99.
14. Stephen David and I have discussed other factors affecting machine-reform conflict in American politics in David and Peterson 1976, pp. 11–18.
15. Dahl 1961, pp. 34–36.
16. Wolfinger 1974, chapter 3; Parenti 1967; Glazer and Moynihan 1963.
17. Wolfinger 1974, p. 36.
18. Ibid.
19. Lowi 1964b, p. 46.
20. Clark 1975.
21. Converse 1966.

22. Lane 1959, p. 239. A study of St. Louis found that 77 percent of the German community in the city and 80 percent of residents of southern and eastern European ancestry had voted at least once in municipal elections, whereas only 61 percent of "old stock" Americans and 62 percent of blacks reported having ever voted in such an election. Lineberry and Sharkansky 1971, p. 60.

23. Greenstone and Peterson 1976, chapter 2.

24. Molotch 1972.

25. Katznelson 1973.

26. Thompson 1975, chapter 6.

27. Peterson and Greenstone 1977, p. 272.

28. Browning, Marshall, and Tabb 1978.

29. The study is cited in Caputo 1976, p. 85.

30. Tompson 1975, pp. 170–71.

31. Peterson 1979b.

32. Tingsten 1937, chapter 3; Lipset 1960.

33. For example, the issue is not discussed in Campbell et al. 1960, nor in Nie, Verba, and Petrocik 1976.

34. Ziegler, Jennings, and Peak 1974.

35. Miner 1963.

36. La Noue and Smith 1973, pp. 187–95.

37. Lowi 1976. The estimate of the percentage of voters who are also employees is given in Long 1972, p. 114.

38. Lowi 1976, p. 34.

39. Williams and Adrian 1963, p. 73.

40. Wolfinger 1974, pp. 380–81.

41. Banfield and Wilson 1963, p. 215.

42. Wirt 1974, p. 144.

43. Levine, Perry, and De Marco 1977.

44. Levi 1977, p. 155.

45. Piven 1976.

46. O'Connor 1973; Levi 1977.

47. Peterson 1976, p. 255.

48. Ibid.

49. The quotation is from Levine, Perry, and De Marco 1977. Details are to be found in Lipsky and Drotning 1973; Ashenfelter 1971; Ehrenberg 1973; and Freund 1974.

50. Clark and Ferguson (forthcoming).

Chapter Nine

1. Peterson 1975.

2. Crenson 1971.

3. Bachrach and Baratz 1962.

4. Agger, Goldrich, and Swanson 1964, chapter 11.

5. Crenson 1971, p. 130.

6. Ibid., p. 117.

7. Ibid., p. 55.

8. Ibid.

9. Ibid., p. 10.

10. Banfield and Wilson 1963, chapter 19; Reichley 1959; Greenstone 1969.

11. On Great Britain, see Beer 1969.

12. Greenstone 1969, chapters 2, 11.

13. On national-local differences in housing policy, see Freedman 1969; on poverty, see Greenstone and Peterson 1976, pp. 77–78.

14. Banfield and Wilson 1963, p. 279.

15. Greenstone 1969, pp. 170–71.

16. McConnell 1966, p. 345.

17. Greenstone 1969, p. 170.

18. Dye 1966; Brazer 1959; Lewis-Beck 1977.

19. Fried 1975, p. 345.

20. This instance is taken from Lipsky and Olson 1976, p. 279.

21. Lipsky 1970. The following paragraphs draw freely from this case study, though Lipsky's own interpretation relies on a bargaining framework within which the rent strikers are said to be a relatively powerless group.

22. Lipsky and Olson 1976.

23. One can find illustrations of such strategies in the emerging Marxist literature on local politics. See Castells 1977; Cockburn 1977.

24. Greenstone and Peterson 1976, pp. 41–42.

25. Wilson 1973.

26. Marris and Rein 1967.

27. Crawford 1974.

28. Piven and Cloward 1971.

29. This analysis is taken from Peterson and Greenstone 1977.

30. Greenstone and Peterson 1976, chapter 10.

31. On school politics in the United States, see La Noue and Smith 1973; Rogers 1968; Peterson 1976; Crain 1968.

32. Bachrach and Baratz 1962.

33. Wolfinger 1971.

34. Schattschneider 1960.

Chapter Ten

1. Ferretti 1976, p. 403.

2. In October 1975, Mayor Abraham Beame wrote to Governor Hugh Carey that New York "has achieved greatness because of the rich variety of its services and institutions—not just for its citizens, but for the citizens of the world. If we are to preserve these precious assets, we must be relieved of the accumulating, unjust burdens placed upon us during the preceding decades." Ibid., p. 337.

3. United States Congress, Congressional Budget Office 1975, p. 11.

4. For instance, in October 1975, Gerald Ford said the following: "Responsibility for New York City's financial problems is being left on the front doorstep of the Federal Government—unwanted and abandoned by its real parents...most other cities in America have faced these very same chal-

lenges, and are still financially healthy today. They have not been luckier than New York; they have simply been better managed." Ferretti 1976, pp. 350–51.

5. Temporary Commission on City Finances 1978, p. 90.

6. Piven 1976, p. 321.

7. Ibid., p. 338.

8. Ibid., p. 329.

9. Shefter 1977, p. 98.

10. Ibid., pp. 105–6.

11. Ibid., p. 106.

12. Ibid.

13. Ibid.

14. David and Kantor 1979, p. 199.

15. Ibid.

16. Ibid., p. 200.

17. Ibid., p. 201.

18. Shefter 1977, p. 98.

19. United States Congress, Congressional Budget Office 1975, pp. 7–9.

20. David and Kantor 1979, p. 208.

21. First National City Bank 1970, p. 19.

22. Ibid., p. 22.

23. Temporary Commission on City Finances 1978, pp. 73, 181.

24. Ibid., p. 83.

25. Shefter 1977, p. 108.

26. Temporary Commission on City Finances 1976, p. 5.

27. The careful reader will note that the average annual percentage increase for New York is reported as only 3.6 percent in table 10.8, while in table 10.5 it is reported as hovering between 4 and 5 percent during this same time period. This difference is due to the following: (1) table 10.5 uses changes in the New York City consumer price index to calculate changes in constant dollars, while table 10.8 uses the national consumer price index, the more appropriate indicator for intercity comparisons; and (2) table 10.5 is taken from New York City sources, while table 10.8 is taken from Census Bureau data. Somwehat different classification systems may partially account for these differences.

28. Temporary Commission on City Finances 1978, p. 95.

29. Temporary Commission on City Finances 1977, p. 6.

30. Temporary Commission on City Finances 1966, p. vi.

31. Greenstone and Peterson 1976, pp. 39–41.

32. First National City Bank 1970, p. 22.

33. Wood 1961, p. 84.

34. New York Chamber of Commerce 1960, p. 2.

35. Ibid., p. 6. Although those dollar figures were attained more quickly than the Chamber of Commerce anticipated, their prediction was essentially correct. Calculated in 1961 dollars with the changes due to increases in intergovernmental assistance removed, the New York City budget did in fact reach a level of $3.081 billion in 1965 and by 1970 had increased to $3.733 billion, just short of the $4 billion that had been anticipated.

36. Ibid., p. 19.
37. Ibid., p. 25.
38. David and Kantor 1979, p. 210.

Chapter Eleven

1. Executive Office of the President 1979, p. 71.
2. Yates 1977, p. 45.
3. Peterson and Greenstone 1977.
4. Wilson 1978.
5. Clark and Ferguson (forthcoming).
6. O'Connor 1973.
7. Alcaly and Mermelstein 1976.
8. Castells 1977; Harvey 1973; Cockburn 1977; Mollenkopf 1977.
9. Piven and Cloward 1977.
10. This line of inquiry owes much to the writings of Antonio Gramsci. See Clark 1977.
11. Griffith 1966, p. 76.
12. Ibid., p. 165.
13. As long as localities were allowed to levy differential tax rates, differing economic bases would still yield certain fiscal dividends. If a community wished to provide services at a higher rate than federal subsidies allowed, it could expand its services above the federal minimum more easily the larger its economic base. In other words, egalitarian objectives could be easily undermined if federal minimums were set very low and most communities provided services above them. State foundations programs in education have failed to equalize local fiscal resources for this very reason. Coons, Clune and Sugarman 1970.
14. Griffith 1966, p. 74.
15. In Britain, the coefficient of variation for total spending in 1965–66 by county boroughs for welfare, children's services, health, education, and libraries per ten thousand residents was .11 (Boaden 1971, p. 14). The coefficient of variation of expenditure for primary school education per thousand residents by all local authorities, 1961–63, was .14; for secondary education the coefficient was .11 (Davies 1968, pp. 277, 283). Although larger coefficients of variation occur when less expensive public services are examined, there is little variation in expenditures for education, the largest of the local authority services, and for overall expenditure totals. In other words, local authorities have a fairly fixed amount of resources available (as compared with states and localities in the United States) but they vary in their allocation of resources among public services. Information on the United States is presented in chapter 3.
16. Alt 1971 found negative associations between wealth and expenditures on education, housing, and fire services; he found positive correlations between wealth and expenditures on police, children's services, libraries, highways, local health facilities, and welfare. Partial coefficients never attained a value larger than .21; in other words, for no public service did the

wealth of the community account for more than 4 percent of the variance in expenditures.

After an extensive review of British literature on determinants of expenditure, Newton 1976, pp. 70–71, concludes that "there is no statistically significant relationship between community wealth, however it is measured, and community spending or performance for a great many services." He says that, although wealthier communities tend to spend "marginally more on planning and parks," they "tend to spend rather less on the aged, mothers and young children, and special education, and to have a lower total per capita expenditure."

17. Even if fully implemented, my proposals still leave localities marginally dependent on their own economic base. In addition, the fiscal incentive is only one of several factors that discourage local officials from attending to the needs of low-income minorities. Even in Britain there is less enthusiasm for redistributive programs on the part of local authorities. Griffith 1966, pp. 256–57, reports that "only in the rarest cases do the Department of Education and Science need to persuade a local education authority to build more schools or the Ministry of Transport to cajole city engineers . . . to produce bigger and better highway proposals . . . . In housing the difference is fundamental . . . . In this area the sense of urgency and the need for a continuing drive for slum clearance have come from the Department."

Appendix

1. Brazer 1959.

2. Findings within the states of Ohio and Massachusetts run along similar lines; the findings for California are heavily influenced by the growth spurt that California cities were experiencing in the late 1940s and are probably not generalizable to other times and places.

3. Bahl 1969.

4. Because Bahl included state aid as one of the independent variables in an analysis where the dependent variables included expenditures from both state and local revenue sources, there is reason to believe that the beta coefficient between density and highway expenditures is an underestimate of the actual relationship.

5. Weicher 1970.

6. Ibid., pp. 392–93.

7. Schmandt and Stephens 1963.

8. Adams 1967.

9. Sharkansky 1971.

References

Adams, R. F. 1967. On the variation in the consumption of public services. In *Essays in state and local finance*, ed. by H. E Brazer, pp. 9–16. Ann Arbor, Michigan: Institute of Public Administration.

Agger, R.; Goldrich, B.; and Swanson, B. 1964. *The rulers and the ruled.* New York: John Wiley.

Alcaly, R. E. and Mermelstein, D., eds. 1976. *The fiscal crisis of American cities.* New York: Vintage Books.

Alexander, K. L., and McDill, E. L. 1976. Selection and allocation within schools: Some causes and consequences of currriculum placement. *American Sociological Review* 41:963–80.

Alford, R. R., and Lee, E. C. 1968. Voting turnout in American cities. *American Political Science Review* 62:796–813.

Alt, J. E. 1971. Some social and political correlates of county borough expenditures. *British Journal of Political Science* 1:49–62.

Ashenfelter, O. 1971. The effect of unionization on wages in the public sector: The case of fire fighters. *Industrial and Labor Relations Review* 24:191–202.

Babcock, R. F. 1966. *The zoning game.* Madison: University of Wisconsin Press.

Bachrach, P., and Baratz, M. S. 1962. Two faces of power. *American Political Science Review* 56:947–52.

———. 1970. *Power and poverty: Theory and practice.* New York: Oxford University Press.

Bahl, R. W. 1969. *Metropolitan city expenditures: A comparative analysis.* Lexington: University of Kentucky Press.

Bahl, R. W.; Campbell, A. K.; and Greytak, D. 1974. *Taxes, expenditures, and the economic base: Case study of New York City.* New York: Praeger.

Banfield, E. C. 1961. *Political influence.* Glencoe, Illinois: Free Press.

Banfield, E. C., and Wilson, J. Q. 1963. *City politics.* Cambridge, Massachusetts: Harvard University Press.

References

Barber, J. D. 1965. *The lawmakers.* New Haven: Yale University Press.

Bauer, R. A.; Pool, I. de Sola; and Dexter, L. A. 1972. *American business and public policy.* Chicago: Aldine-Atherton.

Becker, G. S. 1964. *Human capital.* Princeton, New Jersey: Princeton University Press.

Beer, S. 1969. *British politics in the collectivist age.* Westminster, Maryland: Random House.

Bellush, J., and David, S. M., eds. 1971. *Race and politics in New York City: Five studies in policy-making.* New York: Praeger.

Berg, I. 1970. *Education and jobs: The great training robbery.* New York: Praeger.

Boaden, N. 1971. *Urban policy-making.* Cambridge: Cambridge University Press.

Brazer, S. 1959. *City expenditures in the United States.* Occasional papers no. 66. New York: National Bureau of Economic Research.

Brown, L. D. 1978. In *American politics and public policy,* ed. by W. D. Burnham and M. W. Weinberg. Cambridge, Massachusetts: Massachusetts Institute of Technology Press.

Browning, R. P.; Marshall, D. R.; and Tabb, D. H. 1978. Responsiveness to minorities: A theory of political change in cities. Paper prepared for the annual meeting of the American Political Science Association.

Bryce, J. 1891. *The American commonwealth.* Vol. 1. New York: Macmillan.

————. 1910. *The American commonwealth.* Vol. 1. New edition. New York: Macmillan.

Burkhead, J., with Fox, T. G., and Holland, J. W. 1967. *Input and output in large city high schools.* Syracuse, New York: Syracuse University Press.

Burnham, W. D. 1970. *Critical elections and the mainsprings of American politics.* New York: Norton.

Callahan, R. E. 1962. *Education and the cult of efficiency.* Chicago: University of Chicago Press.

Campbell, A., et al. 1960. *The American voter.* New York: John Wiley.

Caputo, D. A. 1976. *Urban America: The policy alternatives.* San Francisco: W. H. Freeman.

Caraley, D. 1977. *City governments and urban problems.* Englewood Cliffs, New Jersey: Prentice-Hall.

Caro, R. A. 1974. *The power broker: Robert Moses and the fall of New York.* New York: Alfred Knopf.

Castells, M. 1977. *The urban question.* London: Edward Arnold.

Cebula, R. J. 1974. Local government policies and migration: An analysis for SMSAs in the United States. *Public Choice* 19:85–93.

Chicago Urban League. 1977. The current economic status of Chicago's black community. Mimeographed. Chicago.

Citizens' Budget Commission. 1979. *Twenty-five year pocket summary of New York City finances for the fiscal year 1977–78.* New York: Citizens' Budget Commission.

Clark, M. 1977. *Antonio Gramsci and the revolution that failed.* New Haven: Yale University Press.

References

Clark, P. 1959. Chicago's big businessmen. Doctoral dissertation, University of Chicago.

Clark, T. N. 1968. Community structure, decision making, budget expenditures, and urban renewal in fifty-one American communities.

———. 1975. The Irish ethic and the spirit of patronage. *Ethnicity* 2:305–59.

Clark, T. N., and Ferguson, L. C. *Political leadership and urban fiscal strain.* Forthcoming.

Clelland, D. A., and Form, W. H. 1968. Economic dominants and community power: A comparative analysis. In *The search for community power,* ed. by W. D. Hawley and F. M. Wirt, pp. 78–87. Englewood Cliffs, New Jersey: Prentice-Hall.

Cnudde, C. F., and McCrone, D. J. 1969. Party competition and welfare policies in the American states. *American Political Science Review* 63:858–66.

Cockburn, C. 1977. *The local state.* London: Pluto Press.

Coleman, J. S., et al. 1966. *Equality of educational opportunity.* Washington, D. C.: Government Printing Office.

Converse, P. E. 1966. Religion and politics: The 1960 election. In *Elections and the political order,* ed. by A. Campbell et al., pp. 96–124. New York: John Wiley.

Coons, J. E.; Clune, W. H.; and Sugarman, S. D. 1970. *Private wealth and public education.* Cambridge, Mass.: Harvard University Press.

Counts, G. 1928. *School and society in Chicago.* New York: Harcourt, Brace.

Cox, H., and Morgan, D. 1973. *City politics and the press.* Cambridge: Cambridge University Press.

Crain, R. 1968. *The politics of school desegregation.* Chicago: Aldine.

Crawford, R. 1974. The politics of hospital utilization. Doctoral dissertation, University of Chicago.

Crecine, J. P. 1969. *Governmental problem-solving.* Chicago: Rand McNally.

Crenson, M. 1971. *The un-politics of air pollution.* Baltimore, Maryland: Johns Hopkins University Press.

Cronin, J. M. 1973. *The control of urban schools: Perspective on the power of educational reformers.* New York: Free Press.

Dahl, R. 1961. *Who governs?* New Haven: Yale University Press.

———. 1976. Equality and power in American society. In *Urban politics and public policy,* ed. by S. M. David and P. E. Peterson, 2d ed., pp. 28–35. New York: Praeger.

Danielson, M. N. 1965. *Federal-metropolitan politics and the commuter crisis.* New York: Columbia University Press.

David, S. M., and Kantor, P. 1979. Political theory and transformations in urban budgetary arenas: The case of New York City. In *Urban policy making,* ed. by D. R. Marshall, pp. 183–220. Beverly Hills, California: Sage.

David, S. M., and Peterson, P. E., eds. 1976. *Urban politics and public policy.* 2d ed. New York: Praeger.

Davies, B. 1968. *Social needs and resources in local services.* London: Joseph.

References

Derthick, M. 1968. Intercity differences in administration of the public as-
    sistance program: The case of Massachusetts. In *City politics and public
    policy*, ed. by J. Q. Wilson, pp. 243–66. New York: John Wiley.
———. 1972. *New towns in town: Why a federal program failed*. Washing-
    ton, D.C.: Urban Institute.
Diamond, M. 1969. On the relationship of federalism and decentralization.
    In *Cooperation and conflict: Readings in American federalism*, ed. by D. J.
    Elazar et al., pp. 72–80. Itasca, Illinois: F. E. Peacock.
Doig, J. W. 1966. *Metropolitan transportation politics and the New York
    region*. New York: Columbia University Press.
Downs, A. 1957. *An economic theory of democracy*. New York: Harper.
Dye, T. R. 1966. *Politics, economics, and the public: Policy outcomes in the
    American states*. Chicago: Rand McNally.
Eckstein, H. 1960. *Pressure group politics: The case of the British Medical
    Association*. London: Allen & Unwin.
Edel, M., and Sclar, E. 1974. Taxes, spending, and property values: Supply
    adjustment in a Tiebout-Oates model. *Journal of Political Economy* 82:
    941–54.
Ehrenberg, R. G. 1973. Municipal government structure, unionization, and
    the wages of fire fighters. *Industrial and Labor Relations Review* 27:36–48.
Elazar, D. J. 1966. *American federalism: A view from the states*. New York:
    Thomas Y. Crowell.
———. 1970. *Cities of the prairie*. New York: Basic Books.
Elazar, D. J.; Carroll, R. B.; Levine, E. L.; and St. Angelo, D. 1969. *Coopera-
    tion and conflict: Readings in American federalism*. Itasca, Illinois: F. E.
    Peacock.
Eulau, H., and Prewitt, K. 1973. *Labyrinths of democracy*. Indianapolis:
    Bobbs-Merrill.
Executive Office of the President. 1979. *The U.S. budget in brief: Fiscal year
    1980*. Washington, D.C.: Government Printing Office.
Fabricant, S. 1952. *The trend of government activity in the United States
    since 1900*. New York: National Bureau of Economic Research.
Ferretti, F. 1976. *The year the big apple went bust*. New York: G. P. Putnam's
    Sons.
Fiorina, M. P. 1977. *Congress*. New Haven: Yale University Press.
First National City Bank (George Roniger). 1970. *The financial position of
    the city of New York in long-term perspective*. New York: First National
    City Bank.
Fisher, D. 1967. Local determinants of per pupil expenditures in suburban
    high school districts. Doctoral dissertation, University of Chicago.
Fisher, G. W. 1964. Interstate variation in state and local government expen-
    diture. *National Tax Journal* 17:57–74.
Flathman, R. E. 1966. *The public interest*. New York: John Wiley.
Fletcher, P. 1967. The results analyzed. In *Voting in cities*, ed. by L. J.
    Sharpe, pp. 298–303. London: Macmillan & Co.
Forrester, J. 1969. *Urban dynamics*. Cambridge, Massachusetts: Massachu-
    setts Institute of Technology Press.

References

Freedman, L. 1969. *Public housing: The politics of poverty.* New York: Holt, Rinehart, & Winston.
Freund, J. L. 1974. Market and union influences on municipal employee wages. *Industrial and Labor Relations Review* 27:391–404.
Fried, R. C. 1975. Comparative urban policy and performance. In *Handbook of political science*, vol. 6, ed. by F. Greenstein and N. Polsby, pp. 305–79. Reading, Massachusetts: Addison-Wesley.
Frohlich, N.; Oppenheimer, J.; and Young, O. R. 1971. *Political leadership and collective goods.* Princeton, New Jersey: Princeton University Press.
Froman, L. 1967. An analysis of public policies in cities. *Journal of Politics* 29:94–108.
Gardiner, J. 1968. Police enforcement of traffic laws: A comparative analysis. In *City politics and public policy*, ed. by J. Q. Wilson, pp. 151–72. New York: John Wiley.
Gerth, H. H., and Mills, C. W., trans. 1946. *From Max Weber.* New York: Oxford University Press.
Gilbert, C. E. 1964. National political alignments and the politics of large cities. *Political Science Quarterly* 79:25–51.
Gittell, M. 1973. Professionalism and public participation in educational policy-making: New York City, a case study. In *Urban policies and public policy*, ed. by S. M. David and P. E. Peterson, pp. 192–217. New York: Praeger.
Glazer, N., and Moynihan, D. 1963. *Beyond the melting pot.* Cambridge, Massachusetts: Massachusetts Institute of Technology Press and Harvard University Press.
Goetell, R. J. 1978. Federal assistance to national target groups: The ESEA Title I experience. In *The federal interest in financing schooling*, ed. by M. Timpane, pp. 173–208. Cambridge, Massachusetts: Ballinger.
Greenstone, J. D. 1969. *Labor in American politics.* New York: Alfred Knopf.
Greenstone, J. D., and Peterson, P. E. 1976. *Race and authority in urban politics.* Phoenix edition. Chicago: University of Chicago Press.
Griffith, J. A. 1966. Toronto: University of Toronto Press.
Grodzins, M. 1966. *The American system,* ed. by D. J. Elazar. Chicago: Rand McNally.
Grubb, W. N., and Michelson, S. 1974. *States and schools.* Lexington, Massachusetts: Lexington Books.
Hansen, A. H., and Perloff, H. S. 1944. *State and local finance in the national economy.* New York: Norton.
Hansen, S. B. 1975. Participation, political structure, and concurrence. *American Political Science Review* 69:1181–1199.
Hanushek, E. 1972. *Education and race.* Lexington, Massachusetts: Lexington Books.
Hartman, C., et al. 1974. *Yerba Buena: Land grab and community resistance in San Francisco.* San Francisco: Glide Publications.
Harvey, D. 1973. *Social justice and the city.* Baltimore: Johns Hopkins University Press.
Harvey, L. E. 1969. Property tax determinants of education expenditure.

251

Doctoral dissertation, Stanford University.

Hawley, W. D. 1973. *Nonpartisan elections and the case for party politics.* New York: John Wiley.

Hawley, W. D., and Wirt, F. M., eds. 1968. *The search for community power.* Englewood Cliffs, New Jersey: Prentice-Hall.

Hayes, E. C. 1972. *Power structure and urban policy: Who rules in Oakland?* New York: McGraw-Hill.

Hays, S. P. 1964. The politics of reform in municipal government in the progressive era. *Pacific Northwest Quarterly* 55:157–69.

Heidenheimer, A. J.; Heclo, H.; and Adams, C. T. 1976. *Comparative public policy: The politics of social choice in Europe and America.* London: Macmillan & Co.

Heyns, B. 1974. Social selection and stratification within schools. *American Journal of Sociology* 79:1434–51.

Hibbs, D., Jr. 1977. Political parties and macroeconomic policy. *American Political Science Review* 71:1467–87.

Hickrod, G. A. 1971. Local demand for education: A critique of school finance and economic research circa 1959–1969. *Review of Educational Research* 41:35–49.

Hirsch, W. Z. 1960. Determinants of public education expenditures. *National Tax Journal* 13:29–40.

Hirschman, A. O. 1970. *Exit, voice, and loyalty.* Cambridge, Massachusetts: Harvard University Press.

Hofstadter, R. 1955. *The age of reform.* New York: Oxford University Press.

Holli, M. G. 1969. *Reform in Detroit.* New York: Oxford University Press.

Hughes, J. F., and Hughes, A. O. 1972. *Equal education: A new national strategy.* Bloomington: Indiana University Press.

Hunter, F. 1953. *Community power structure.* Chapel Hill: University of North Carolina Press.

James, H. T.; Kelly, J.; and Garms, W. 1966. *Determinants of educational expenditures in large cities of the United States.* Stanford, California: Stanford University School of Education.

James, H. T.; Thomas, J. A.; and Dyck, H. J. 1963. *Wealth, expenditure, and decision-making for education.* Stanford, California: Stanford University School of Education.

Jencks, C. S. 1972. The conventional wisdom. In *On equality of educational opportunity,* ed. by F. Mosteller and D. P. Moynihan, pp. 72–81. New York: Random House.

Jencks, C. S., et al. 1972. *Inequality.* New York: Basic Books.

Jennings, M. K. 1964. *Community influentials: The elites of Atlanta.* New York: Free Press.

Katzman, M. T. 1971. *The political economy of urban schools.* Cambridge, Massachusetts: Harvard University Press.

Katznelson, I. 1973. *Black men, white cities.* New York: Oxford University
———. *City trenches.* New York: Pantheon. Forthcoming.

Kaufman, H. 1960. *The forest ranger.* Baltimore, Maryland: Johns Hopkins University Press.

References

Key, V. O., Jr. 1949. *Southern politics.* New York: Alfred Knopf.

———. 1964. *Politics, parties, and pressure groups.* 5th ed. New York: Thomas Y. Crowell.

King, A. T. 1977. Estimating property tax capitalization: A critical comment. *Journal of Political Economy* 85:425–31.

Kramer, R. 1969. *Participation of the poor: Comparative case studies in the war on poverty.* Englewood Cliffs, New Jersey: Prentice-Hall.

Ladd, E. C. 1970. *American political parties.* New York: Norton.

Lane, R. E. 1959. *Political life.* Glencoe, Illinois: Free Press.

La Noue, G. R., and Smith, B. L. R. 1973. *The politics of school decentralization.* Lexington, Massachusetts: Lexington Books.

Latham, E. 1952. *The group basis of politics.* Ithaca, New York: Cornell University Press.

Lee, E. C. 1960. *The politics of nonpartisanship.* Berkeley and Los Angeles: University of California Press.

———. 1963. City elections: A statistical profile. In *The municipal yearbook 1963,* pp. 74–84. Chicago: International Managers' Association.

Levi, M. 1977. *Bureaucratic insurgency: The case of police unions.* Lexington, Massachusetts: Lexington Books.

Levin, H. M. 1977. A decade of policy developments in improving education and training for low-income populations. In *A decade of federal antipoverty programs,* ed. by R. H. Haveman, pp. 123–88. New York: Academic Press.

Levine, C. H.; Perry, J. L.; and De Marco, J. 1977. Collective bargaining in municipal governments: An interorganizational perspective. In *Managing human resources,* ed. by C. H. Levine, pp. 159–200. Urban Affairs Annual Review, vol. 13. Beverly Hills, California: Sage.

Levy, F.; Meltsner, A. J.; and Wildavsky, A. 1974. *Urban outcomes: Schools, streets, and libraries.* Berkeley and Los Angeles: University of California Press.

Lewis-Beck, M. S. 1977. The relative importance of socioeconomic and political variables for public policy. *American Political Science Review* 71:559–66.

Liebert, R. J. 1974. Municipal functions, structure, and expenditures: A reanalysis of recent research. *Social Science Quarterly* 54:765–83.

Lineberry, R., and Fowler, E. P. 1967. Reformism and public policies in American cities. *American Political Science Review* 61:701–16.

Lineberry, R., and Sharkansky, I. 1971. *Urban politics and public policy.* New York: Harper & Row.

Lipset, S. M. 1960. *Political man.* Garden City, New York: Doubleday.

Lipsky, D. B., and Drotning, J. E. 1973. The influence of collective bargaining on teachers' salaries in New York State. *Industrial and Labor Relations Review* 27:18–35.

Lipsky, M. 1970. *Protest in city politics: Rent strikes, housing, and the power of the poor.* Chicago: Rand McNally.

Lipsky, M., and Olson, D. J. 1977. *Commission politics: The processing of racial crisis in America.* New Brunswick, New Jersey: Transaction Books.

References

Long, N. E. 1972. *The unwalled city.* New York: Basic Books.
Lowi, T. 1964*a*. American business, public policy, case studies, and political theory. *World Politics* 16:677–715.
———. 1964*b*. *At the pleasure of the mayor.* New York: Free Press.
———. 1969. *The end of liberalism.* New York: Norton.
———. 1976. Gosnell's Chicago revisited via Lindsay's New York. In *Urban politics and public policy,* ed. by S. M. David and P. E. Peterson, 2d ed., pp. 28–35. New York: Praeger.
Lupo, A.; Colcord, F.; and Fowler, E. P. 1971. *Rites of way: The politics of transportation in Boston and the U.S. city.* Boston: Little, Brown.
McConnell, G. 1966. *Private power and American democracy.* New York: Alfred Knopf.
McDougall, G. S. 1976. Local public goods and residential property values: Some insights and extensions. *National Tax Journal* 29:436–47.
McFarland, A. S. 1969. *Power and leadership in pluralist systems.* Stanford, California: Stanford University Press.
Macmahon, A. W. 1972. *Administering federalism in a democracy.* New York: Oxford University Press.
Marris, P., and Rein, M. 1967. *Dilemmas in social reform.* New York: Atherton.
Marsh, P. E., and Gortner, R. A. 1963. *Federal aid to science education: Two programs.* Syracuse, New York: Syracuse University Press.
Maxwell, J. A., and Aronson, R. 1977. *Financing state and local governments.* Washington, D. C.: Brookings Institution.
Meadows, G. R. 1976. Taxes, spending, and property values: A comment and further results. *Journal of Political Economy* 84:869–80.
Meltsner, A. J. 1971. *The politics of city revenue.* Berkeley and Los Angeles: University of California Press.
Merton, R. K. 1957. *Social theory and social structure.* New York: Free Press.
Meyerson, M., and Banfield, E. C. 1955. *Politics, planning, and the public interest.* Glencoe, Illinois: Free Press.
Miller, D. C. 1958. Decision-making cliques in community power structures: A comparative study of an American and an English city. *American Journal of Sociology* 64:299–310.
———. 1970. *International community power structures.* Bloomington: Indiana University Press.
Mills, E. S., and Oates, W. E. 1975. *Fiscal zoning and land use controls.* Lexington, Massachusetts: Lexington Books.
Minar, D. W. 1964. Community characteristics, conflict, and power structures. In *The politics of education in the local community,* ed. by R. S. Cahill and S. P. Hencley, pp. 125–44. Danville, Illinois: Interstate.
Miner, J. 1963. *Social and economic factors in spending for public education.* Syracuse, New York: Syracuse University Press.
Mollenkopf, J. 1977. Southwestern urban development and the flight from political conflict and adaptation. Mimeographed. Palo Alto, California: Stanford University Graduate School of Business.
Molotch, H. 1972. *Managed integration.* Berkeley and Los Angeles: University of California Press.

Morgan, J. N., et al. 1962. *Income and welfare in the United States.* New York: McGraw-Hill.

Morss, E. R. 1966. Some thoughts on the determinants of state and local expenditures. *National Tax Journal* 19:95–103.

Muller, Thomas. 1975. *Growing and declining urban areas: A fiscal comparison.* Washington, D.C.: Urban Institute.

Murnane, R. J. 1975. *The impact of school resources on the learning of inner city children.* Cambridge, Massachusetts: Ballinger.

Murphy, J. T. 1971. Title I of ESEA: The politics of implementing federal education reform. *Harvard Educational Review* 41:35–63.

Musgrave, R. A. 1959. *The theory of public finance.* New York: McGraw-Hill.

Netzer, D. 1966. *Economics of the property tax.* Washington, D.C.: Brookings Institution.

Newton, K. 1976. Community performance in Britain. *Current Sociology* 26:49–84.

New York Chamber of Commerce. 1960. *The coming crisis in New York City finances.* New York: New York Chamber of Commerce.

Nie, N. H.; Verba, S.; and Petrocik, J. R. 1976. *The changing American voter.* Cambridge, Massachusetts: Harvard University Press.

Oates, W. E. 1969. The effects of property taxes and local public spending on property values: An empirical study of tax capitalization and the Tiebout hypothesis. *Journal of Political Economy* 77:957–71.

————. 1972. *Fiscal federalism.* New York: Harcourt Brace Jovanovich.

————. 1973. The effects of property taxes and local spending on property values: A reply and further results. *Journal of Political Economy* 81:1004–8.

O'Connor, J. 1973. *The fiscal crisis of the state.* New York: St. Martin's Press.

Olson, M. 1968. *The logic of collective action.* New York: Schocker.

Orfield, G. 1969. *The reconstruction of southern education: The schools and the 1964 Civil Rights Act.* New York: John Wiley, Interscience.

O'Shea, D. 1970. The impact of political leadership on educational policy. Doctoral dissertation, University of Chicago.

Ostrogorski, M. 1910. *The organization and development of political parties II: The United States.* New York: Macmillan.

Ostrom, E.; Baugh, W.; Guarasci, R.; Parks, R.; and Whitaker, G. 1973. *Community organization and the provision of public services.* Beverly Hills, California: Sage.

Owen, J. D. 1972. The distribution of educational resources in large American cities. *Journal of Human Resources* 7:26–38.

Parenti, M. 1967. Ethnic politics and the persistence of ethnic identification. *American Political Science Review* 61:717–26.

Peterson, P. E. 1975. Incentive theory and group influence: James Wilson's *Political Organizations* and the end of group theory. Paper prepared for the annual meeting of the American Political Science Association.

————. 1976. *School politics Chicago style.* Chicago: University of Chicago Press.

————. 1979a. A unitary model of local taxation and expenditure policies in

References

the United States. *British Journal of Political Science* 9:281–314.

———. 1979b. Organizational imperatives and ideological change: The case of black power. *Urban Politics Quarterly* 14:465–84.

Peterson, P. E., and Greenstone, J. D. 1976. The community action controversy as a test of two competing models of the policy-making process. In *Theoretical perspectives on urban politics*, ed. by M. Lipsky and W. Hawley, pp. 67–99. New York: Prentice-Hall.

———. 1977. Racial change and citizen participation: The mobilization of low-income communities through community action. In *A decade of federal antipoverty programs*, ed. by R. H. Haveman, pp. 241–78. New York: Academic Press.

Peterson, P. E., and Kantor, P. 1977. Political parties and citizen participation in English city politics. *Comparative Politics* 9:197–217.

Peterson, P. E., and Karpluss, S. 1978. The impact of property taxes and educational expenditures on property values in central cities and suburban communities. Mimeographed. Chicago: University of Chicago Department of Political Science.

Piven, F. F. 1976. The urban crisis: Who got what, and why. In *Urban politics and public policy*, ed. by S. M. David and P. E. Peterson, 2d ed., pp. 318–38. New York: Praeger.

Piven, F. F., and Cloward, R. 1971. *Regulating the poor.* New York: Pantheon.

———. 1977. *Poor people's movements.* New York: Pantheon.

Pollakowski, H. O. 1973. The effects of property taxes and local public spending on property values: A comment and further results. *Journal of Political Economy* 81:994–1003.

Polsby, N. W. 1980. *Community power and political theory.* 2d ed. New Haven: Yale University Press.

Pressman, J. L. 1972. Preconditions of mayoral leadership. *American Political Science Review* 66:511–24.

———. 1975. *Federal programs and city politics.* Berkeley and Los Angeles: University of California Press.

Pressman, J. L., and Wildavsky, A. 1973. *Implementation.* Berkeley and Los Angeles: University of California Press.

Presthus, R. 1964. *Men at the top: A study in community power.* New York: Oxford University Press.

Prewitt, K. 1970. Political ambitions, volunteerism, and electoral accountability. *American Political Science Review* 64:5–17.

Psacharopoulos, G. 1973. *Returns to education: An international comparison.* New York: Elsevier.

Rafuse, R. W., Jr. 1965. Cyclical behavior of state-local finances. In *Essays in fiscal federalism*, ed. by R. A. Musgrave, pp. 63–120. Washington, D. C.: Brookings Institution.

Reagan, M. D. 1972. *The new federalism.* New York: Oxford University Press.

Reichley, J. 1959. *The art of government: Reform and organization politics in Philadelphia.* New York: Fund for the Republic.

Riesman, D. 1950. *The lonely crowd.* New Haven and London: Yale University Press.

References

Rogers, D. 1968. *110 Livingston Street*. New York: Random House.

Rosen, H. S., and Fullerton, D. J. 1977. A note on local tax rates, public benefit levels, and property values. *Journal of Political Economy* 85:433–40.

Sacks, S., and Harris, R. 1964. The determinants of state and local government expenditure and intergovernmental flows of funds. *National Tax Journal* 17:75–85.

Sacks, S.; Harris, R.; and Carroll, J. J. 1963. *State and local government: The role of state aid in New York*. Albany, New York: Department of Audit and Control.

Sacks, S., and Hellmuth, W. F., Jr. 1961. *Financing government in a metropolitan area*. New York: Free Press.

Salisbury, R. H. 1970. Schools and politics in the big city. In *The politics of education at the local, state, and federal levels*, ed. by M. W. Kirst, pp. 17–32. Berkeley: McCutchan Publishing.

Savas, E. S. 1976. Solid waste collection in metropolitan areas. In *The delivery of urban services*, ed. by E. Ostrom, pp. 207–30. Urban Affairs Annual Review, vol. 10. Beverly Hills, California: Sage.

Sayre, W., and Kaufman, H. 1960. *Governing New York City*. New York: Russell Sage.

Schattschneider, E. E. 1960. *The semi-sovereign people*. New York: Holt, Rinehart, & Winston.

Schmandt, H. J., and Stephens, G. R. 1963. Local government expenditure patterns in the United States. *Land Economics* 39:397–406.

Schulze, R. O. 1961. The bifurcation of power in a satellite city. In *Community political systems*, ed. by M. Janowitz, pp. 19–80. New York: Free Press.

Schulze, R. O., and Blumberg, L. U. 1957. The determination of local power elites. *American Sociological Review* 63:290–96.

Scott, J. C. 1972. *Comparative political corruption*. Englewood Cliffs, New Jersey: Prentice-Hall.

Sharkansky, I. 1968. *Spending in American states*. Chicago: Rand McNally.

———. 1970. *Regionalism in American politics*. Indianapolis: Bobbs-Merrill.

———. 1971. Economic theories of public policy: Resource-policy and need-policy linkages between income and welfare benefits. *Midwest Journal of Political Science* 15:722–40.

Sharkansky, I., and Hofferbert, R. I. 1969. Dimensions of state politics, economics, and public policy. *American Political Science Review* 63:867–79.

Sharp, A. M. 1965. The behavior of selected state and local government fiscal variables during the phases of the cycles, 1949–61. In *Proceedings of the National Tax Association*, pp. 599–613. New York: National Tax Association.

Shefter, M. 1976. The emergence of the political machine: An alternative view. In *Theoretical perspectives on urban politics*, ed. by M. Lipsky and W. Hawley, pp. 14–44. Englewood Cliffs, New Jersey: Prentice-Hall.

———. 1977. New York City's fiscal crisis: The politics of inflation and retrenchment. *Public Interest* 48:98–127.

Smith, M. P. 1972. Basic findings reconsidered. In *On equality of educa-*

tional opportunity, ed. by F. Mosteller and D. P. Moynihan, pp. 254–69. New York: Random House.

Stokes, D. E. 1967. Parties and the nationalization of electoral forces. In *The American party systems*, ed. by W. N. Chambers and W. D. Burnham, pp. 182–202. New York: Oxford University Press.

Strange, J. H. 1972. Citizen participation in community action and model cities programs. *Public Administration Review* 32:457–70.

Summers, A. A., and Wolfe, B. L. 1977. Do schools make a difference? *American Economic Review* 67:639–52.

Temporary Commission on City Finances. 1966. *Financing the City University: Fiscal issues of public higher education in New York City*. Staff paper 1, February. New York: Temporary Commission.

————. 1976. *An historical and comparative analysis of expenditures in the city of New York*. Eighth interim report to the mayor, October. New York: Temporary Commission.

————. 1977. *The effects of personal taxes in New York City: Some proposals for a more rational system*. Eleventh interim report to the mayor, February. New York: Temporary Commission.

————. 1978. *The City in transition: Prospects and policies for New York*. New York: Arno Press.

Thompson, F. 1975. *Personnel policy in the city*. Berkeley and Los Angeles: University of California Press.

Thompson, W. R. 1965. *A preface to urban economics*. Baltimore, Maryland: Johns Hopkins University Press.

Thurow, L. C. 1972. Education and economic equality. *Public Interest* 28:66–81.

Tiebout, C. M. 1956. A pure theory of local expenditures. *Journal of Political Economy* 64:416–24.

Tingsten, H. 1937. *Political behavior*. London: P. S. King & Son.

Tompkins, G. L. 1975. A causal model of state welfare expenditures. *Journal of Politics* 37:392–416.

Truman, D. 1951. *The governmental process*. New York: Alfred Knopf.

Tyack, D. B. 1974. *The one best system*. Cambridge, Massachusetts: Harvard University Press.

United States Advisory Commission on Intergovernmental Relations. 1964. *The role of equalization in federal grants*. Washington, D.C.: Government Printing Office.

————. 1974. *Local revenue diversification: Incomes, sales tax, and user charges*. Washington, D.C.: Government Printing Office.

United States Congress, Congressional Budget Office. 1975. *New York City's fiscal problem: Its origins, potential repercussions, and some alternative policy responses*. Background paper no. 1, 10 October. Washington, D.C.: Government Printing Office.

United States Department of Commerce, Bureau of the Census. 1977. *Local government finances in selected metropolitan areas and large counties: 1975–76*. Government finances: GF 76, no. 6.

————. 1977. *Survey of current business: Business statistics*. Washington, D.C.: Government Printing Office.

References

United States House of Representatives, Subcommittee on Elementary, Secondary, and Vocational Education of the Committee on Education and Labor. 1977. *Title I—funds allocation: Hearing on H.R. 15*. 95th Congress, 1st Session.

United States Senate, Committee on Government Operations, Subcommittee on Intergovernmental Relations. 1969. The federal system as seen by federal aid officials. In *Cooperation and conflict: Readings in American federalism*, ed. by D. J. Elazar et al., pp. 331–38. Itasca, Illinois: F. E. Peacock.

Verba, S., and Nie, N. H. 1972. *Participation in America*. New York: Harper & Row.

Vidich, A. J., and Bensman, J. 1958. *Small town in mass society*. Princeton, New Jersey: Princeton University Press.

Ways, M. 1969. Creative federalism and the great society. In *Cooperation and conflict: Readings in American federalism*, ed. by D. J. Elazar et al., pp. 619–31. Itasca, Illinois: F. E. Peacock.

Weber, M. 1921. *The city*. New York: Collier Books.

Weicher, J. C. 1970. Determinants of central city expenditures: Some overlooked factors and problems. *National Tax Journal* 23:379–96.

White, T. H. 1969. *The making of the president 1968*. London: Jonathan Cape.

Wiebe, R. H. 1962. Businessmen and reform: A study of the progressive movement. Cambridge, Massachusetts: Harvard University Press.

Wildavsky, A. 1964. *Leadership in a small town*. Totowa, New Jersey: Bedminster Press.

Williams, O. P. 1971. *Metropolitan political analysis*. New York: Free Press.

Williams, O. P., and Adrian, C. R. 1963. *Four cities: A study of comparative policy making*. Philadelphia: University of Pennsylvania Press.

Wilson, J. Q. 1973. *Political organizations*. New York: Basic Books.

Wilson, W. J. 1978. *The declining significance of race*. Chicago: University of Chicago Press.

Wirt, F. M. 1974. *Power in the city: Decision making in San Francisco*. Berkeley and Los Angeles: University of California Press.

Wirt, F. M., and Kirst, M. W. 1972. *The political web of American schools*. Boston: Little, Brown.

Wolfinger, R. E. 1960. Reputation and reality in the study of community power. *American Sociological Review* 25:636–44.

———. 1971. Nondecisions and the study of local politics. *American Political Science Review* 65:1063–80.

———. 1974. *The politics of progress*. Englewood Cliffs, New Jersey: Prentice-Hall.

Wolfinger, R. E., and Field, J. O. 1966. Political ethos and the structure of city government. *American Political Science Review* 60:306–26.

Wood, R. C. 1958. *Suburbia*. Boston: Houghton Mifflin.

———. 1961. *1400 governments: The political economy of the New York metropolitan region*. Cambridge, Massachusetts: Harvard University Press.

Wright, D. S. 1975. Revenue sharing and structural features of American federalism. *Annals of the American Academy of Political and Social Science* 419:100–119.

Yates, D. 1977. *The ungovernable city: The politics of urban problems and policymaking.* Cambridge, Massachusetts: Massachusetts Institute of Technology Press.

Zeigler, H. M.; Jennings, M. K.; with Peak, G. W. 1974. *Governing American schools.* North Scituate, Massachusetts: Duxbury.

Index

Ability-to-pay principle, 71, 75, 77. *See also* Redistributive policies

Adams, R. F., 226–27

Adrian, C. R., 30, 31, 133, 163

Advisory Commission on Intergovernmental Relations, United States, 72

Affirmative action programs, 160–61, 212–13

AFL–CIO, 121, 163

Agger, R., 140

Alioto, Joseph Lawrence, 126

All-City Employees' Association (Los Angeles), 163

Allocational policies, 44–46, 52, 64–65, 150–66; and benefit tax ratios, 45–46, 49, 151; defined, 41, 44, 132; by federal government, 77, 78; by local governments, 77, 78; New York City, 195; as response to redistributive demands, 179, 181–82; by state governments, 77, 78; and trade unions, 173. *See also* Costs of services, local governments; Demand, economic; Fiscal capacity, local governments

Aptitude tests for employment, 151–52

Atlanta: education policies, 98; power structure, 140, 141

Average taxpayer, defined, 34, 35–36. *See also* Benefit/tax ratios

Bachrach, P., 87, 88, 91

Bahl, R. W., 223, 225

Baltimore, antipoverty programs, 87–88

Banfield, Edward, 18, 117–18, 172

Bankruptcy, 210, 218. *See also* New York City fiscal crisis

Baratz, M. S., 87, 88, 91

Beame, Abraham, 199, 242n.2

Benefit/tax ratios, 34–36, 38, 104; allocational policies, 45–46, 49, 151; and benefits-received principle, 71–72; developmental policies, 42, 49; and fiscal capacity, 46–47; redistributive policies, 37–38, 44, 49, 50, 77, 215

Benefits-received principle, 71–72, 75, 77. *See also* Developmental policies

Blacks, 118, 189; and Democratic party, 113, 159; and education policies, 94–104, 181–82; in government, 87–88, 160–62; redistributive demands of, 70, 158–60, 161, 178–79, 181–82, 212–13; and redistributive policy expenditures, 53, 55–56, 57

Boeing Aircraft, 23

Index

developmental policies, 49–50,
55–63 passim, 223, 225, 226; and
redistributive policies, 48–49, 53,
226, 227
Democratic party, 110–11, 113,
115, 153, 155, 207; and blacks,
113, 159; in New Haven, 112–13;
and redistributive issues, 173,
174; and trade unions, 171, 172
Denver, Colorado, 25
Depression, 111
Derthick, M., 90–91, 118
Detroit: decentralized power, 182;
political parties, 113; unions, 172
Developmental policies, 41–43,
51–52, 64–65, 131–49, 182–83;
and benefit/tax ratios, 42, 49; in
central cities, 98–99, 104–5;
defined, 44, 131–32; by federal
government, 68, 69, 70, 77,
78–79; implementation of, 82–84,
143–48; and independent authorities, 133–36; by local governments, 68, 69, 77, 78; in New
York City, 133–35, 145, 195; and
political leadership, 143–48; and
power structure, 136–43; by state
governments, 77, 78; in suburbs,
95–97, 104–5; and trade unions,
173. See also Costs of city services, local governments; Demand, economic; Education
policies; Fiscal capacity, local
governments
Diamond, Martin, 14–15
Dilworth, Richardson, 126, 143, 145
Duluth, Minnesota, 25
Dye, Thomas, 10, 12, 61–62, 64

East Chicago, Indiana: Pollution
politics, 168–70
Eckstein, H., 131
Economic Development Administration (EDA), 89
Economic interests of cities: exports' role in, 21–23, 24, 26; and
local government, 29–30; and
local service infrastructure,

23–24; and political participation,
129; and production factors,
24–29; and status interests,
30–32. See also Interests of cities
Education, United States Department of, 85
Education, United States Office of,
83, 84, 85, 99
Educational Testing Service,
236n.27
Education and Science, Department
of (Britain), 219, 245n.17
Education policies, 21, 42, 52, 69,
81, 93–106; and blacks, 99–104,
181–82; central cities, 94, 97–99;
and Coleman study, 99–104; and
fiscal capacity, 53, 55, 57, 63,
95–96, 223; implementation of,
83–85; and property values, 95,
96–97; suburban, 94–97, 98; and
verbal ability, 96, 97, 99. See also
Developmental policies; Redistributive policies
Eisenhower, Dwight D., 211
Elazar, Daniel, 14, 15, 25
Elections, voter turnouts, 115, 119,
163
Elementary and Secondary Education Act (ESEA) Title I, 83, 84–85
Emergency Financial Control Board
(New York City), 209
Employees, public, political power,
162–65
Employment policies, 45, 151; in
federal system, 68. See also
Allocational policies; Patronage
Ethnic groups, 6–7, 152, 156–58,
211
Eulau, H., 30, 31
Excise taxes, 71, 74, 75, 76
Expenditures, local government:
and economic demand, 48; and
fiscal capacity, 46–47, 48; and
internal politics model, 9–13; by
policy type, see Allocative
policies; Developmental policies;
Education policies; Redistributive
policies; problem of unit defini-

penditures, 95–96; median, decline in New York City, 203; median, and fiscal capacity of community, 52, 53, 55, 57
Income taxes, 71, 74, 75; corporate, 71, 75, 76; in New York City, 206
Interests of cities, 17–38; as sum of individual interests, 17–18; Tiebout optimal size theory, 18–20. See also Economic interests of cities
Intergovernmental programs, 82–85, 217–22. See also Great Society programs
Intergovernmental transfers, 29, 67, 68, 72; in Great Society programs, 86; in New York City budget, 196–97; and policy choices, 58–59, 75–76, 81, 231n.31; and tax rates, 47

Johnson, Lyndon B., 85–86, 89, 125, 211. See also Great Society programs

Kantor, P., 191, 194, 209
Katzman, M. T., 98
Kaufman, H., 14, 98
Kennedy, John F., 125, 158, 163
Key, V. O., 110
King, Martin Luther, 160

Labor, as production factor, 23, 25–27
Labour party (Britain), 111, 112
Land, as production factor, 24–25
Lane, Robert, 158
Lee, Richard, 126, 144–45, 146, 147
Levi, M., 164
Levy, F., 98
Liberal party (Britain), 111, 112
Lindsay, John, 111–12, 126, 176, 190, 194, 199
Lineberry, R., 229n.12
Lipsky, Michael, 175, 177, 178
Lobbyists, 117
Local educational authority (Britain), 219

Los Angeles, 96; public union, 163; trade unions, 172
Lowi, Theodore, 131, 157, 163
Low-income individuals, and redistributive expenditure levels, 53, 56, 57, 64. See also Poor, and local policies

McConnell, G., 90, 172
McCrone, D. J., 62
McGovern, George, 125
Machine politics, 6–9, 152–56
Maier, Henry, 174–75
Manpower programs, 86, 160, 235n.2
Marshall, D. R., 161
Marxists, xi–xiii, 164, 216–17
Massachusetts Port Authority, 134
Massachusetts Turnpike Authority, 134
Matching formulae, 58
Media, and local politics, 115, 123–25
Meltsner, A. J., 98
Michelson, S., 95, 98
Migration: controls, 25–27, 69–70; and optimal city size, 20; and optimal service distribution, 32–33
Miller, D. C., 136
Milwaukee, open housing legislation, 174–75
Miner, J., 95
Minimum standards of service provision, 221
Minneapolis, Minnesota, taxes, 206
Minorities, 31, 158, 189. See also Blacks
Moses, Robert, 134–35, 145
Multiplier effect of city exports, 23
Municipal Assistance Corporation (New York City), 209
Municipality, problem of defining, 10–11

Naftalin, Arthur, 126
National Center for Education Statistics, 236n.27

Index